CODING
KIDS

2 BOOKS IN 1: PYTHON FOR KIDS AND SCRATCH CODING FOR KIDS. A BEGINNERS GUIDE TO COMPUTER PROGRAMMING. HAVE FUN AND LEARN TO CODE QUICKLY, EVEN IF YOU'RE NEW TO PROGRAMMING

CHRISTIAN MORRISON

Copyright - 2020 -

All rights reserved.

The content contained within this book may not be reproduced, duplicated or transmitted without direct written permission from the author or the publisher.

Under no circumstances will any blame or legal responsibility be held against the publisher, or author, for any damages, reparation, or monetary loss due to the information contained within this book. Either directly or indirectly.

Legal Notice:

This book is copyright protected. This book is only for personal use. You cannot amend, distribute, sell, use, quote or paraphrase any part, or the content within this book, without the consent of the author or publisher.

Disclaimer Notice:

Please note the information contained within this document is for educational and entertainment purposes only. All effort has been executed to present accurate, up to date, and reliable, complete information. No warranties of any kind are declared or implied. Readers acknowledge that the author is not engaging in the rendering of legal, financial, medical or professional advice. The content within this book has been derived from various sources. Please consult a licensed professional before attempting any techniques outlined in this book.

By reading this document, the reader agrees that under no circumstances is the author responsible for any losses, direct or indirect, which are incurred as a result of the use of information contained within this document, including, but not limited to, - errors, omissions, or inaccuracies.

PYTHON FOR KIDS

LEARN TO CODE QUICKLY WITH THIS BEGINNER'S GUIDE TO COMPUTER PROGRAMMING. HAVE FUN WITH MORE THAN 40 AWESOME CODING ACTIVITIES, GAMES AND PROJECTS, EVEN IF YOU ARE A NOVICE.

CHRISTIAN MORRISON

Copyright - 2020 -

All rights reserved.

The content contained within this book may not be reproduced, duplicated or transmitted without direct written permission from the author or the publisher.

Under no circumstances will any blame or legal responsibility be held against the publisher, or author, for any damages, reparation, or monetary loss due to the information contained within this book. Either directly or indirectly.

Legal Notice:

This book is copyright protected. This book is only for personal use. You cannot amend, distribute, sell, use, quote or paraphrase any part, or the content within this book, without the consent of the author or publisher.

Disclaimer Notice:

Please note the information contained within this document is for educational and entertainment purposes only. All effort has been executed to present accurate, up to date, and reliable, complete information. No warranties of any kind are declared or implied. Readers acknowledge that the author is not engaging in the rendering of legal, financial, medical or professional advice. The content within this book has been derived from various sources. Please consult a licensed professional before attempting any techniques outlined in this book.

By reading this document, the reader agrees that under no circumstances is the author responsible for any losses, direct or indirect, which are incurred as a result of the use of information contained within this document, including, but not limited to, - errors, omissions, or inaccuracies.

TABLE OF CONTENTS

INTRODUCTION   9

CHAPTER - 1
GETTING STARTED WITH PYTHON   19

CHAPTER - 2
WHERE TO START: THE BASICS   37

CHAPTER - 3
THE MAGIC REIGN OF LISTS   49

CHAPTER - 4
FUN WITH LOOPS, LOOPS, LOOPS...   65

CHAPTER - 5
BETTER THE QUESTION BETTER THE ANSWER: IF STATEMENT   75

CHAPTER - 6
THE TURTLE GRAPHICS OF YOUR DREAMS   89

CHAPTER - 7
WORKING WITH PYTHON FUNCTIONS   99

CHAPTER - 8
PYTHON'S BUILT-IN FUNCTIONS   111

CHAPTER - 9
RESOURCES: USEFUL MODULES   117

CHAPTER - 10
GAME PROGRAMMING   123

CHAPTER - 11
MORE GAMES   133

CHAPTER - 12
    HOW TO DEAL WITH ERRORS?   **145**

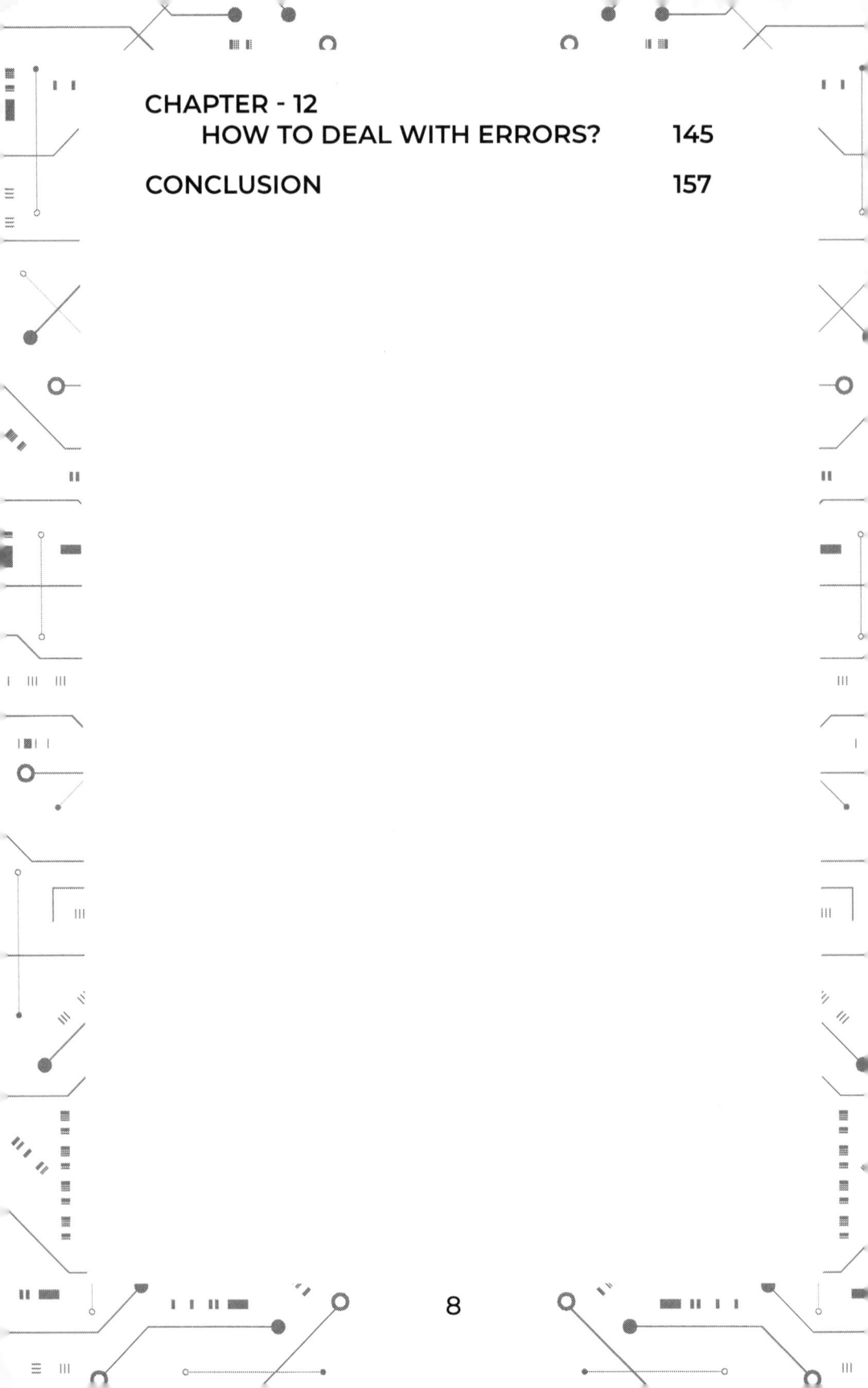

CONCLUSION   **157**

INTRODUCTION

What is coding? Coding is the process of putting together the segments of your data that seem to illustrate an idea or concept. In this way, coding is a way of making abstractions from the existing data in their resources to build a greater understanding of the forces involved.

Remember that it is possible to code any portion of the content of a resource on any number of nodes to show that it is related to each of its concepts or categories.

Why Learn to Code?

The coding of the content of your resources can contribute significantly to your analysis in several ways:

- Coding allows you to gather and view all the material related to a category or case through all its resources. Viewing all this material allows you to review the coded segments in context and create new and more refined categories as you gain a new understanding of the meaning of the data.

- The codification of its resources facilitates the search for patterns and theories. It is possible to browse the encoded content of your resources using queries and search functionality to test theories and find new patterns in your data.

Example: When coding in C the algorithm of the program Add, seen in the Design, something similar to:

```c
#include <stdio.h>
int main ()
{
    int a, b, c;
    printf ("\n first n% number (integer):", 163);
    scanf ("% d", & a);
printf ("\n second n% number (integer):", 163);
    scanf ("% d", & b);
    c = a + b;
    printf ("\n The sum is:% d", c);
    return 0;
```

To encode an algorithm, you have to know the syntax of the language to which it will be translated. However, regardless of the programming language in which a program is written, it will be its algorithm that determines its logic. The logic of a program establishes what its actions are and in what order they should be executed. Therefore, it is convenient for every programmer to learn to design algorithms before moving on to the coding phase.

Programming Languages

A programming language can be defined as an artificial language that allows you to write the instructions of a computer program or put another way. A programming language allows the programmer to communicate with the computer to tell it what it has to do. Many programming languages have invented by man. We can classify into three main types: the machine, low level, and high level.

Machine language is the only one that understands the digital computer. it is its "natural language". Only two symbols can be used on it: zero (0) and one (1). Therefore, machine language is also called binary language. The computer can only work with bits. However, it is not easy for the programmer to write instructions such as:

10100010

```
11110011

00100010

00010010
```

For this reason, more understandable programming languages were invented for the programmer.

Thus, low-level languages appeared, also called assembly languages, which allow the programmer to write the instructions of a program using English abbreviations, also called mnemonic words, such as ADD, DIV, SUB, etc., instead of use zeros and ones. For example, the instruction:

```
ADD a, b, c
```

It could be the translation of the action:

$$c \leftarrow a + b$$

This action is present in the Add algorithm of the Design, which indicated that in the memory space represented by the variable c the sum of the two numbers stored in the memory spaces represented by the variables a and b must be stored.

A program written in an assembly language has the disadvantage that it is not understandable to the computer since it is not composed of zeros and ones. To translate the instructions of a program written in an assembly language to instructions of a machine language, you must use a program called an assembler.

An added difficulty to binary languages is the fact that they are dependent on the machine, or rather, the processor, that is, each processor uses a different machine language, a different set of instructions, which is defined in its hardware. Consequently, a program written for a type of processor cannot be used on other equipment that uses a different processor, since the program will not be portable. For this program to work on a second computer, all instructions written in the machine language of the first computer must be translated into the binary language of the second computer, which is a very expensive and complex job for the programmer.

Likewise, since the instructions that can be written in an assembly language are always associated with the binary instructions of a particular computer, assembly languages are also processor dependent. However, high-level languages are independent of the processor, that is, a program written on any computer with high-level language can be transported to any other computer, with small changes or even none.

A high-level language allows the programmer to write the instructions of a program using words or syntactic expressions. For example, in C you can use words such as case, if, for, while, etc. to build with the instructions like:

```
if (n0> 0) printf ("The number% is positive", 163);
```

This translated into English comes to say that, if the number is greater than zero, then write the message on the screen: "The number is positive."

Another important feature of high-level languages is that, for most of the instructions in these languages, several instructions in an assembly language would be needed to indicate the same. In the same way that, most of the instructions of an assembly language, also groups several instructions of a machine language.

On the other hand, a program is written in a high-level language also does not get rid of the inconvenience of the fact that it is not understandable to the computer and, therefore, to translate the instructions of a program written in a high-level language to instructions of a machine language, you have to use another program that is called a compiler.

What Can You Make with Code?

You can do many things with codes. For example, let's see what can be done with JavaScript code.

The things that can be done with Code are very varied, among the most prominent are:

1. You can obtain the information about the browser that the user is using, the version of it, the operating system on which it is running, and even the screen resolution that you have configured on your computer.

2. You can work with pop-up and interactive dialogs created with div elements, instead of pop-up windows, which have stopped being used for security and design reasons.

3. You can create sophisticated menu systems with pop-up submenus that are activated with the user action.

4. Values entered in form fields can be validated before they are sent to the server.

5. You can create navigation trees to make it easier for users to move from one page to another through your website.

6. You can create substitution effects for images controlled by the action of placing or removing the mouse pointer.

7. You can create some animations such as transitions of images and objects from a web page.

8. You can change the position of HTML elements on the web page dynamically or controlled by the movement of the mouse pointer.

9. You can redirect the user from one page to another, without the need for a static link.

10. You can perform some calculations with the values entered in the form fields.

11. You can get the date of the operating system where the web page is running on the client.

12. Sophisticated calendar controls can be created to select a date, instead of being manually entered by users in form fields.

Types of Errors

When a syntax error exists in any instruction of the source code of a program, this error will prevent both the compiler and the interpreter from translating said instruction, since neither of them will understand what the programmer is telling you. For example, if instead of the instruction:

```
printf ("\ n first n% number (integer):", 163);
```

When the compiler or the interpreter reads this line of code, neither of them will understand what prrintf is and, therefore, they will not know how to translate this instruction into machine code, therefore, both will stop the translation and notify the programmer with a message of error.

In summary, syntax errors are detected in the process of translating the source code into binary code. On the contrary that it happens with the errors of execution and of logic that can only be detected when the program is running.

A runtime error occurs when the computer cannot execute any instructions correctly. For example, the instruction:

```
c = 5/0;
```

It is syntactically correct and will be translated into binary code. However, when the computer tries to perform the division:

```
5/0
```

An execution error will occur, since, mathematically, it cannot be divided by zero.

As for logic errors, they are the most difficult to detect. When a program has no syntax or execution errors but still does not work well, this is due to the existence of some logical error. So, a logic error occurs when the results obtained are not as expected. For example, if instead of the instruction:

```
c = a + b;
```

A programmer would have written:

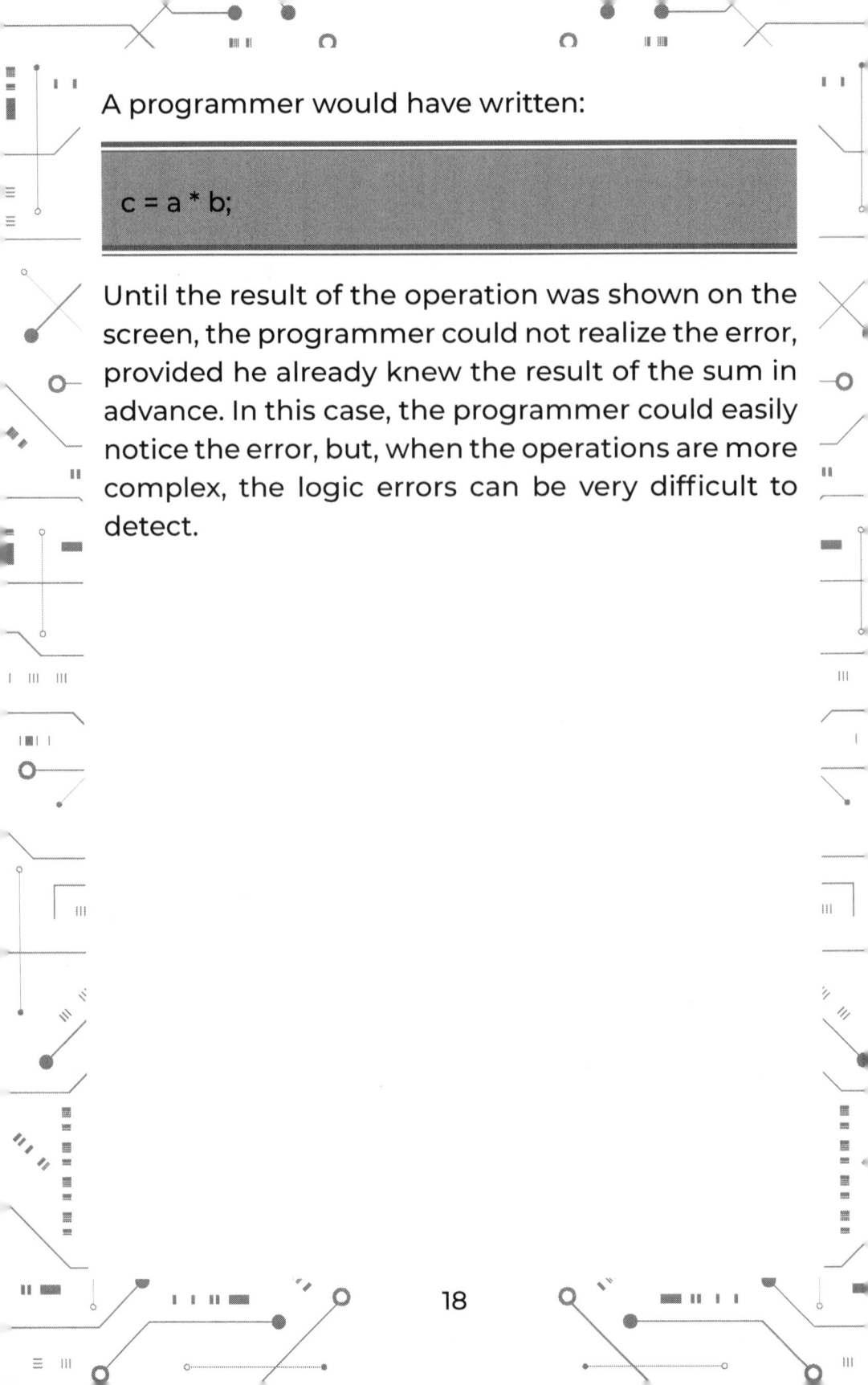

```
c = a * b;
```

Until the result of the operation was shown on the screen, the programmer could not realize the error, provided he already knew the result of the sum in advance. In this case, the programmer could easily notice the error, but, when the operations are more complex, the logic errors can be very difficult to detect.

CHAPTER - 1
GETTING STARTED WITH PYTHON

What is Python?

Python is a minimalist programming language, which contains a syntax that makes it quite simple. It is an interpreted language, that is to say, not compiled, in addition this serves for all types of development specially to give dynamics to objects in different programs and / or paradigms.

Undoubtedly Python is one of the best options to develop a website, especially when you know the basic elements of language.

Let's see Python what offers us.

Python Features

Before continuing, we will point out some important Python features and why you should learn it.

Minimalist Code

Yes, the code and the simple syntax are perfect for developing websites, facilitating the work and writing of it.

Well Paid

That's right, if you are going to develop a Python website, prepare your bank account, since the benefit you will receive from developing a Python website will be very profitable, as you can see in Medium.

Multiplatform

Python can not only run it in an operating system, so you can take it anywhere, from free operating systems such as Linux and through the already known Windows or Mac, in addition to other devices that have systems based on the aforementioned distributions.

Extensive Libraries

An advantage that comes very well from Python is the number of libraries or libraries you can find to develop.

There is a wide variety of reusable code, from game creation to large websites and quality.

Installing Python

On a PC

If you are using Windows machine, you can follow the procedure below.

Step1. Let us begin by opening up our web browser and going straight to the source. In the address bar, type in www.python.org and you will be greeted by a simplistic website as shown here:

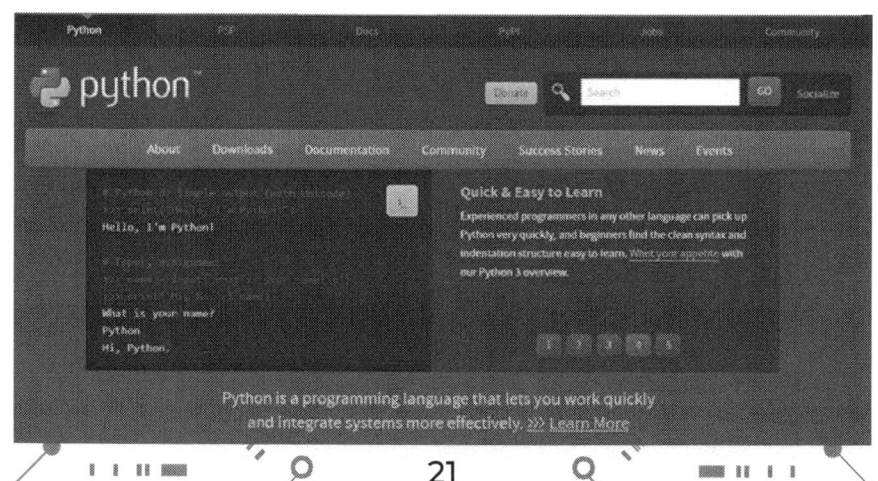

Step2. Mouse cursor over 'Downloads' and the website should be able to detect your platform and present the corresponding version accordingly automatically.

Step3. Click on the button to commence the download.

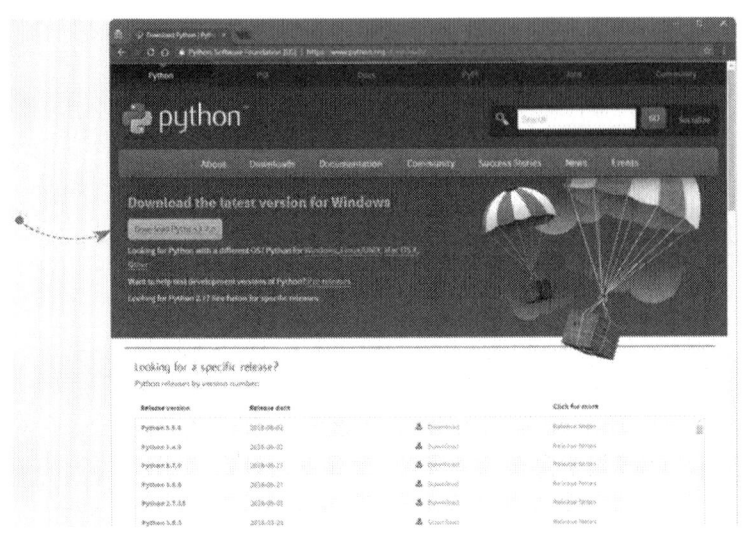

Step4. Once your download is complete, click on it to begin installation. There will be a pop up window.

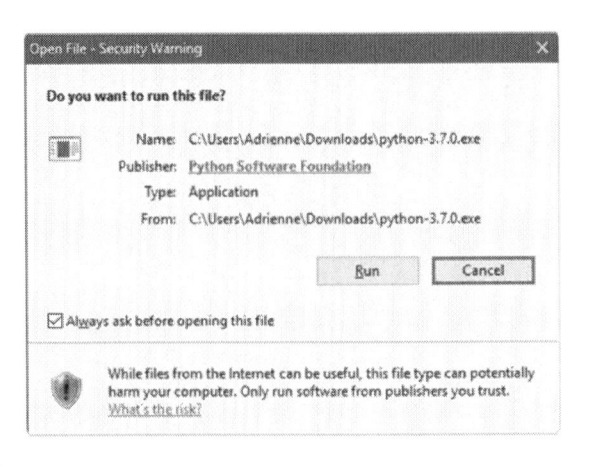

Step5. After download and installation, you can simply run the downloaded file, by double-clicking on the Python file. A dialog box will appear that looks like this:

Step6. Make sure the check the ADD PYTHON 3.7 TO PATH checkbox.

Step7. Then just click Install Now. Python will begin installation. A pop-up Window below will appear.

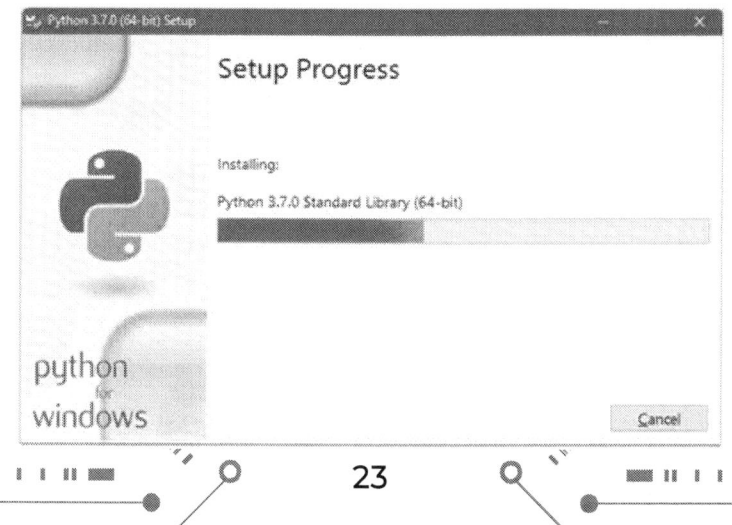

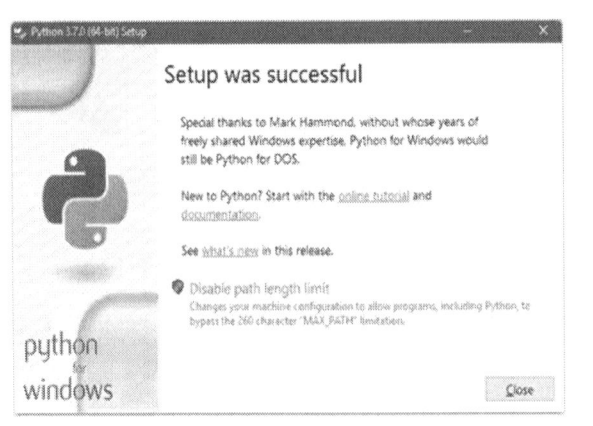

Step8. A few minutes later you should have a working Python installed on your system.

Step9. Yehey! You're done installing and you are ready to start your python journey on windows!

On Mac

Step1. On your computer, open an Internet browser like Google Chrome or Mozilla Firefox.

Step2. In the address bar, type "https://www.python.org/downloads/" to go to the official Python website's Downloads section.

Step3. Through the magic of coding, the website will probably know what type of computer you are using, and the DOWNLOAD button will show you the correct version of Python to install! In our case, we want the latest version, which was Python 3.7.0. Don't worry if it tells you to download a newer version. You can also find the installer for your specific machine in the Files section.

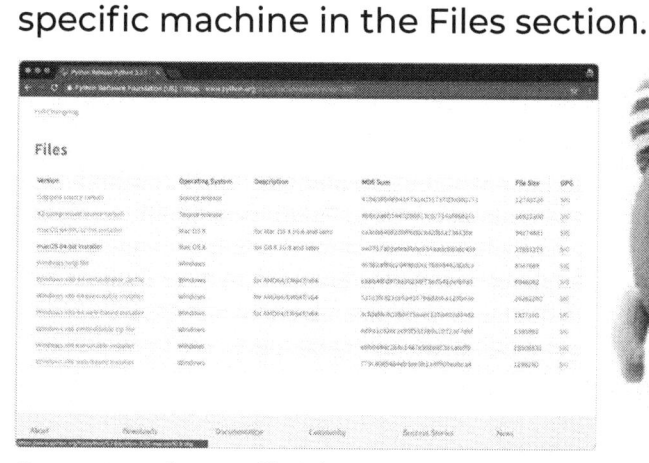

Step4. After clicking on the version, a download should start. Wait for it to finish before starting the installer.

Step5. When you start the installer, you should see a window like this one:

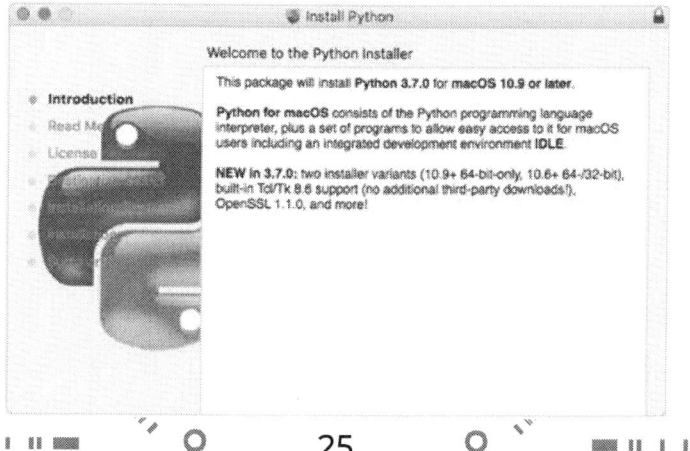

25

Step6. Click the CONTINUE button. You'll then be presented with some important information that you can choose to read or not.

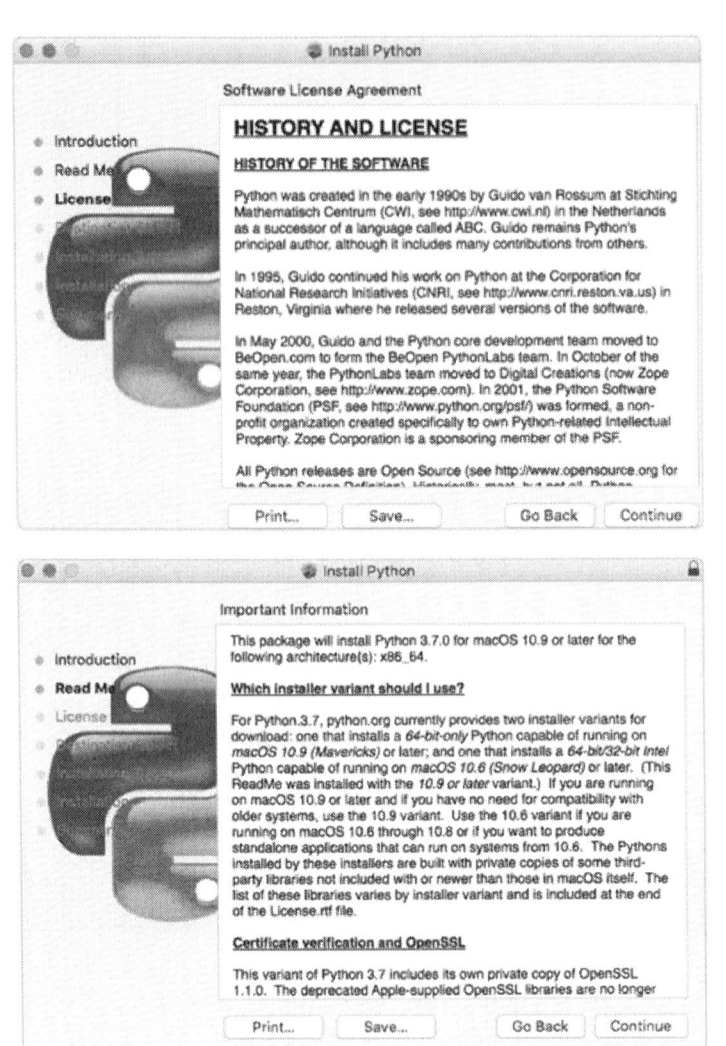

Step7. Click the CONTINUE button. Next you will see the license information.

Step8. Click the CONTINUE button. You'll be asked to agree to the terms of the software license agreement.

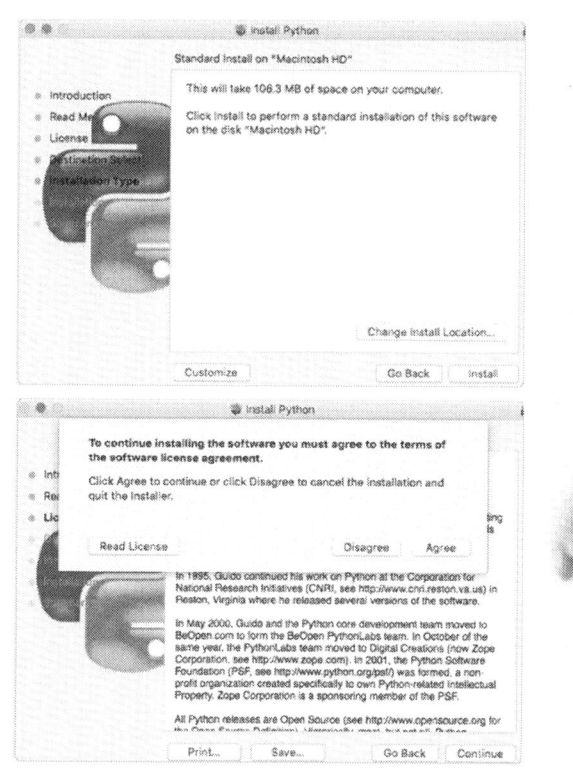

Step9. Click the AGREE button. You'll reach this final window:

Step10. Click the INSTALL button. If you need to, enter your personal user name and password for your account on your computer. Mac OS sometimes asks for this to make sure you want to install something. If you don't see this pop-up window, you can skip to the next step.

Step11. Installation should begin.

Step12. Wait for the installation to finish. Once it is done, you should see this:

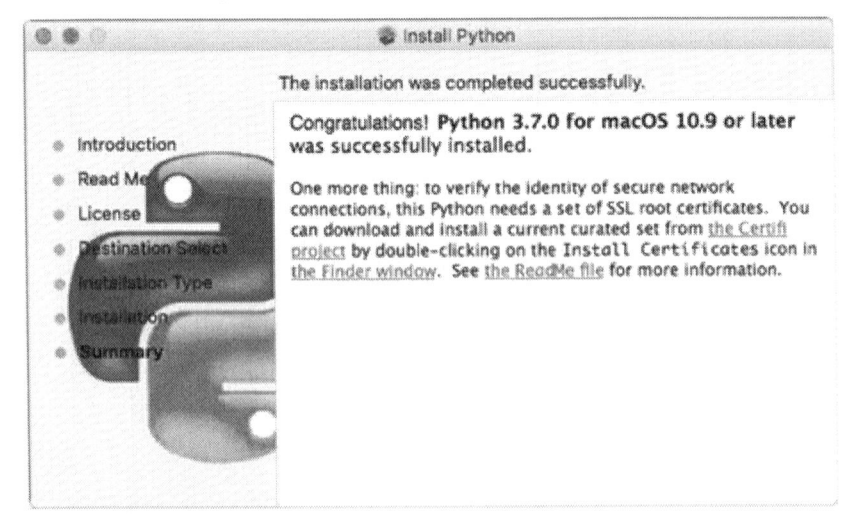

Step 14. Congratulate yourself! You've just installed Python on your Mac!

After Installation

How to Run Python

Before we start running our first Python program,

it is important that we understand how we can run python programs. Running or executing or deploying or firing a program simply means that we are making the computer process instructions/lines of codes. For instance, if the lines of codes (program) require the computer to display some message, then it should. The following are the ways or mode of running python programs. The interpreter is a special program that is installed when installing the Python package and helps convert text code into a language that the computer understands and can act on it (executing).

Immediate Mode

It is a way of running python programs that are not written in a file. We get into the immediate mode by typing the word python in the command line and which will trigger the interpreter to switch to immediate mode. The immediate mode allows typing of expressions directly, and pressing enter generates the output. The sign below is the Python prompt:

>>>

The python prompt instructs the interpreter to accept input from the user. For instance, typing 2+2 and pressing enter will display 4 as the output. In a way, this prompt can be used as a calculator. If you need to exit the immediate mode, type quit() or exit().

Now type 5 +3, and press enter, the output should be 8. The next mode is the Script Mode.

Script Mode

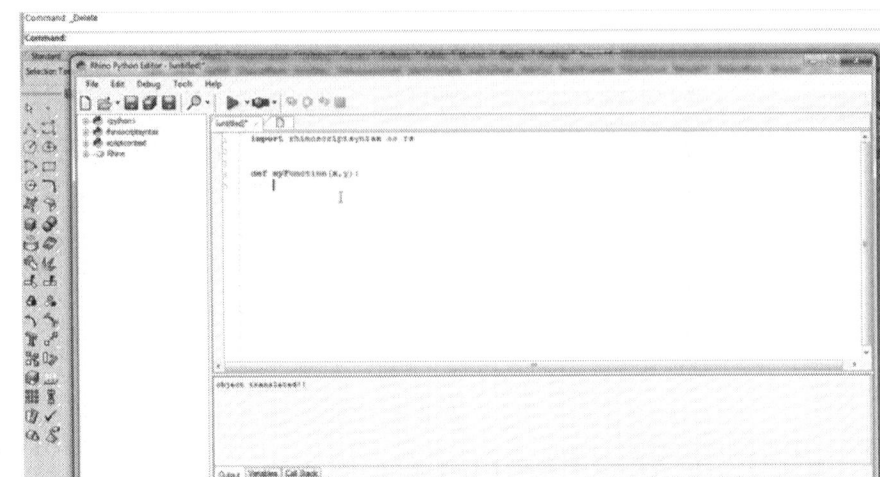

The script mode is used to run a python program written in a file; the file is called a script.

Integrated Development Environment (IDE)

An IDE provides a convenient way of writing and running Python programs. One can also use text editors to create a python script file instead of an IDE by writing lines of codes and saving the file with a .py extension. However, using an IDE can simplify the process of writing and running Python programs. The IDEL present in the Python package is an example of an IDE with a graphical user interface and gets installed along with the Python language. The advantages of IDE include helping getting rid of repetitive tasks and simplify coding for beginners. IDE provides syntax highlighting, code hinting, and syntax checking among other features. There also commercial IDE such as the PyScripter IDE that performs most of the mentioned functions.

Note

We have presented what Python is, how to download and install Python, the immediate and script modes of Python IDE, and what is an IDE.

Your First Program in Python

The rest of the illustrations will assume you are running the python programs in a Windows environment.

1. Start IDLE

2. Navigate to the File menu and click New Window

3. Type the following:

4. Print ("Hello World!")

5. On the file, menu click on Save. Type the name of myProgram1.py

6. Navigate to Run and click Run Module to run the program.

The first program that we have written is known as the "Hello World!" and is used to not only provide an introduction to a new computer coding language but also test the basic configuration of the IDE. The output of the program is "Hello World!" Here is what has happened, the Print() is an inbuilt function, it is prewritten and preloaded for you, is used to display whatever is contained in the () as long as it is between the double quotes. The computer will display anything written within the double quotes.

First Try!

Assignment

Now write and run the following python programs:

a) print("I am now a Python Language Coder!")

b) print("This is my second simple program!")

c) print("I love the simplicity of Python")

d) print("I will display whatever is here in quotes such as owyhen2589gdbnz082")

Now we need to write a program with numbers, but before writing such a program, we need to learn something about Variables and Types.

Remember python is object-oriented and it is not statically typed which means we do not need to declare variables before using them or specify their type. Let us explain this statement; an object-oriented language simply means that the language supports viewing and manipulating real-life scenarios as groups with subgroups that can be linked and shared mimicking the natural order and interaction of things. Not all programming languages are object-oriented; for instance, Visual C programming language is not object-oriented. In programming, declaring variables means that we explicitly state the nature of the variable. The variable can be declared as an integer, long integer, short integer, floating integer, a string, or as a character including if it is accessible locally or globally. A variable is a storage location that changes values depending on conditions.

For instance, number1 can take any number from 0 to infinity. However, if we specify explicitly that int number1 it then means that the storage location will only accept integers and not fractions for instance, fortunately or unfortunately, python does not require us to explicitly state the nature of the storage location (declare variables) as that is left to the python language itself to figure out that.

Before tackling types of variables and rules of writing variables, let us run a simple program to understand what variables when coding a python program are.

Start IDLE

Navigate to the File menu and click New Window

Type the following:

```
num1=4
num2=5
sum=num1+num2
print(sum)
```

On the file, menu click on Save. Type the name of myProgram2.py

Navigate to Run and click Run Module to run the program.

The expected output of this program should be "9" without the double quotes.

Explanation

At this point, you are eager to understand what has just happened and why the print(sum) does not have double quotes like the first programs we wrote. Here is the explanation.

The first line num1=4 means that variable num1(our shortened way of writing number1, first number) has been assigned 4 before the program runs.

The second line num2=5 means that variable

num2(our shortened way of writing number2, second number) has been assigned 5 before the program runs.

The computer interprets these instructions and stores the numbers given

The third line sum=num1+num2 tells the computer that takes whatever num1 has been given and add to whatever num2 has been given. In other terms, sum the values of num1 and num2.

The fourth line print(sum) means that display whatever sum has. If we put double quotes to sum, the computer will display the word sum and not the sum of the two numbers! Remember that cliché that computers are garbage in and garbage out. They follow what you give them!

Note

+ is an operator for summing variables and has other users.

Now let us try out three Assignments involving numbers before we explain types of variables and rules of writing variables so that you get more freedom to play with variables. Remember variables values vary for instance num1 can take 3, 8, 1562, 1.

Follow the steps of opening the Python IDE and do the following:

The output should be 54

num1=43

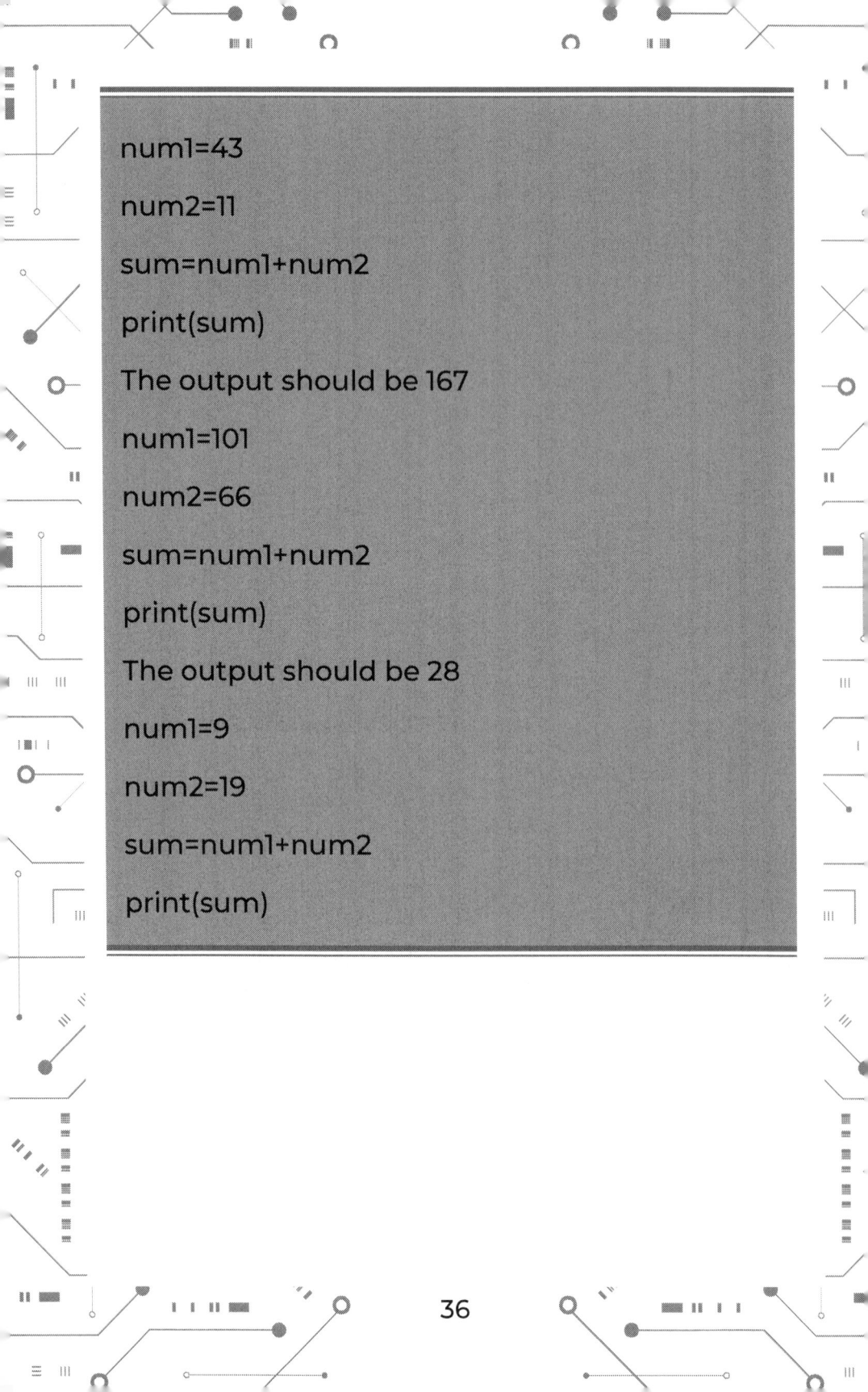

num2=11

sum=num1+num2

print(sum)

The output should be 167

num1=101

num2=66

sum=num1+num2

print(sum)

The output should be 28

num1=9

num2=19

sum=num1+num2

print(sum)

CHAPTER - 2
WHERE TO START: THE BASICS

Variables

Variables are names for values. In Python the = symbol assigns the value on the right to the name on the left. The variable is created when a value is assigned to it. Here is a Python program that assigns an age to a variable age and a name in quotation marks to a variable first_name.

```
age = 42
first_name = 'Eunice'
```

Types of Variables

Now that we have defined what are variables are and the rules to write variable names, let us explore different types of variables.

A) Numbers

The Python accommodates two kinds of numbers, namely floating-point numbers and integer numbers. Python also supports complex numbers. When you sign a value to a number, then a number object is created. For example:

```
number3 = 9
number4 = 12
```

Different Numerical Types Supported in Python

- long for example 681581903L
- int for example 11, 123, -151
- float for example 0.5, 23.1, -54.2
- complex for example 4.12j

Exercise

Identify the type of numerical below:

a. 234, 19, 312

b. 4.56, 2.9, 9.3

c. 76189251468290127624471

Identify the numerical type suitable for the following contexts:

d. Salary amount.

e. Counting the number of students in a class.

f. Getting the census figure in an entire country of China.

B) Strings

A sequence of characters. The character is just a symbol. For example, the English language contains 26 characters.

Computers do not deal with characters, but rather numbers (binary). Although you may see characters on your screen, it is internally stored and processed as a combination of 0 and 1.

Transforming a character into a cipher number is called, and the inverse process is decoding. ASCII and Unicode are some popular codecs used.

In Python, the string is a string of Unicode characters. Unicode was introduced to include every letter in all languages and bring uniformity into coding. You can learn more about Unicode here.

How to create a string in Python?

Strings can be created by enclosing characters within a single quotation mark or double quotation marks. Even triple quotes can be used in Python but are generally used to represent multi-line strings and lines.

```python
# all of the following are equivalent

my_string ='Hello'

print(my_string)

my_string ="Hello"

print(my_string)

my_string ='''Hello'''

print(my_string)
```

```python
# triple quotes string can extend multiple lines

my_string ="""Hello, welcome to
   the world of Python"""

print(my_string)
```

How To Use The Variables?

Now that you know how to assign variables to different values, the next step is understanding how to use them right. Let's create a scenario running from a previous one of calculating how much you'll have to save daily to be able to buy yourself a present at the end of the year. Imagine at the end of the year, you're unable to save the exact amount of money to buy yourself the dream gift, but your dad, seeing your efforts, asks you for the amount left so he can add up to it to get you your gift.

You only have to use your Python shell and assign variables to calculate it. Let's see...

> Amount_needed= $40
>
> Amount_in_hand=$33.75

Since regular math makes us understand that you'd have to subtract the amount you have from the amount needed to know how much will be left, then you have...

> Amount_left=Amount_needed – Amount_in_hand

We have assigned our chosen variables to the values we have. All we have to do next is to input this into the Python shell and print the answer you're looking to get (i.e. print Amount_left) and see the outcome it gives. Just in case your saving goals are the same as mine, you should get $6.25. This means that your dad is going to give you $6.25 extra. Remember that while calculating with Python, you don't need to include the units (miles, sheets, dollars, or $) they stand for, just the numbers.

In the case that you get to the store, and you find out that your dream present has increased to $43, you can still use the same variable, only that you'll change it to contain the new value. Here's how you can input it in your Python shell. On a new line, enter Amount_needed= $43. Then, copy and paste the equation to calculate the answer again, to give you:

Amount_left=Amount_needed – Amount_in_hand

Then, go ahead to print your new answer.

Calculating With Python: Numbers And Operators

Python Numbers: Are they different from regular numbers?

Because you want to ask our program to solve the right equations (because computer language isn't 100% human language), you need to know the basic types of numbers that exist in the Python language. The first is the integers. They are the regular whole numbers that we use when counting, doing basic math, or telling our age like 0, 1, 89, 20225, and negatives like -88. The other is the floating-point numbers or floats for short, which are the decimal numbers like 0.8, 2.0, and 7.888 used to describe fractions.

Basic Python Operators

When you want to make mathematical calculations, the most common operations you perform are addition, subtraction, multiplication, and division, right? Those basic symbols we use to represent this operation are what we call operators in Python. The + (plus), - (minus), * (multiply by), and / (divide) represent the effect and calculations we want our set of numbers to have in that particular equation. So, if you input 3*4, you want to multiply your first number 3 by 4, which gives you 12.

Less Basic Python Operators

With Python, you can go further and perform mathematical calculations that your basic calculators don't provide for you. They are the exponent and modulus. As technical as they may sound, they are pretty straightforward operations. Not to worry, the only reason they are referred to as 'less basic' is because they are not the regular ones you're exposed to. Imagine you have to multiply a particular number by itself a number of times, say multiply 5 by itself 6 times. You do this using the exponent operator, which is the double asterisk (**). Now instead of typing 5*5*5*5*5, you only have to type 5**6 and get the same answer. It is the same as when you have 56 in a math problem.

In regular math, when you divide integers by other integers (remember integers?) and the numbers don't divide evenly, you have a remainder. In Python, going through the normal division route doesn't show you what remainder is left. You only get the whole number answer. For instance, 5/2 gives you 2 in Python. In the actual sense, there's a remainder of 1. To fix this, Python provides a special operator that allows you to check the remainder of your division equation. We call it modulus. It's represented by the percent (%) symbol. So, to get the remainder of 5/2, you input 5%2 and get 1.

Order of Operations

Now that you understand the basic and not so basic operators that can be used when calculating with Python, you should also know that there's a particular order that the operators have to follow to get correct answers and program right. There's only one way you can input your different operators in whichever order you wish to have them and still get the right answer. But before going into that exception, it's important that you're reminded about the order that the math rule (and Python in turn) follows. It is exponent first, then multiplication and division, then addition and subtraction. So, if you input 2 + 2 * 4 into a Python program, you'll be getting 10. If your intention is for the program to add up 2 and 2 before multiplying the answer by 4 and get 16, you'll have to go a little mile further.

Here's where the exception we spoke about a few words ago comes in. You have the option of adding parentheses or round brackets as they're regularly called. The parentheses indicate that you want the operation inside the brackets to go first before the others follow. So, in this case, when you input

(2+2)*4, you'll get 16 instead of the 10 when you carry out the operation without a round bracket. You can also have parentheses inside another parentheses. Say, ((5 + 10) * 20) / 10. With this, you're telling the computer to operate on the innermost bracket first, then go into the outer bracket, and then the rest of the equation according to the basic math rules. In this case, you get 30. This works because all the mathematical rules that you know apply to Python, and other programming languages.

CALCULATING IN THE PYTHON SHELL

You sure do know how to do regular calculations on pen and paper or on calculators. But how do you do math with Python? Here's how you go about it:

You start a Python shell by double-clicking the IDLE icon on your desktop. You get a >>> symbol which is the command prompt where you can input whatever it is you want your computer to process, which in this case is a math calculation. Try typing in a basic calculation like 7+6, and press ENTER. You should see the answer to your equation, which is 13.

You can also use the Python program to solve your daily mathematical problems, like knowing how much you'd need to save daily to achieve your goal of buying yourself a present at the end of the year. You can try this out on your own Python shell and see how much you should put into your piggy bank daily.

Comments

When writing python programs and indeed any programming language, comments are very important. Comments are used to describe what is happening within a program. It becomes easier for another person taking a look at a program to have an idea of what the program does by reading the comments in it. Comments are also useful to a programmer as one can forget the critical details of a program written. The hash (#) symbol is used before writing a comment in Python. The comment extends up to the newline character. The python interpreter normally ignores comments. Comments are meant for programmers to understand the program better.

Example

i. Start IDLE

ii. Navigate to the File menu and click New Window

iii. Type the following:

```
#This is my first comment

#The program will print Hello World

Print('Hello World')   #This is an inbuilt function to display
```

On the file, menu click on Save. Type the name of myProgram5.py

Navigate to Run and click Run Module to run the program

Assignment

This Assignment integrates most of what we have covered so far.

Write a program to sum two numbers 45, and 12 and include single line comments at each line of code.

Write a program to show the names of two employees where the first employee is "Daisy" and the second employee is "Richard." Include single comments at each line of code.

Write a program to display the student registration numbers where the student names and their registration are: Yvonne=235, Ian=782, James=1235, Juliet=568.

Multi-line Comments

Just like multi-line program statements we also have multi-line comments. There are several ways of writing multi-line comments. The first approach is to type the hash (#) at each comment line starting point.

For Example

Start IDLE.

Navigate to the File menu and click New Window.

Type the following:

```
#I am going to write a long comment line
#the comment will spill over to this line
#and finally end here.
```

The second way of writing multi-line comments involves using triple single or double quotes: ''' or ". For multi-line strings and multi-line comments in Python, we use the triple quotes. Caution: When used in docstrings they will generate extra code, but we do not have to worry about this at this instance.

Example

Start IDLE.

Navigate to the File menu and click New Window.

Type the following:

```
"This is also a great
illustration of
a multi-line comment in Python."
```

CHAPTER - 3
THE MAGIC REIGN OF LISTS

What Is A List?

In your Python shell, you'll input it as favorite_colors= ['red', 'blue', 'purple', 'green']. You then ask your computer to print(favorite_colors), and you get all the items on your list as [red, blue, purple, green].

You may be wondering what the list and a string is. A list has a number of features that a string doesn't have. It allows you to add, remove, or pick one or some of the characters in the list. Imagine over the next few years, you decide you have one more favorite color you want to add to your existing list, or you no longer like a particular color, a list in Python allows you manipulate it.

A string can't allow you to add or remove without changing the entire characters in it. We could print the second item in the favorite_colors (blue) by entering its position in the list (called the index position) inside square brackets ([]). Index position is the position the computer sees the items in the list as. To computers, index positions begin from 0 (instead of the regular 1 we're all used to). So, the first item on your list is in index position 0, the second item is in index position 1, and so on.

You'll enter something like, print(favorite_colors[1]) in your Python shell. You'll get blue after hitting ENTER.

To change an item in your existing list, you'll enter it this way:

```
favorite_colors[1]= 'yellow'

print(favorite_colors)
```

You'll now have:

['red', 'yellow', 'purple', 'green'] as your list.

You have successfully removed the item 'blue' and replaced it with 'yellow' at index position 1.

You may also wish to show only some part of your list. You do this by using a colon (:) inside square brackets. For example, enter the following in your command prompt to see the second and third items on your list.

```
print(color_list[1:3])
```

Writing [1:3] is the same as saying, 'show the items from index position 1 up to (but not including) index position 3' – or in other words, items 2 and 3. This process is called slicing.

In this case, append adds an item to the end of a list. It goes this way:

```
color_list.append('white')

print(color_list)

['red', 'yellow', 'purple', 'green', 'white']
```

To remove items from a list, use the del command (short for delete). To remove the third item on your list, it's:

```
del color_list[2]

print(color_list)

['red', 'yellow', 'green', 'white']
```

We can also join lists by adding them, just like adding numbers, using a plus (+) sign.

If your first list includes numbers 1 to 3, and your second list includes random words, you can join them as one list. Here's how:

```
second_list=['buckle', 'my', 'shoes']

print(first_list + second_list)

After hitting ENTER, you get:

[1, 2, 3, 'buckle', 'my', 'shoes']
```

Working With Lists

Now, we have obtained one piece of information. Moving to the next one, let us find out what is at the start of this list. To do that, we will call up the first element, and this is where the concept of index position comes in.

An index is the position of a component. Here, the first component is 'Joey' and to find out that, we will do this:

```
friends = ["Joey", "Chandler", "Ross", "Phoebe", "Rachel", "Monica"]

print(friends[0])
```

Here, we will use the square brackets and use the value of zero. Why zero and not one? In Python, and in quite a few languages as well, the first position is always a zero. Here, "friends[0]" essentially tells the program to print the component with the first index position. The output, obviously, is:

Joey

Similarly, let's print the rest out accordingly!

```
friends = ["Joey", "Chandler", "Ross", "Phoebe", "Rachel", "Monica"]
print(friends[0])
print(friends[1])
print(friends[2])
print(friends[3])
print(friends[4])
print(friends[5])
```

Output:

Joey

Chandler

Ross

Phoebe

Rachel

Monica

There is another way to do this. Suppose you do not know the length of the list, and you wish to print out the last recorded entry of the same, you can do that by using the following method:

```
friends = ["Joey", "Chandler", "Ross", "Phoebe", "Rachel", "Monica"]

print(friends[-1])
```

Output:

Monica

The '-1' will always fetch you the last entry. If you use '-2' instead, it will print out the second to last entry as shown here:

```
friends = ["Joey", "Chandler", "Ross", "Phoebe", "Rachel", "Monica"]

print(friends[-2])
```

Output:

Rachel

There are other variations involved here, as well. You can call the items from a specific starting point. Using the same list above, let's assume we wish the prompt to print out the last three entries only. We can do that easily by using the starting index number of the value we wish to print. In this case, it would be the index number '3':

```
friends = ["Joey", "Chandler", "Ross", "Phoebe", "Rachel", "Monica"]

print(friends[3:])
```

Output:

```
['Phoebe', 'Rachel', 'Monica']
```

You can also limit what you wish to see on the screen further by setting a range of index numbers. The first number, the one before the colon, represents the starting point. The number that you input after the colon is the endpoint. In our list of friends, we have a range from zero to five, let us narrow our results down a little:

```
friends = ["Joey", "Chandler", "Ross", "Phoebe", "Rachel", "Monica"]

print(friends[2:5])
```

Output:

> ['Ross', 'Phoebe', 'Rachel']

Remember, the last index number will not be printed; otherwise, the result would have also shown the last entry.

You can modify the values of a list quite easily. Suppose you wish to change the entry at index number five of the above list, and you wish to change the entry from 'Monica' to 'Geller,' this is how you would do so:

> friends = ["Joey", "Chandler", "Ross", "Phoebe", "Rachel", "Monica"]
>
> friends[5] = "Geller"
>
> print(friends)

Output:

> ['Joey', 'Chandler', 'Ross', 'Phoebe', 'Rachel', 'Geller']

It is that easy! You can use lists with loops and conditional statements to iterate over random elements and use the ones which are most suitable to the situation. Practice a little, and you should soon get the hang of them.

What about if you wish to add numbers or values to the existing lists? Do we have to scroll all the way up and continue adding numbers manually? No! There are things called methods, which you can access at any given time to carry out various operations.

Here's a screengrab to show just how many options you have available to you once you press the '.' Key:

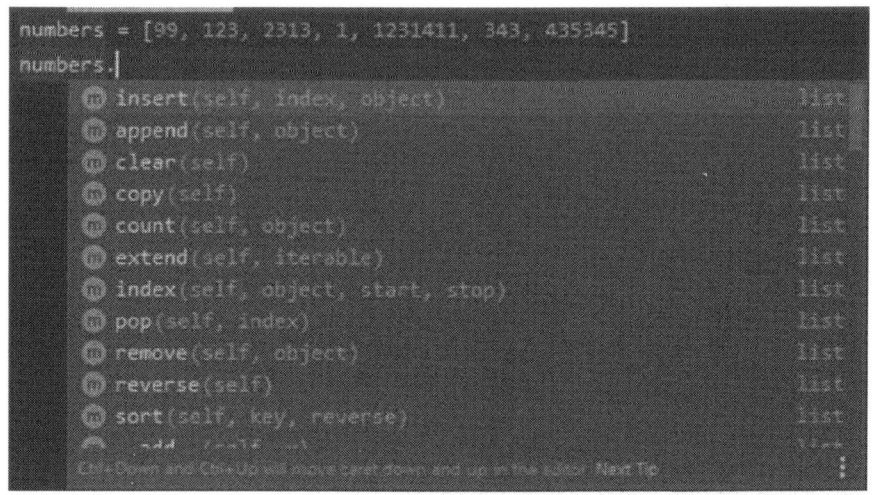

```
numbers = [99, 123, 2313, 1, 1231411, 343, 435345]
numbers.
    insert(self, index, object)                list
    append(self, object)                       list
    clear(self)                                list
    copy(self)                                 list
    count(self, object)                        list
    extend(self, iterable)                     list
    index(self, object, start, stop)           list
    pop(self, index)                           list
    remove(self, object)                       list
    reverse(self)                              list
    sort(self, key, reverse)                   list
```

We will not be talking about all of these, but we will briefly look at some basic methods that every programmer should know.

Straight away, the 'append' method is what we use to add values. Simply type in the name of the list you wish to recall, followed by ".append" to let the program know you wish to add value. Type in the value, and that is it!

The problem with using the append method is that it adds the item randomly. What if you wish to add value to a specific index number? To do that, you will need to use the insert method.

Using an insert method, you will need to do this:

```
numbers = [99, 123, 2313, 1, 1231411, 343, 435345]

numbers.insert(2, 999)

print(numbers)
```

Output:

```
[99, 123, 999, 2313, 1, 1231411, 343, 435345]
```

The number was added right where I wanted. Remember to use an index position that is valid. If you are unsure, use the len() function to recall how many components are within a list. That should then allow you to know the index positions available.

You can also remove items from a list as well. Simply use the remove() method and input the number/value you wish to remove. Please note that if your list has more than one value that is exactly the same, this command will only remove the first instance only.

Let us assume you are presented with a list of mixed entries. There is no order that they follow. The numbers are just everywhere, disregarding the order. If you wish, you can sort the entire list to look more appealing by using the sort() method.

```
numbers = [99, 123, 2313, 1, 1231411, 99, 435345]
numbers.sort()
print(numbers)
```

Output:

```
[1, 99, 99, 123, 2313, 435345, 1231411]
```

You know, you can also have it the other way around by using the reverse() method. Try it!

To completely empty a list, you can use the clear() method. This specific method will not require you to pass any argument as a parameter. There are other methods such as pop() (which takes away the last item on the list only) that you should experiment with. Do not worry; it will not crash your system down or expose it to threats. The IDE is like a safe zone for programmers to test out various methods, programs, and scripts. Feel free and feel at ease when charting new waters.

Tuples

As funny as the name may be, tuples are pretty much like lists. The only major difference is that these are used when you do not wish for certain specialized values to change throughout the program. Once you create a tuple, it cannot be modified or changed later on.

Tuples are represented by parenthesis (). If you try and access the methods, you will no longer have access to the methods that you did when you were using lists. These are secure and used only in situations where you are certain you do not wish to change, modify, add, or remove items. Normally, we will be using lists, but it is great to know we have a safe way to do things as well.

Dictionaries

Unlike tuples and lists, dictionaries are different. To begin with, they work with "key-value pairs," which sounds confusing, I know. However, let us look at what exactly a dictionary is and how we can call, create, and modify the same.

To help us with the explanation, we have our imaginary friend here named James, who has graciously accepted to volunteer for the exercise. We then took some information from him such as his name, email, age, the car he drives, and we ended up with this information:

Name – James

Age – 58

Email – james@domain.com

Car – Tesla T1

What we have here are called key pairs. To represent the same within a dictionary, all we need is to create one. How do we do that? Let's have a look.

friend = {

"name": "James",

"age": 30,

"email": "james@domain.com",

"car": "Tesla T1"

}

We define a dictionary using {} braces. Add each pair as shown above with a colon in the middle. Use a comma to separate items from one another. Now, you have a dictionary called 'friend' and you can access the information easily.

Now, to call up the email, we will use square brackets as shown here:

```
friend = {
"name": "James",
"age": 30,
"email": "james@domain.com",
"car": "Tesla T1"
}
print(friend["email"])
```

Output:

james@domain.com

Similarly, try recalling the other elements to try it out yourself. Once again, I remind you that Python is case sensitive. If you recall 'age' as 'Age', it will not work at all.

Suppose you wish to recall an item without knowing the key pairs within a dictionary. If you type in a key named 'dob', the program is going to return an error like this:

Traceback (most recent call last):

```
    File "C:/Users/Programmer/PycharmProjects/
PFB/Lists2.py", line 7, in <module>
print(friend["dob"])
KeyError: 'dob'
```

There is a way you can check for values without the program screaming back at you with red/pink fonts. Use the .get() method instead, and the program will simply say 'None,' which represents the absence of value.

You can also give any keypair, that may not have existed before, a default value as well.

```
friend = {
"name": "James",
"age": 30,
"email": "james@domain.com",
"car": "Tesla T1"
}
print(friend.get("dob", "1, 1, 1900"))
Output:
1, 1, 1900
```

Unlike tuples, you can add, modify, or change values within a dictionary. I have already shown you how to do that with lists, but just for demonstration purposes, here's one way you can do that.

```
friend["age"] = 60

print(friend["age"])

Output:

60
```

CHAPTER - 4

FUN WITH LOOPS, LOOPS, LOOPS...

What Is A Loop?

Loops are going to be another great topic that we are able to work with when it comes to Python. Loops are a good way to clean up some of the code that you want to work with so that you can make sure that enough shows up in your code, without having to write out as many lines. For example, if you have a code that you would like to work with that lists out the numbers gong one from fifty, you do not want to actually write out that many lines of code in the process. You can work with these loops instead to make sure that it is able to write out the lines, but it is really just a short amount of code. These loops are then able to hold onto a ton of information and will only use a few lines of code to make it happen.

There are a lot of things and a ton of data that we are then able to add into the loop, but you will find that these are actually pretty easy for us to work with anyway. These loops are going to be there to tell the compiler that it needs to continue reading through one or two lines of code over and over again until the conditions that you add into it are met.

So, if you are working on a program where you ask the compiler to write out numbers that go from one to ten, then the loop will tell your compiler to read through the numbers going from one to ten, then the loop will be set to go through the same line of code until it reaches ten. This can simplify the code while making sure that you are still able to get the things done that you would like.

When you work with all of these loops, it is important to remember to set up so that you have the condition in place before you ever try to work on the program. If you just go through and write out your loop, without adding in the condition that is needed, then the loop will start, but it will not know when to stop. The loop will just keep going through itself and will freeze the computer. Double-check before you run the program that the condition is in place before starting.

As you go through and create some of your own code with Python, there is going to be a few different loop types that you are able to work with. There are actually going to be many options, but we need to focus on the three main ones known as the while loop, the for loop, and the nested loop.

Using For Loops

The while loop can help us out with a lot of the different things that you want to accomplish when you are working on loops in this part of the code. In addition to handling some of the work with loops that the while loop can do, it is possible to work with them for a loop. When you are working with the for loops, you are working with the method that is considered the more traditional out of the two, and you can even make this the option that you use all of the time.

When you work with one of the for loops, your user will not go in and provide information to the code and then the loops start. Rather, with the for loop, Python is set up to go through an iteration in the order that it shows up on the screen. There is no need for input from the user because it just continues through the iteration until the end occurs. An example of a code that shows how a for loop works is the following:

Measure some strings:

```
words = ['apple', 'mango', 'banana', 'orange']
for w in words:
    print(w, len(w))
```

Write this code into your compiler and then execute it. The for loop is going to make sure that all the words in the line above it are shown up on the screen, exactly how you wrote them out. If you want them in a different order, you need to do that as you work on the code, not later on. You can add in any words or other information that you want to show up in this kind of loop, just make sure that you have it in the right order from the beginning.

Using While Loop

The first type of loop that we are going to work on is the while loop. This loop is one that you can choose for your code when you know the specific number of times you want the code to cycle through that loop. You would use it to finish counting to ten for example. This one will need to have a condition, in the end, to make sure that it stops at the right point and doesn't keep going forever. It is also a good option if you want to ensure that your loop occurs at least one time before it moves on to the next part of the code. A good example of the while loop is the following code:

#calculation of simple interest. Ask the user to input the principal, rate of interest, number of years.

```
counter = 1

while(counter <= 3):

principal = int(input("Enter the principal amount:"))

numberofyeras = int(input("Enter the number of years:"))

rateofinterest = float(input("Enter the rate of interest:"))

simpleinterest = principal * numberofyears * rateofinterest/100

print("Simple interest = %.2f" %simpleinterest)

#increase the counter by 1

counter = counter + 1

print("You have calculated simple interest for 3 time!")
```

With the example that we did above, you will find that the user is able to place in the information that makes the most sense for them and the program. The code is then going to give them the interest rate based on the information that the user provides to it. For this one, we are going to set up the while at the beginning of the code and then told it to only go through the loop a maximum of three times. You will then be able to change up the code as well to make sure that it will go through the loops as many times as you would like.

Nested Structures

We can also finish this out with a look at how the nested loop is going to work. This is a more advanced type of loop that is going to combine two of the other loop types together in order to get them to run at the same time. There are a number of instances where you can work with this nested loop, and it is often going to depend on the kind of code that you would like to complete and what you are hoping to get out of it.

The third type of loop that we are able to work with here is going to be known as the nested loop. Any time that you are working with this loop, you are basically going to take one of the other types of loops and then you will place it inside of a different loop. Both of these loops will end up running in the code at the same time, and they will both continue on until they are complete. There are a number of situations where you will want to focus on these nested loops to help you finish your code.

For example, you may find that you would like to work on a nested loop that can create a new multiplication table, the nested loop is going to be a good one to get it done. The code that we need to use in order to make this one work for our needs and to see how a nested loop is going to work will include:

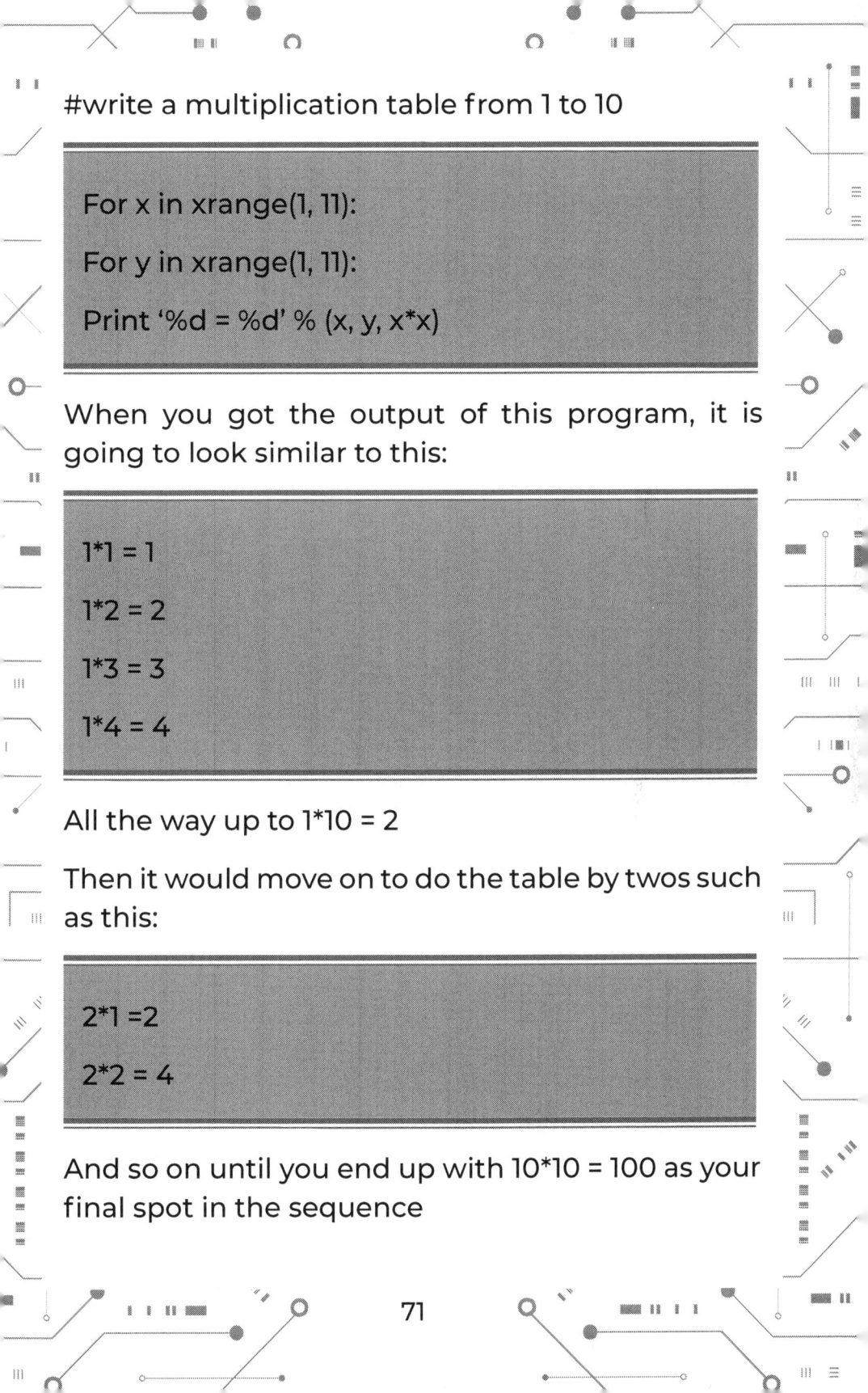

#write a multiplication table from 1 to 10

```
For x in xrange(1, 11):

For y in xrange(1, 11):

Print '%d = %d' % (x, y, x*x)
```

When you got the output of this program, it is going to look similar to this:

```
1*1 = 1

1*2 = 2

1*3 = 3

1*4 = 4
```

All the way up to 1*10 = 2

Then it would move on to do the table by twos such as this:

```
2*1 =2

2*2 = 4
```

And so on until you end up with 10*10 = 100 as your final spot in the sequence

Any time you need to get one loop to run inside another loop, the nested loop will be able to help you get this done. You can combine together the for loop, the while loop, or each combination based on what you want to get done inside the code. But it definitely shows you how much time and space inside the code that these loops can save. The multiplication table above only took up four lines to write out and you got a huge table. Think of how long this would take if you had to write out each part of the table!

The for loop, the while loop, and the nested loop are going to be some of the most common loops that a beginner is able to focus on when it is time to write out their own codes in this language. You are able to use these codes to make sure that you can get a ton done in some of the programs that you have chosen, without having to focus as much on writing out a ton of lines. You are even able to do this in a manner that will make sure that certain parts of the code will read through themselves again, without you having to rewrite it at all. There are many times when you will want to handle writing loops in your code, and learning how to make each one work can help make your code stronger.

Errors

Syntax Error

When a Python interpreter encounters an error in the program, it terminates the program and displays an error message to the user. Syntax represents the structure of a program and the rules of declaring that structure. If there is a single error, Python will quit and you will not be able to run the program.

If you're new to programming, you may spend a few days tracking syntax errors. Once you become familiar with the language, however, you will make fewer errors, and it will be easy to track them.

Runtime Error

A runtime errors occurs after running the program. That is, the error will not show up until you run the program. Runtime errors are commonly known as exceptions as they indicate something has already happened.

Semantic Errors

If a program has a semantic error, the program will run successfully and the Python interpreter will not generate the error message. The program will run up to the end but will not perform the task it was meant to do.

To correct semantic errors, you have to look at the program output and work backwards by analyzing what each output was supposed to do.

CHAPTER - 5
BETTER THE QUESTION BETTER THE ANSWER: IF STATEMENT

Comparison operators are special operators in Python programming language that evaluate to either True or False state of the condition. Program flow control refers to a way in which a programmer explicitly species the order of execution of program code lines. Normally, flow control involves placing some condition (s) on the program code lines. The most basic form of these conditional statements is the if statement. This one is going to provide us with some problems right from the beginning. But knowing a bit about it will help us to get the if else and other control statements to work the way that we want.

To start, the if statement is going to take the input of the user, and compare it to the condition that you set. If the condition is met here, then the code will continue on, usually showing some kind of message that you set up in the code.

However, if the input does not match up with the condition that you set the returned value will be False.

The If structures

This is the simplest decision structure. It includes a statement or block of statements on the "True" path only.

The general form of the Python statement is

if Boolean_Expression:

Here goes

a statement or block of statements

In the next example, the message "You are underage!" displays only when the user enters a value less than 18. Nothing is displayed when the user enters a value that is greater than or equal to 18.

```
file_13 _1 a

age = int(input( "Enter your age: " ))

if age < 18:

print( "You are underage!" )
```

The If-Then-Else Structure

The "if...else" statement will execute the body of if in the case that the tests condition is True. Should the if...else tests expression evaluate to false, the body of the else will be executed. Program blocks are denoted by indentation. The if...else provides more maneuverability when placing conditions on the code. The if...else syntax

if test condition:

Statements

else:

Statements

A program that checks whether a number is positive or negative

Start IDLE.

Navigate to the File menu and click New Window.

Type the following:

```
number_mine=-56
if(number_mine<0):
print(number_mine, "The number is negative")
else:
print(number_mine, "The number is a positive number")
```

Assignment

Write a Python program that uses if..else statement to perform the following

1. Given number=9, write a program that tests and displays whether the number is even or odd.

2. Given marks=76, write a program that tests and displays whether the marks are above pass mark or not bearing in mind that pass mark is 50.

3. Given number=78, write a program that tests and displays whether the number is even or odd.

4. Given marks=27, write a program that tests and displays whether the marks are above pass mark or not bearing in mind that pass mark is 50.

Assignment

Write a program that accepts age input from the user, explicitly coverts the age into integer data types, then uses if...else flow control to tests whether the person is underage or not, the legal age is 21. Include comments and indentation to improve the readability of the program.

Other follow up work: Write programs in Python using if statement only to perform the following:

1. Given number=7, write a program to test and display only even numbers.

2. Given number1=8, number2=13, write a program to only display if the sum is less than 10.

3. Given count_int=57, write a program that tests if the count is more than 45 and displays, the count is above the recommended number.

4. Given marks=34, write a program that tests if the marks are less than 50 and display the message, the score is below average.

5. Given marks=78, write a program that tests if the marks are more than 50 and display the message, great performance.

6. Given number=88, write a program that tests if the number is an odd number and displays the message, Yes it is an odd number.

7. Given number=24, write a program that tests and displays if the number is even.

8. Given number =21, write a program that tests if the number is odd and displays the string, Yes it is an odd number.

The If-elif structure

Now think of scenarios where we need to evaluate multiple conditions, not just one, not just two but three and more. Think of where you have to choose team member, if not Richard, then Mercy, if not Richard and Mercy then Brian, if not Richard, Mercy, and Brian then Yvonne. Real-life scenarios may involve several choices/conditions that have to be captured when writing a program.

Remember that the elif simply refers to else if

and is intended to allow for checking of multiple expressions. The if the block is evaluated first, then elif block(s), before the else block. In this case, the else block is more of a fallback option when all other conditions return false. Important to remember, despite several blocks available in if..elif..else only one block will be executed.. if...elif..else Syntax:

if test expression:

Body of if

elif test expression:

Body of elif

else:

Body of else

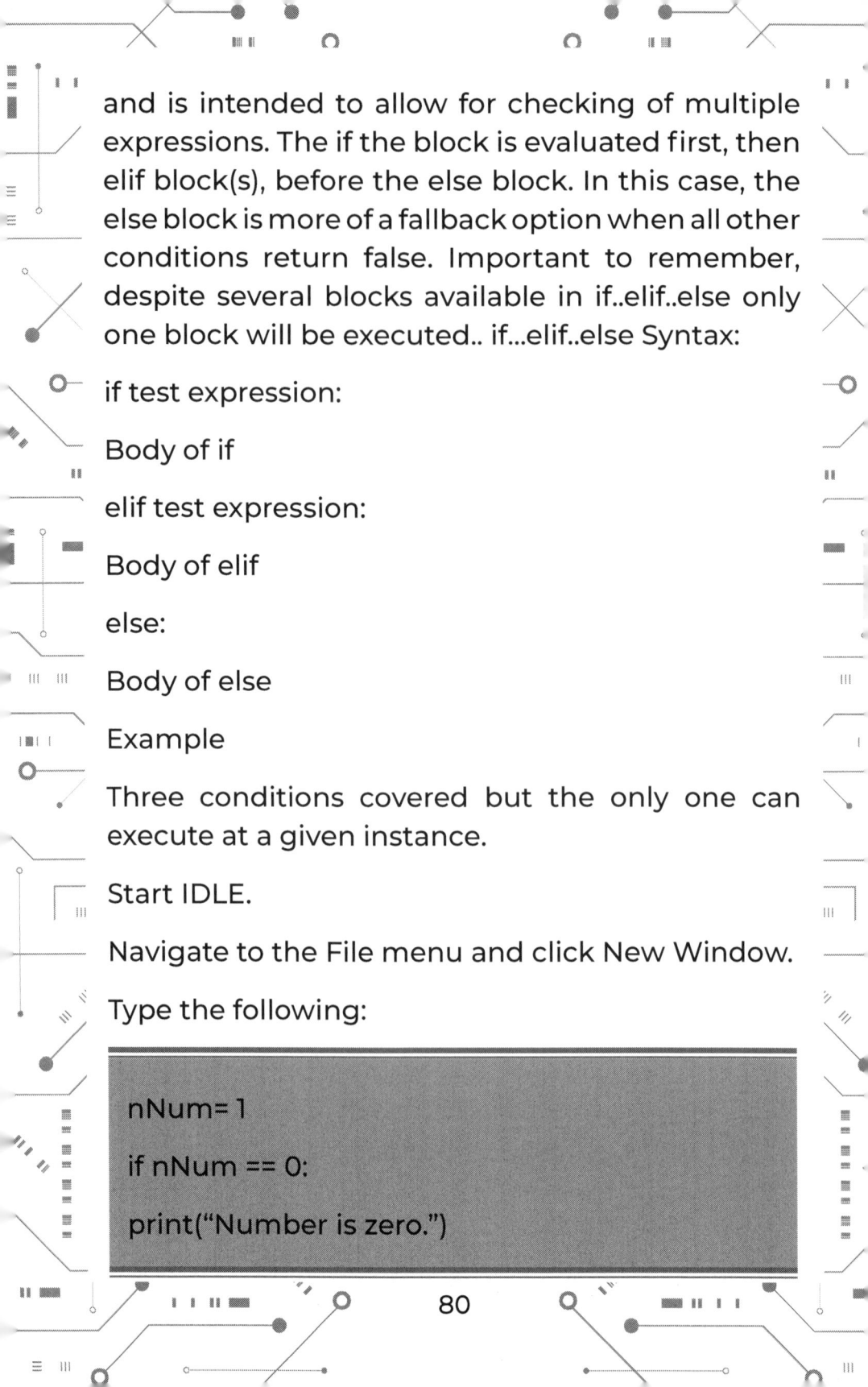

Example

Three conditions covered but the only one can execute at a given instance.

Start IDLE.

Navigate to the File menu and click New Window.

Type the following:

```
nNum= 1

if nNum == 0:

print("Number is zero.")
```

```
elif nNum > 0:

    print("Number is a positive.")

else:

    print("Number is a negative.")
```

Incidental using the If Statement

There are many things that you can do with values and variables, but the ability to compare them is something that will make it much easier for you to try and use Python. It is something that people will be able to do no matter what type of values that they have, and they can make sure that they are doing it in the right way so that their program will appear to be as smooth-running as possible.

To compare your variables is one of the many options that Python offers you, and the best way to do it is through an "if statement."

Now, you can create a new file. This is what you will need to be able to do. Do not forget indentation!

Here is the way that an incidental will look:

```
apples=6

bus = "yellow"
```

```
if apples == 0:

print ("Where are the apples?" )

else:

print ("Did you know that busses are %s?", bus)
```

Run the code through your python program. It will look like this.

```
Did you know that busses are yellow?
```

The easiest way to understand why the output looked like this is because the apples were not included with the variation. There were not zero apples, and that was something that created a problem with the code. For that reason, it wasn't put in the output because there was no way to do it and no way to make it look again.

To make sure that you are going to be able to use it with a not statement, you can use another if statement in combination with that not.

```
if not apples == 0
```

Now, you can try to run the code again through the program that you created.

Did you know that busses are yellow?

Both of the things that you wrote in the code are included with the statements, and then, you will be able to try different things. If you do not want to write out the not statement, you can simply use the "!"

```
apples=5
if apples!= 0:
    print("How about apples!")
```

When there is an input in your program, such as the number of apples that someone wants or a fact that they have that they can teach you about, the output will look the same. Either they will get a statement about the apples, or they will get a statement about the bus being yellow. If there are no apples that are put into the equation, then you will have the output show up as "Where are the apples"

The conditionals that you use are made up of simple expressions. When you break them down into even smaller pieces, it is easy to understand how they can be used and what you will be able to do with the expressions that you have in the things that you do. It will also give you the chance to be able to show that there is so much more than what you initially had with the variables and values.

Nested if Statements in Python

Sometimes it happens that a condition exists but there are more sub-conditions that need to be covered and this leads to a concept known as nesting. The amount of statements to nests is not limited but you should exercise caution as you will realize nesting can lead to user errors when writing code. Nesting can also complicate maintaining of code. The only indentation can help determine the level of nesting.

Example

Start IDLE.

Navigate to the File menu and click New Window.

Type the following:

```
my_charact=str(input("Type a character here either 'a', 'b' or 'c':"))

if (my_charact='a'):

if(my_charact='a'):

print("a")

else if:

(my_charact='b')

print("b")
```

```
else:

    print("c")
```

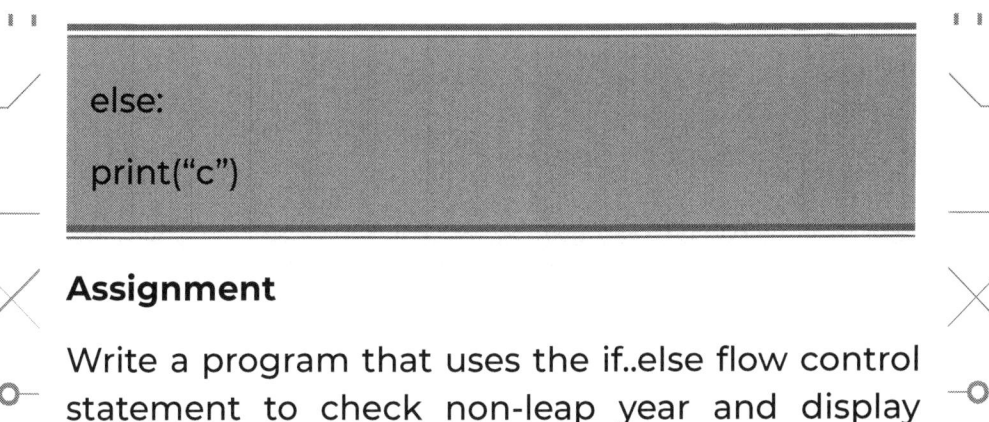

Assignment

Write a program that uses the if..else flow control statement to check non-leap year and display either scenario. Include comments and indentation to enhance the readability of the program.

Absolutes

There is a way to create the conditionals so that there is a block of codes that will show you whether or not there is a conditional, and it has something that it can do even if the conditional is not true and cannot be verified with the different things that you do.

That is where the absolute conditionals come into play.

You will need to see whether or not there are different things that you can put in.

Create the variable

apples

Now, you will need to put the input in with the different things that you have created a version of the file that you saved.

```
print "What is your age?"

age = input()
```

That is the way that you will be able to see how old someone is. But, how exactly does that relate to the number of apples you have?

It doesn't, it just shows you how the variable works so that people can put things in.

You'll create

```
apples = input ("What number of apples are there?/n")
```

That is the easiest part of it and will help you to create the variable that you need for the rest of it.

```
if apples == 1:

print ("I don't know what to do with just one apple!")
```

You'll get an error though because applesis actually just a string and you need to make it an integer.

Simple:

```
int(string)
```

Now it will look like this:

```
apples = input("What number of apples are there?/n")
apples = int(apples)
if apples == 1:
    print ("I don't know what to do with just one apple!")
```

Put this whole string into your file or change the wording around a bit so that you can figure out what you want to do with it (that is truly great practice for you). When you have put it in, run it through.

The code will work because you created a variable, you added different elements to it, and you allowed for the input of the "apples" in the sequence so that you would be able to show how things worked with it.

This was one of the greatest ways that you could do new things, and it also allowed you the chance to be able to try new things so that you were doing more with it. While you are creating strings of integers, you will need to make sure that you are transforming them into integers instead of simple strings so that you can make sure that they show up and there are no error codes.

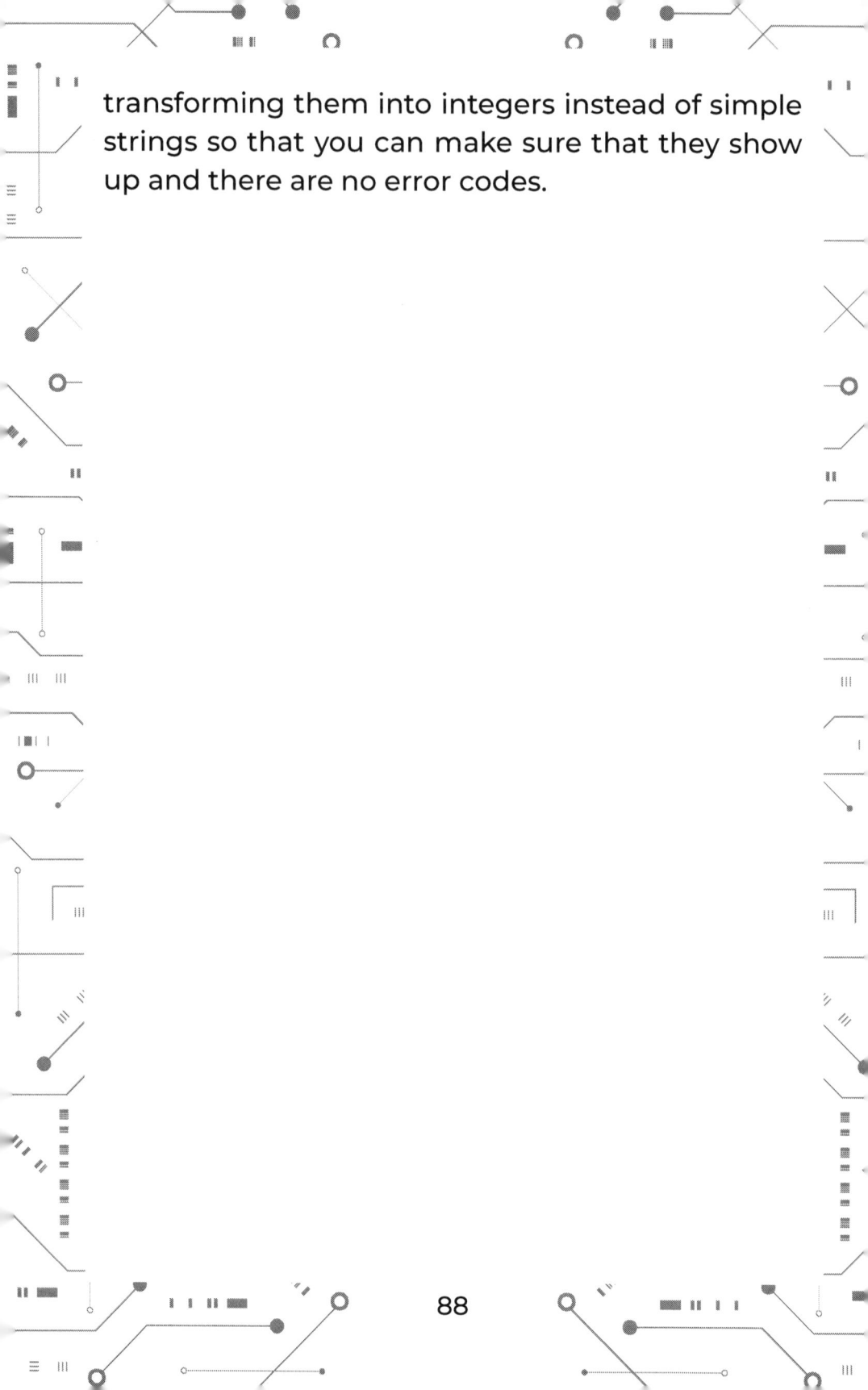

CHAPTER - 6
THE TURTLE GRAPHICS OF YOUR DREAMS

What is Turtle

Turtle is a very handy Python tool. It is a module —we shall discuss what a module later— that helps us draw in Python.

Before we can use the turtle module, we need to import it. To import a module into Python, we use import <module name>

```
>>> import turtle
>>>
```

It looks like nothing happened; this is a good thing since we did not get an error. For example, if you try to import a module that does not exist, Python will return an error as shown below:

```
>>> import unknown_module
Traceback (most recent call last):
  File "<pyshell#2>", line 1, in <module>
    import unknown_module
ModuleNotFoundError: No module named 'unknown_module'
```

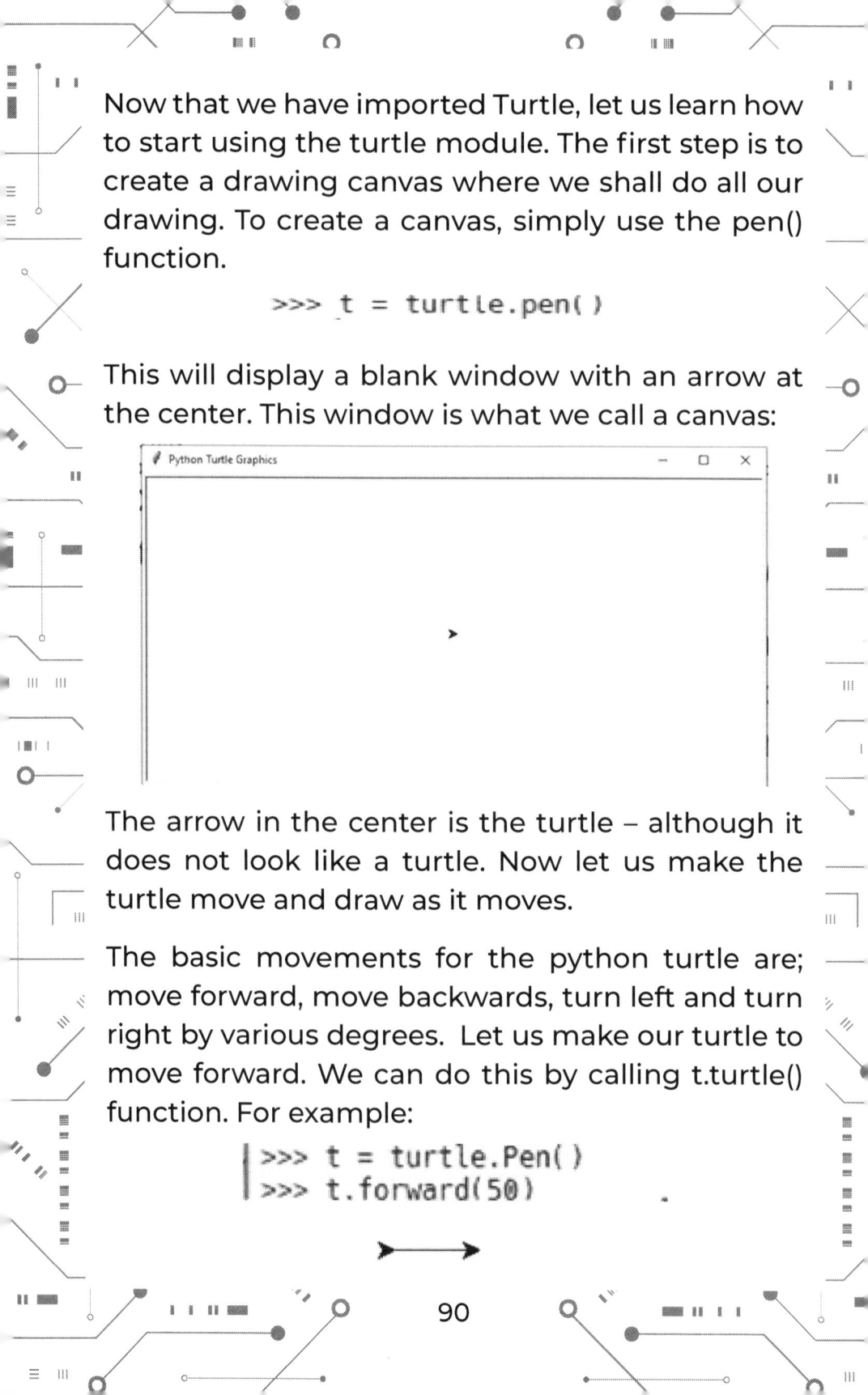

Now that we have imported Turtle, let us learn how to start using the turtle module. The first step is to create a drawing canvas where we shall do all our drawing. To create a canvas, simply use the pen() function.

```
>>> t = turtle.pen()
```

This will display a blank window with an arrow at the center. This window is what we call a canvas:

The arrow in the center is the turtle – although it does not look like a turtle. Now let us make the turtle move and draw as it moves.

The basic movements for the python turtle are; move forward, move backwards, turn left and turn right by various degrees. Let us make our turtle to move forward. We can do this by calling t.turtle() function. For example:

```
>>> t = turtle.Pen()
>>> t.forward(50)
```

From the above command, we tell Python to make t, which in this case refers to the turtle, to move forward by 50 pixels or by 50 points. In a computer, a pixel is the smallest point on the computer screen –your computer screen consists of very tiny dots called as pixels. This is an example of a highly magnified number on a computer screen.

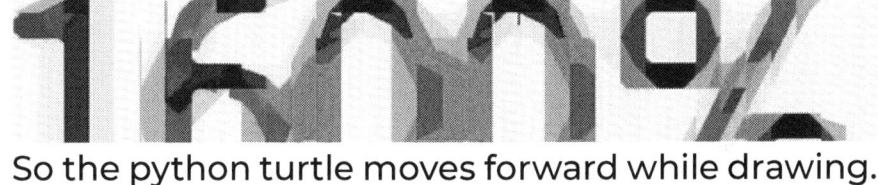

So the python turtle moves forward while drawing. Let us make it go to the left using t.left() function.

```
>>> t.left(90)
```

This tells the turtle to move left by 90 degrees. Now, if we want the turtle to turn right, we just change it to right(90). The diagram below shows which directions the turtle will take after angle variations.

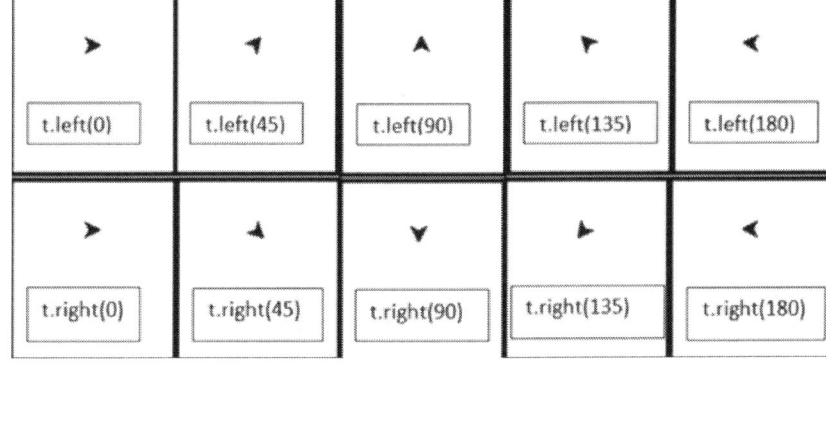

t.left(0)	t.left(45)	t.left(90)	t.left(135)	t.left(180)
t.right(0)	t.right(45)	t.right(90)	t.right(135)	t.right(180)

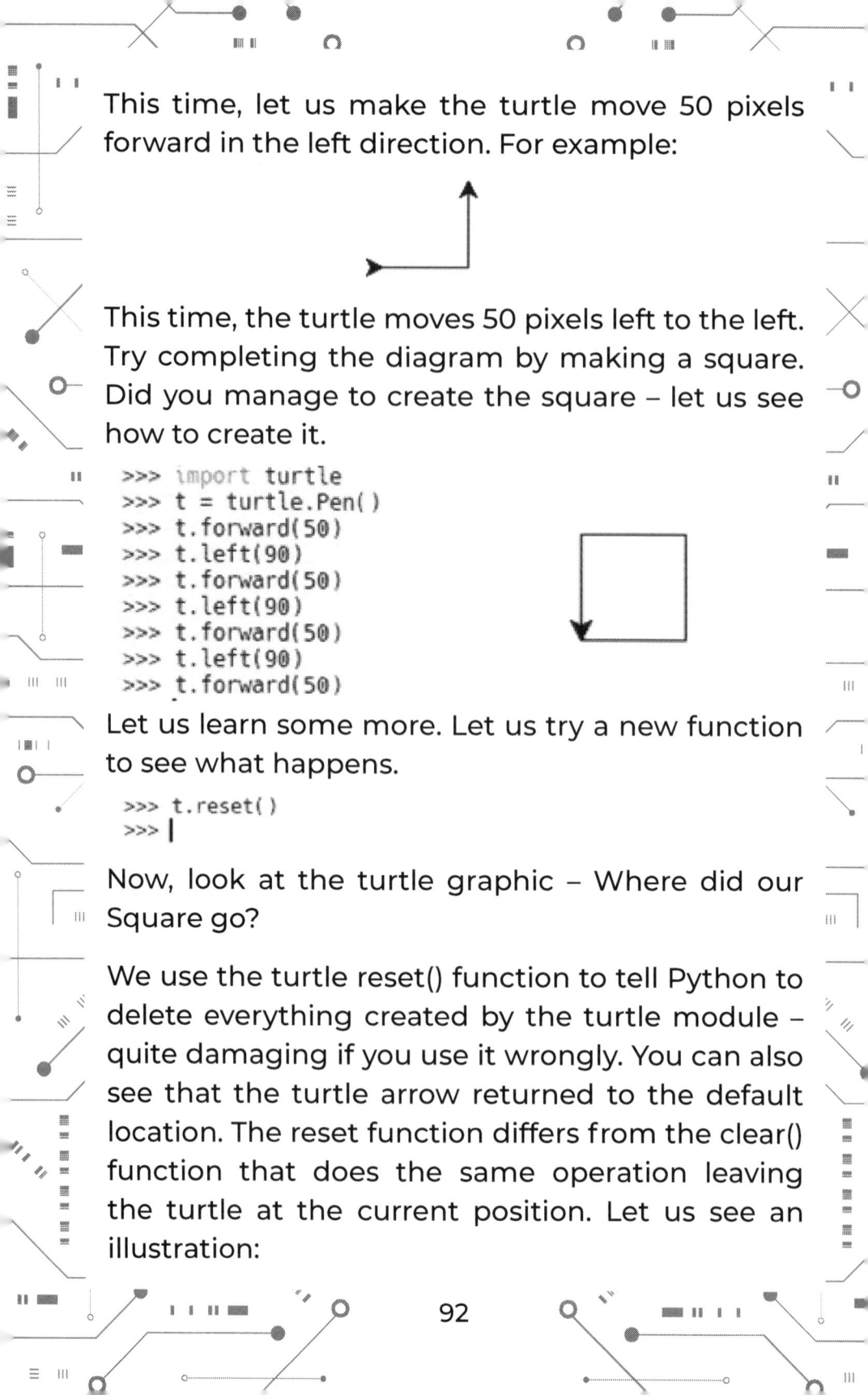

This time, let us make the turtle move 50 pixels forward in the left direction. For example:

This time, the turtle moves 50 pixels left to the left. Try completing the diagram by making a square. Did you manage to create the square – let us see how to create it.

```
>>> import turtle
>>> t = turtle.Pen()
>>> t.forward(50)
>>> t.left(90)
>>> t.forward(50)
>>> t.left(90)
>>> t.forward(50)
>>> t.left(90)
>>> t.forward(50)
```

Let us learn some more. Let us try a new function to see what happens.

```
>>> t.reset()
>>>
```

Now, look at the turtle graphic – Where did our Square go?

We use the turtle reset() function to tell Python to delete everything created by the turtle module – quite damaging if you use it wrongly. You can also see that the turtle arrow returned to the default location. The reset function differs from the clear() function that does the same operation leaving the turtle at the current position. Let us see an illustration:

```
>>> t.clear()
>>>
```

What if we wanted our turtle to do a moonwalk, which is moving backwards while drawing? To get the python turtle to move backwards, we use the backward function(). For example:

```
>>> t.backward(200)
>>>
```

What if we wanted the turtle to go up or down without making any drawings. What would we do then? First, reset your turtle using the reset function. To make the turtle move up without drawing, we can use the up() function. The up() function makes the turtle move upwards by 30 pixels.

To make the turtle go down without drawing, we use the down() function. This also makes the turtle go down by 30 pixels. If you want to hide the turtle so that you can see what you have created, you can use the hideturtle() function.

Diagrams with straight lines are not the only thing you can create using turtle. To create a circle, we use the circle() function while entering the radius of the circle –the operation of entering values in a function is called parameter passing.

Here is how we create a circle – reset the turtle first before creating a circle:

```
>>> import turtle
>>> t = turtle.Pen()
>>> t.circle(60)
```

This time, look at the following lines of code and try to guess what they do. If you get them right, Pizza is on me

```
>>> t.reset()
>>> t.color("Green")
>>> t.circle(100)
>>> t.hideturtle()
```

Let us find out what the above lines of code actually do. The first line resets the turtle, the second line sets the color of the turtle to Green, the third creates a circle with a radius of 100, and the third line hides the turtle – I know I owe you a pizza🍕.

We change the color of the turtle by simply using the color() function and passing the name of the color we want as the parameter.

We can also fill the drawing we created using the begin_tfill() and end_fill() functions. Let us fill our circle with the color Green.

```
>>> t.begin_fill()
>>> t.circle(100)
>>> t.end_fill()
```

We do not need to pass the color green in the begin_fill() function as we are already using color green – but in case we want another color, we have to enter the color.

NOTE: You MUST end the fill for the filling to be completed. Again, the filling works only if you close your drawing to prevent the color of the drawing from leaking out in the canvas.

Exercise

Try out the following exercise:

Question 1

Draw a red rectangle of length 40 pixels and 80 pixels. You should first import the turtle module, create canvas named my_pen, then draw the rectangle, and finally hide the turtle.

Question 2

Write a python program that creates three circles one inside the other. The first circle should have a radius of 60 pixels, the second one should have a radius of 40 pixels, and the last one a radius of 30 pixels. Each circle should have a different color fill from the others.

Question 3

Write a program that creates box that does not have corners as shown below:

Solutions

Let us look at sample solutions for the above questions – you can solve them in any way you find appropriate.

Solution 1

```
>>> import turtle
>>> my_pen = turtle.Pen()
>>> my_pen.color("Red")
>>> my_pen.forward(80)
>>> my_pen.left(90)
>>> my_pen.forward(40)
>>> my_pen.left(90)
>>> my_pen.forward(80)
>>> my_pen.left(90)
>>> my_pen.forward(40)
>>> my_pen.hideturtle()
```

Solution 2

```
>>> import turtle
>>> C = turtle.Pen()
>>> C.fillcolor("blue")
>>> C.begin_fill()
>>> C.circle(60)
>>> C.end_fill()
>>> C.fillcolor("yellow")
>>> C.begin_fill()
>>> C.Circle(40)
Traceback (most recent call last):
  File "<pyshell#8>", line 1, in <module>
    C.Circle(40)
AttributeError: 'Turtle' object has no attribute 'Circle'
>>> C.circle(40)
>>> C.end_fill()
>>> C.fillcolor("red")
>>> C.begin_fill()
>>> C.circle(30)
>>> C.end_fill()
>>> C.hideturtle()
```

Solution 3

```
>>> import turtle
>>> box = turtle.Pen()
>>> box.up()
>>> box.forward(10)
>>> box.down()
>>> box.forward(50)
>>> box.up()
>>> box.forward(10)
>>> box.left(90)
>>> box.forward(10)
>>> box.down()
>>> box.forward(50)
>>> box.up()
>>> box.forward(10)
>>> box.left(90)
>>> box.forward(10)
>>> box.down()
>>> box.forward(50)
>>> box.up()
>>> box.forward(10)
>>> box.left(90)
>>> box.forward(10)
>>> box.down()
>>> box.forward(50)
>>> box.hideturtle()
```

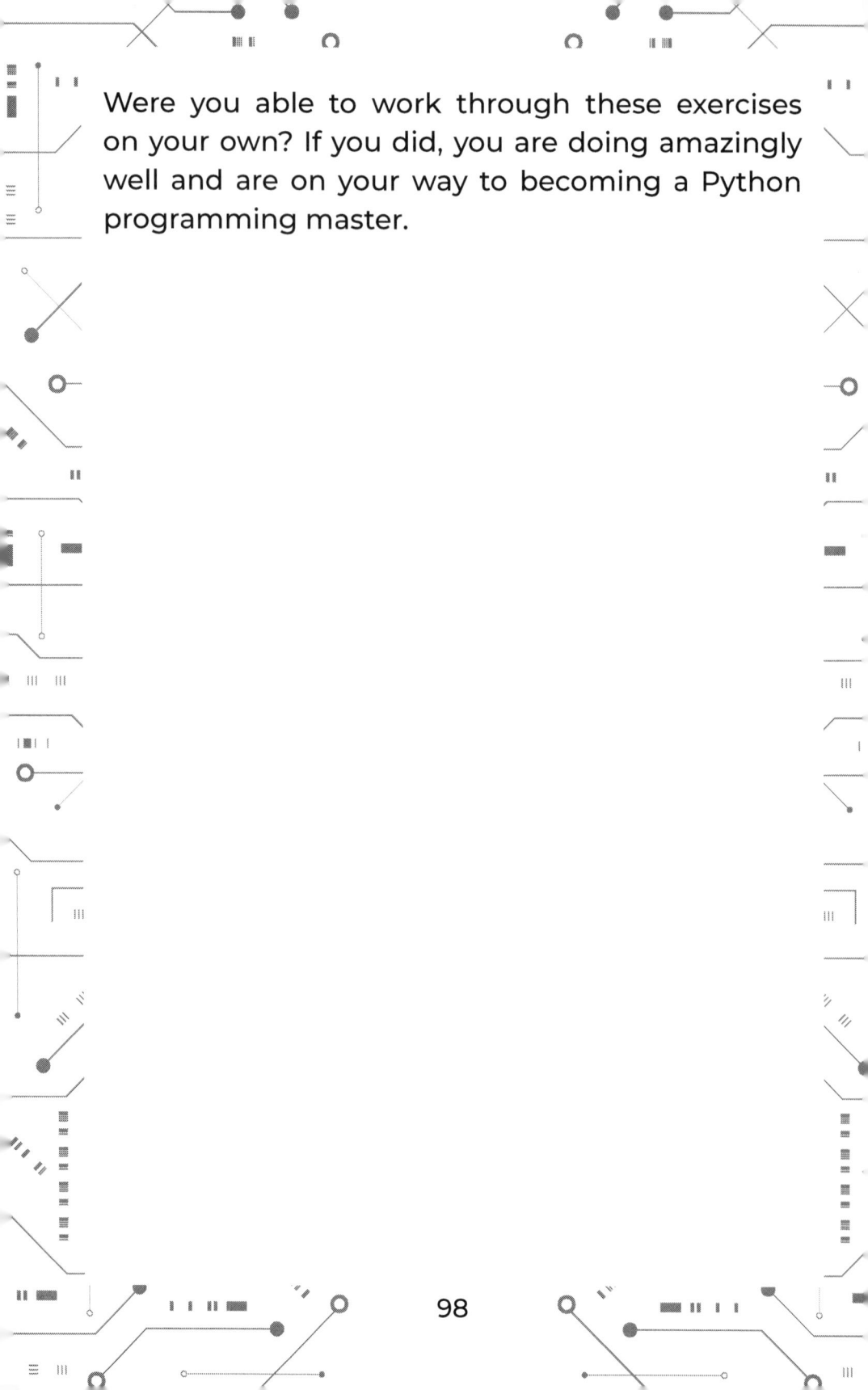

Were you able to work through these exercises on your own? If you did, you are doing amazingly well and are on your way to becoming a Python programming master.

CHAPTER - 7
WORKING WITH PYTHON FUNCTIONS

In this section, we are going to learn a very important programming technique known as Reduce, Reuse, and Recycle that falls under the category of functions in programming.

Loops are very effective if we are repeating an action many times over. However, if we want to repeat lines of code, we must use functions. A function is a block of code that contains other code within it to perform a task. We have used functions before.

In the background, without functions, we would have to enter a code like this every time we need to print out something on the screen:

```python
import collections as _collections
import re
import sys as _sys
import types as _types
from io import StringIO as _StringIO

__all__ = ["pprint","pformat","isreadable","isrecursive","saferepr",
           "PrettyPrinter"]


def pprint(object, stream=None, indent=1, width=80, depth=None, *,
           compact=False):
    """Pretty-print a Python object to a stream [default is sys.stdout]."""
    printer = PrettyPrinter(
        stream=stream, indent=indent, width=width, depth=depth,
        compact=compact)
    printer.pprint(object)

def pformat(object, indent=1, width=80, depth=None, *, compact=False):
    """Format a Python object into a pretty-printed representation."""
    return PrettyPrinter(indent=indent, width=width, depth=depth,
                         compact=compact).pformat(object)

def saferepr(object):
    """Version of repr() which can handle recursive data structures."""
    return _safe_repr(object, {}, None, 0)[0]

def isreadable(object):
    """Determine if saferepr(object) is readable by eval()."""
    return _safe_repr(object, {}, None, 0)[1]

def isrecursive(object):
    """Determine if object requires a recursive representation."""
    return _safe_repr(object, {}, None, 0)[2]

class _safe_key:
    """Helper function for key functions when sorting unorderable objects.

    The wrapped-object will fallback to a Py2.x style comparison for
    unorderable types (sorting first comparing the type name and then by
    the obj ids).  Does not work recursively, so dict.items() must have
    _safe_key applied to both the key and the value.

    """

    __slots__ = ['obj']

    def __init__(self, obj):
```

Once we create a function, we can then use it to perform the specified task whenever needed. Let us look at an example.

If you wanted to create a code for a rectangle and then create 10 other rectangles, you would have to type the code 10 times. The aspect of repeating code is not a fun part of programming.

For the rectangle problem, we can create a function that contains the code for creating the desired rectangle. We can then call the function to create the rectangle as many times as we want.

Example of functions that we already used include: print(), list(), range() —that is why they were using parenthesis. However, the functions we used were built-in functions, meaning they come preinstalled in Python. We can also create our own functions to reuse.

To create a function, we must understand its syntax. A python function has three key components. They include:

- a name
- function parameters
- function body

These three components work together as follows:

```
def function_name(parameters):
    function_body
```

The function structure is similar to the structure of the for and while loops. You must indent the function body. The function name can be any name you like as long it follows the rules on naming a variable.

The next part is the parameters. Parameters are the variables that the function will be taking to perform its specific task. For example, in the print function, we passed either the number, a string, or a variable to print out. Parameters are not always required and you can create a function without parameters.

The function body contains the lines of code that define what the function does. For example, if you have a program that tests the maximum and minimum value between two numbers, you will write the code to test out this problem inside the function body.

Whenever you need to use a function, you just call the function using its name. If the function requires parameters, you MUST pass these parameters during the function call. Let us see an example that prints out the "Hello, I am your first function"

```
def print_me():
    print("I am your first function")
print_me()
```

Note that this is a function without parameters and thus, we did not need to pass them during the function call. Now we can use this function whenever we need it in the entire program.

Here are some of the reasons why functions are important:

- Simplifies the process of coding
- Allows for code reuse
- It makes debugging a lot easier –debugging is the process of finding and fixing errors in a program
- It reduces the code size and makes it clean and readable

Let us now see how to work with a function that has parameters. Use the max and min functions.

```
>>> def min_max(number1, number2):
        if (number1 > number2):
            print("Max number is %s"%number1)
        else:
            print("Maximum number is %s"%number2)
```

```
>>> min_max(10,20)
Maximum number is 20
```

Above, we declared a function called min_max that takes two arguments: number1 and number2. The function checks if the first number is greater than the second number. If it is, the maximum number is the first number; otherwise, the maximum number is the second number. During the function call, we passed in the numbers we wanted to test —in this case 10 and 20. The program then checks for the maximum and returns the value.

If you want to create a function that you can use across all your python programs, we create a file that contains the function code and then import it in other files.

Can you remember the toy business project we worked on earlier? We can create a python function to calculate the amount earned in one day. The parameters required are total number of toys, toys spoilt, and the cost of each toy. Create a new file and save it, making sure you remember the name of the file as well as the function name.

```python
def income_per_day(total_toys, toys_spoilt, cost_per_toy):
    total_money = (total_toys - toys_spoilt) * cost
    print("Total income = %S" %total_money)
```

To use the function in another file, simply create a new file and use the import module.

```python
from daily_income import income_per_day
cost_per_toy = 25
day1_total = input("Enter the total number of toys in that day: ")
day1_total = int(day1_total)
day1_spoilt = input("How many toys were spoilt: ")
day1_spoilt = int(day1_spoilt)
print("Day 1 result: ")

# function call
income_per_day(day1_total, day1_spoilt, cost_per_toy)
```

```
Enter the total number of toys in that day: 200
How many toys were spoilt: 10
Day 1 result:
Total income = 4750
```

Now we can use the income_per_day function in all the required programs. All we have to do is change the required arguments.

Variables created within a function are only visible within a function. For example, if you try to use the variable such as total_money in the main program, it will result in an error. This aspect of variable accessibility is what we refer to as a variable or function scope. Therefore, the variable such as total_money has a scope of its created function. This means that once the function executes, the attendant results is the immediate destruction of the variable.

If you want to use the result of a function call, we use the keyword return followed by the value we want returned. When Python comes across the return keyword in a function, it knows that it has come to the end of the function and returns the current value from the function call. However, you can only return one value from a function. The return keyword also indicates the end of the function execution and any code beyond the return keyword will not execute.

Let us test out your understanding of the various principles learned in this part of this python guidebook:

Exercise

Question 1

Write a python function that asks the user for a name input and the number of times to print the name. Use loops to solve this problem.

Question 2

Expand the toy business program we worked with earlier to calculate the income for five consecutive days —use loops.

Question 3

Write a python program that creates a rectangle using the python turtle module. Use the rectangle function to draw a bookshelf.

Now that we have had tons of practice writing python code and programs, we need to look at another important feature, a feature that you must master before you can master programming —in Python and in other programming languages:

Solution 1

```
def name(name, times):
    name = input("Enter your name: ")
    times = input("Enter the number of times: ")
    times = int(times)
    for in range(0, times):
        print(name)
name()
```

Solution 3

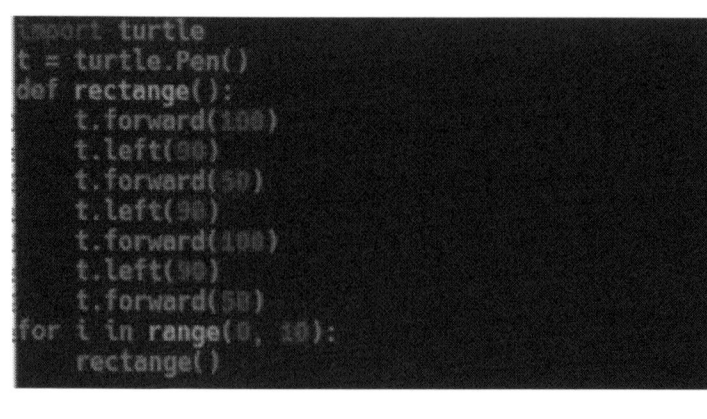

```
import turtle
t = turtle.Pen()
def rectange():
    t.forward(100)
    t.left(90)
    t.forward(50)
    t.left(90)
    t.forward(100)
    t.left(90)
    t.forward(50)
for i in range(0, 10):
    rectange()
```

Creating Your Own Functions

Let's learn how to create our own functions and make use of them within other scripts and programs. In order to tell Python that you would like to create a function, you can use the def keyword. The def keyword tells Python you want to define a function and that it needs to recognize a variety of keywords and values to follow. After using the def keyword, you need to provide the function name and any arguments/parameters your function will make use of. You can then begin writing the commands you'd like your function to carry out. In other words, the syntax for creating a function looks something like this:

```
def name(parameters):
    Code to carry out desired actions
```

Your functions will often require another keyword, the return keyword. The return keyword specifies an expression, variable, or value you'd like the function to pass back out to the main program once the function has finished running. Once the return statement is executed, the function will stop running, and the expression you've designated will be passed back. Here's how to return an expression or value:

```
def name(parameters):
    Code to carry out desired actions
    return desiredExpression
```

If your function returns a value, you can assign that value to a variable by calling the function and assigning it to a variable. You can then manipulate the return value that has been stored in the variable.

returned_value = function_used(list of parameters)

If your function does not need to return a value, you can either just not use the return keyword or use return None.

Here's an example of a function that you can run in PyCharm:

```
def multiply_values(num_1, num_2):
    num_3 = 2
    print("Number 1 is : " + str(num_1))
    print("Number 2 is : " + str(num_2))
    print("Number 3 is: " + str(num_3))
    mult_num = num_1 * num_2 * num_3
```

```
        print("Product of multiplication is: " + str(mult_num))

    return mult_num
```

The function takes in two different numbers as parameters, multiplies these numbers together, and then multiplies the product of those numbers by two. The function then returns the multiplied value. The function also prints out the numerical values that have been passed in, as well as the product of the multiplication.

We can now call the function, assign it to a variable, and then print the variable to make sure that the returned value is what we expect it to be.

```
multiplied = multiply_values(8, 9)

print(multiplied)
```

You may notice that we have called the print function within our own function. Python allows you to call functions within functions like this, even your own custom functions.

CHAPTER - 8
PYTHON'S BUILT-IN FUNCTIONS

By now, you've seen that using functions can save you a huge amount of time and energy. Therefore, it will pay off to know about some commonly used Python functions. The functions listed below are all built-in to Python and can be called simply by invoking them with no imports needed. Also included in this section are methods, which act like functions, but only work on specific data types and structures. The methods are typically invoked using dot notation on the target object.

print() - We've already covered this extensively, but it prints out the provided arguments to your terminal or screen.

abs() - This returns the absolute value of the provided argument, assuming the value is a numerical value (a float or integer).

round() - Rounds the provided numerical value to the nearest integer.

min() - Finds and returns the smallest value in a list of values. It even works on strings, where it will select the earliest alphabetical characters.

max() - The opposite of min, finds the largest or alphabetically last values.

sorted() - Sorts a list in ascending order and works on both numerical values and strings.

sum() - Adds the elements of a list together and returns the sum.

len() - Counts and returns the number of elements in a list. If called on a string, it will return the number of characters in the string.

type() - Returns the data type of the variable that the function has been provided.

String Methods

lower() - Converts all elements of the string to lowercase.

upper() - Converts all elements of the string to uppercase.

strip() - Removes extra whitespace from the beginning or end of the string.

replace() - Takes two arguments and replaces the first string with the second string.

split() - Takes in a specified delimiter as an argument and splits the string on that delimiter (splits strings into a list, splitting whenever the specified character occurs).

join() - Joins elements of a list into a single string, and you can choose the delimiter to join on.

List Methods

append() - Adds the provided argument to a list.

remove() - Removes the provided argument from a list.

count() - Returns the index number of the given value in a list.

clear() - Removes all elements from a list.

Dictionary Methods

keys() - Gives all the keys found in the dictionary.

values() - Gives all the values found in the dictionary.

clear() - Deletes everything from the dictionary.

Functions and Imports Exercise

Functions are an incredibly important part of programming in Python, so let's be sure that we understand. We'll try another programming exercise, and this time, we will focus on functions and imports.

Try doing the following:

- Write a function that takes arguments and manipulates the values of those arguments in some way (bonus points for making use of *args or **kwargs). Return the results of the manipulation. Use local variables in the function.
- Save the file your function is in within your current folder.
- Create a new file.
- Import the function from your original file.
- Create some global variables and pass them into the function.
- Print the resulting value of the function.

After you've attempted this by yourself, you can review the example below to see one way of meeting the requirements for this exercise.

Here's one potential solution:

save this in a file called "shopping_list.py"

```
def shopping_list(store, *args):

    shopping_list = []

    for i in args:

        print("Adding {} to list".format(i))
```

```
        shopping_list.append(str(store) + " - " + str(i))
    return shopping_list
```

In another file in the same directory:

create a new file in the same directory (or alias the import)

```
from shopping_list import shopping_list as SL

grocery_list = SL("Hilltop Grocery", "bread", "milk", "coffee", "apple juice")

computer_list = SL("Top Computer Parts", "RAM", "keyboard", "USB hub")

print(grocery_list)

print(computer_list)
```

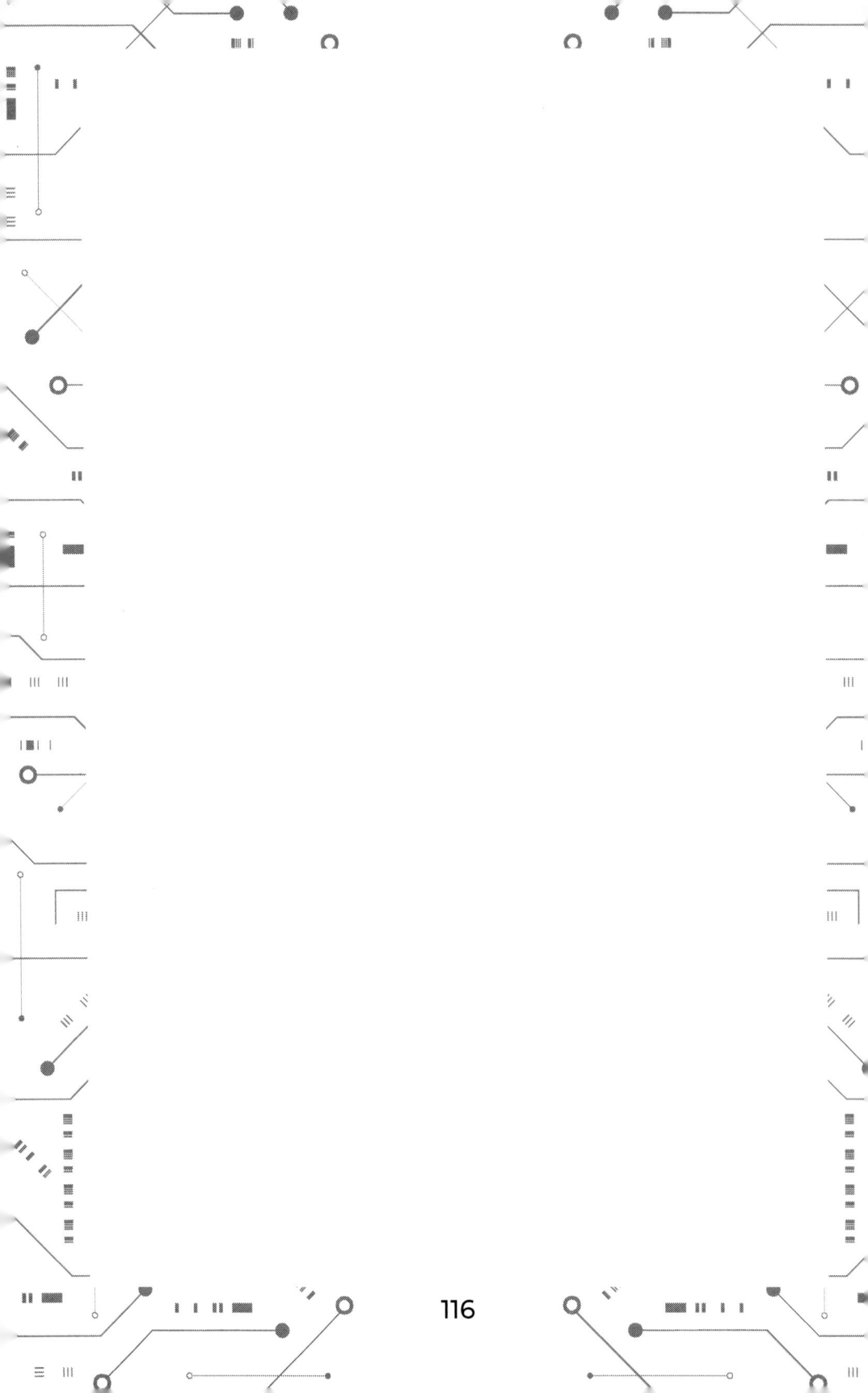

CHAPTER - 9
RESOURCES: USEFUL MODULES

Modules

Let's look at how to use some of Python's built-in functions. We've already gone over some of Python's included functions, like the print() function. These functions are part of the standard Python package. In contrast, some additional functions come with a Python installation but aren't available for use until you import them. Such functions are referred to as "modules."

In order to import a module, you can use one of several different import methods. The entire module can be imported by simply typing:

```
import name_of_module
```

For example, Python comes with a module called random, which can be used to generate random numbers. To import this module, you would just type:

```
import random
```

When you import a module with the above method, in order to use a function that the module possesses, you need to call the function using dot notation. For example, in order to make use of the randrange() function, you can use the following syntax:

```
random_nums = random.randrange(0, 25)
```

You can also assign shorthand or nicknames to a module that you import so that you don't have to write out the name of the module each time. For instance, we can alias random like this:

```
import random as r
```

We can now call the randrange function simply by writing:

```
random_nums2 = r.randrange(0, 25)
```

We can also import specific functions rather than importing an entire module. We can import specific functions by specifying the name of the module with from and then using the import keyword with the name of the functions we want to import.

```
from random import randrange
```

Importing a specific function this way enables us to just refer to the function by name when we want to use it:

```
random_nums3 = randrange(0, 25)
```

You can import multiple functions from a module by separating the name of the functions you wish to import with a comma. In general, if you don't need to use many functions from the module, it's a good idea to import just the functions you need rather than the entire module.

Creating Modules

After you create your own functions, you can package them into modules for use in other programs and scripts. Creating modules out of functions that you commonly use may save you a lot of time, as you can just reuse them for future projects. Python makes it very easy to create a module and import it to another program; all you must do is the following:

- Make sure that the file you created the function in is saved in the ".py" extension.

- Ensure that the file containing the function is in the same folder as the file you are importing the function to.

Here's a practical example of how to do that. Let's say we're creating a function that will join multiple input phrases into a single string. The function might look something like this:

```python
def args_to_string(*args):
    string_1 = ""
    for i in args:
        string_1 += i + " "
    return string_1
```

We can save the function in a file called argtostring.py and after that, we can create another file in the same directory using PyCharm. Next, we import the function for use.

```
from argtostring import args_to_string

string_1 = args_to_string('Hello,', 'this', 'should', 'be', 'one', 'string.')

print(string_1)
```

While using an imported function in the same directory is that simple, you may have to use a function that is in a different directory. Here's a quick look at how you can access a file that is in a different directory. You can use the sys module, which enables Python to change where it searches for files. Let's assume that the file you created was stored in a folder called PythonPrograms saved on the C drive. In this case, you could simply use the sys module to include that folder as part of the "path," the list of directories that Python will search when looking for files.

```
import sys

sys.path.append('C:\\PythonPrograms')
```

Including these commands in your program would be enough for Python to be able to find the argtostring.py file stored there.

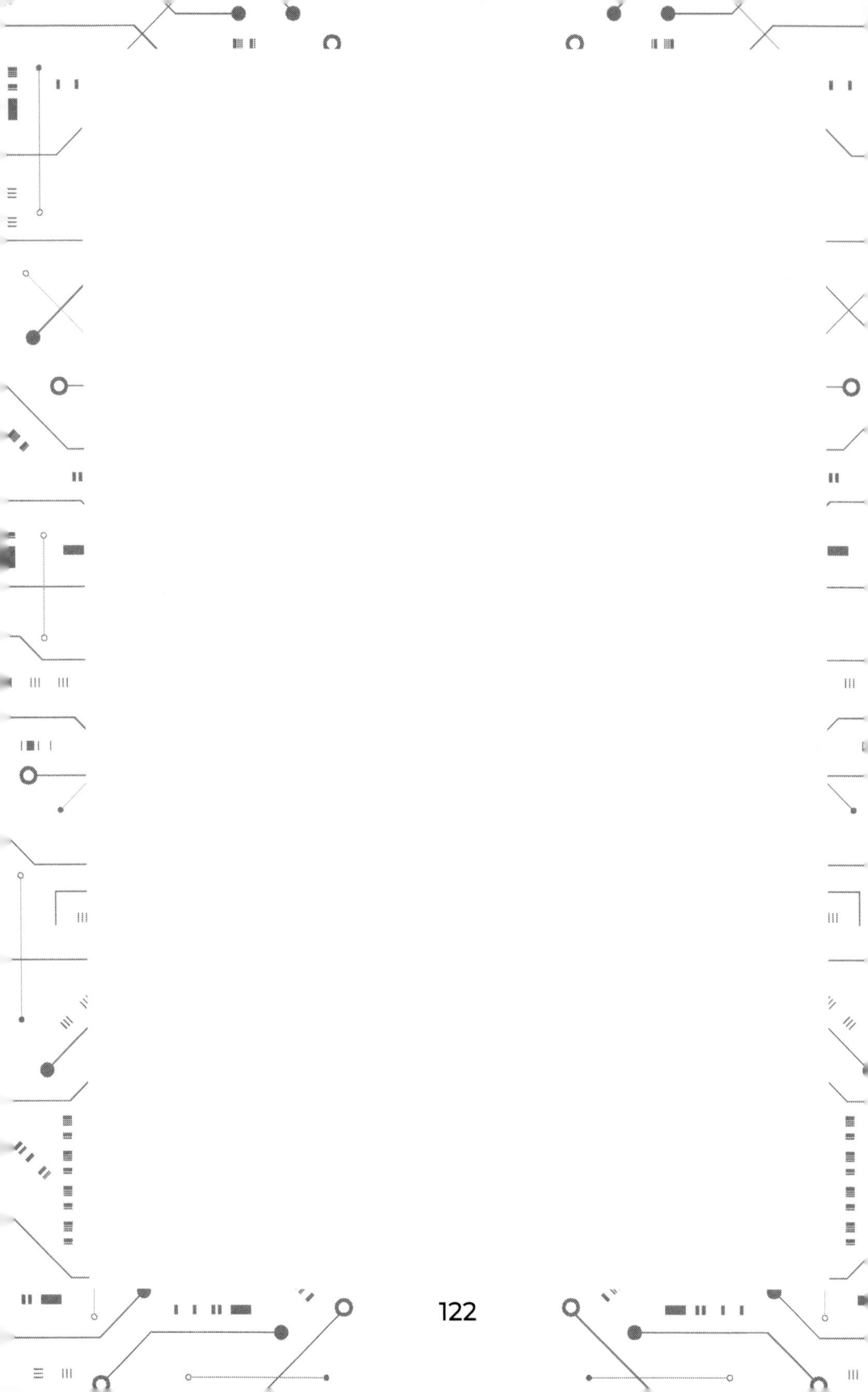

CHAPTER - 10
GAME PROGRAMMING

Now, believe it or not you are almost ready to write your very first game. You already know how to output information to the screen and you also know how to take input from a user.

Well, you can only work on text at the moment but you'll get the hang of it later on. But imagine that with only that know how along with the knowledge of algorithms you can now design your very first game.

We will go over how to design a simple coin flip or coin toss game. We will just go over the design process. The actual programming will follow after the design is complete.

A coin flip or toss represents a certain random element to the results. It's one of those things that you can use to decide how a decision will go.

People sometimes flip or toss a coin when they are not sure what to do given two options.

Why do you have to flip a coin when you can create an app for that?

Now, note that we will not design the graphics for this coin toss game or app. We will only work on pure text. The idea is to ask the user to choose whether a coin will show heads or tails.

You will then make a virtual coin toss. And then display what the result was—either heads or tails. You will then inform the user if his or her guess was right. I bet you can already imagine the Python code that you will use for this game.

Sounds easy, right? Well, there is only one final obstacle (well, two actually) before you can construct this game. You need to learn how to make a virtual coin toss. In other words, how do you mimic the randomness of a coin flip? The other thing is how to make your program choose between two different options—which we will cover after.

Random Number Generators: Mimic a Coin Flip

Now, before we can write a coin flip program, we need a way to produce random numbers. That may sound like something difficult if not impossible. After all, how in the world do you make something random?

Well, the good news is that there is a way for you to generate random numbers with the help of Python programming. As you might have guessed, it requires some really serious math. But don't worry. Someone else has done the math for you.

You don't have to come up with the mathematical formula or the algorithm that will create random numbers. It all has been done for you. In fact, there are several ways to produce random numbers in Python.

We will introduce you to one of these Python language constructs so you can create the coin toss game. To do that we will need to use a function called choice( ). This is only one of several functions in Python that are used to generate random numbers.

Not only do these functions produce random numbers, they can also manipulate the randomness of the numbers being created. In a way, they give you some degree of control so you can decide which set of numbers can be produced.

Note that these functions are used in many games, apps, lottery programs, and many other applications where an element of randomness is needed. They are pretty useful actually.

The choice( ) Function

As it was mentioned earlier, for this coin flip or coin toss game we will use the choice( ) function. So, what is it?

Remember, it is spelled with a small "c" at the beginning. The choice( ) function will output only one random number. That makes things easier for now since all we want is something that will produce either of 2 results.

We can use the choice( ) function to randomly generate either the number 1 or 0—well, we can also choose 1 or 2. It' all up to you which two numbers you will choose. The next question is how does this function work?

Here is an example of how the choice( ) function will look like in a Python program:

```
print (random.choice([5, 4, 3, 2, 1]))
```

You are already familiar with the print( ) function. Next as you can see from the sample above, you use the choice( ) function by using the following line of code:

```
random.choice( )
```

From the said example above you will also notice a set of numbers enclosed within a pair of square brackets, which are the following:

```
[5, 4, 3, 2, 1]
```

This function will choose any of the numbers inside the set contained within the square brackets. Note that only the numbers in this container will be used. That is the control that will be given to you when using this random number generator.

What we have below is called the syntax of a statement. In programming terms, a syntax is the proper arrangement of terms in a programming language so that it can be interpreted correctly (or translated correctly into a language that can be understood by a computer).

The following is the official syntax of the choice( ) function:

```
random.choice([sequence])
```

Here are the parts of this function:

- random.choice – this is the function call or the right way you make use of this function. You need to add the word "random." (followed by a dot) before the word "choice." So you might be thinking what is this "random" part of the statement? Well, that is called the module (we'll talk about modules in a minute). What this part of the code is telling us is that "choice" is part of "random" or contained inside "random."

•[sequence] – this part will contain a sequence of numbers or in the case of our coin toss program it will contain either of two words (i.e. heads, tails). This part of the choice( ) function is the list of items where the output will be selected.

choice( ) is a useful function if you want to specify exactly which numbers will be included in the selection. There are downsides of course. What if you want to choose any number ranging from 1 to 500,000?

Writing all those numbers in your Python code will become way too long if you do it that way. Don't worry. There are other functions that can handle such a task. For now let's just concentrate on using the choice( ) function since we want a limited set of numbers to choose from.

Open your Python console and enter the following lines code:

```
>>> import random
>>> print(random.choice(["heads","tails"]))
```

> **Import Statement**
>
> We used the following statement:
>
> >>> import keyword

And now you have:

> >>> import random

The reserved word "import" is a statement that is used to import or make use or bring in predefined codes. Don't let that technical sounding thing scare you. This statement makes use of the import system in Python programming.

You remember that it was explained earlier that other people have written the algorithms and the Python code for a lot of tasks that you will need in programming. In this case when you need a program that will generate random numbers, there are others who have already done the job for you.

All you need to do is to use their code. That means someone else already wrote the code for the choice( ) function that we were discussing earlier. Now, in order for you to use that function you need to import it from the code that they wrote into your code.

That eliminates the need to write what they already wrote. All you need to do is to import it. In this case you will import something called "random."

In Python programming "random" is something called a module. Think of a module as a collection of programming code that has already been made for you to use. You have now learned two modules in this programming language—random and keyword.

You can't use the choice( ) function without importing the random module first. That is why you start with an import statement first and then use the choice( ) function.

Now, moving forward—notice that when you press enter after this line of code:

```
>>> print(random.choice(["heads","tails"]))
```

The system will display either heads or tails. Press the up arrow key to display that command again. Pressing the up arrow key on the command console of Python will display the last command that you entered. That way you don't have to retype everything over and over again. This only works on the command line console.

Notice that the pattern produced is random. There is no specified number of times the words "heads" or "tails" will be selected.

Coin Flip Game Algorithm

Now we are ready to create the algorithm for the coin flip game. Here it is:

1. Greet the player and mention the name of the game.

2. Explain the rules of this game: a virtual coin will be tossed. There will be no graphics involved. Just an imaginary or virtual coin toss for now.

3. The player will guess whether the coin will show heads or tails.

4. Flip or toss the coin.

5. The player that guesses the side of the coin gets 1 point, the player who doesn't guess, is deducted to him 1 point. The player who gets 3 points, wins.

Programming Exercise

Judging from the algorithm above, you already know how to perform steps 1 to 4. Open your IDLE editor (or if you have installed a different IDE then use that one instead). Write the lines of code for steps 1 to 4.

You will see a complete coin toss/coin flip program later on as we go over the rest of the game design. There are a couple more concepts that you need to learn so that you will be able to complete coding for this project.

CHAPTER - 11
MORE GAMES

Rock, Paper, Scissors

This classic game involves choosing one of three objects, as the name suggests. Once both selections are made, the items are revealed to see who wins. The player who wins is determined by three simple rules. The rock will crush the scissors, while the scissors cut paper and the paper covers rock.

To handle these rules, we are going to create a list of choices, similar to the list of colors we created before in some of our drawing programs. Then we will add a random selection function that will represent the choice the computer makes. Next, the human player will have to make his or her choice. Finally, the winner is decided with the help of a number of if statements.

Have you tried to create your own version of

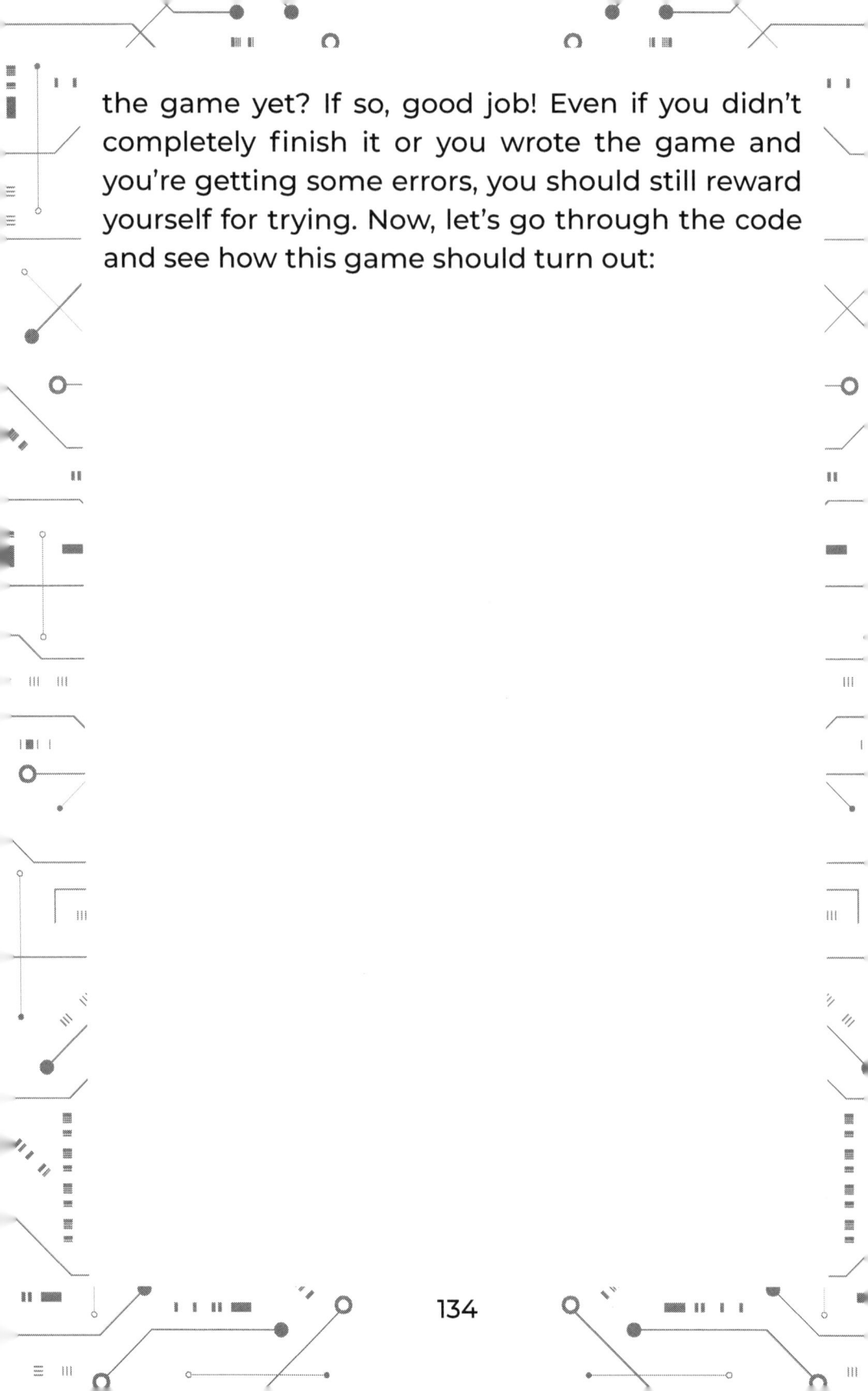

the game yet? If so, good job! Even if you didn't completely finish it or you wrote the game and you're getting some errors, you should still reward yourself for trying. Now, let's go through the code and see how this game should turn out:

```
import random

selectionChoices = [ "rock", "paper", "scissors"]

print ("Rock beats scissors. Scissors cut paper. Paper covers rock.")

player = input ("Do you want to choose rock, paper, or scissors? (or quit) ?"

while player != "quit":
    player = player.lower ()
computer =  random.choice(selectionChoices)
print("You selected " +player+ ",
and the computer selected" +computer+ ".")
if player == computer:
print("Draw!")
elif player == "rock":
if computer == "scissors":
print ("Victory!")
else:
```

```
print("You lose!")
elif  player == "paper":
    if computer == "rock":
        print("Victory!")
    else:
        print("You lose!")
elif  player == "scissors":
    if computer == "paper":
        print("Victory!")
    else:
        print("You lose!")
else:
    print("Something went wrong...")
print()
player = input ("Do you want to choose rock, paper, or scissors? (or quit) ?"
```

Now let's break down the code and discuss each step.

First we import the random package which allows us to use a number of functions that we are going to take advantage of when giving the computer the ability to make random choices. Then we create a list for the three game objects and print the games rules so that the human player knows them. The computer will already know what to do because it is programmed, after all. Next, we ask the player to type his or her choice and then a loop is executed to check the choice of the player. The player also has the option of quitting the prompt window, and when that happens the game is over. Our loop makes sure that if the player doesn't select the quit option, the game will run.

The next step is to ask the computer to select one of the three game objects. This choice is done randomly and the selected item is stored inside a variable called "computer". After the choice is memorized, the testing phase begins to see which player will win. First a check is performed to see whether the two players have chosen the same item. If they did, then the result is a draw and nobody wins. Next, the program verifies whether the player chose rock, and then it looks at the computer to see if it chose scissors. If this is the case, then the rule says rock beats scissors, so the player wins. If the computer didn't select a rock as well, neither did it pick scissors, then it certainly chose paper. In this case the computer will win. Next, we have two elif statements where we perform two more tests that check whether the player selected paper or scissors. Here we also have a statement that checks to see if the player chose something that isn't one of the three possible items. If that is the case, an error message is sent that tells the player he either chose something that he is not allowed, or he mistyped the command.

Lastly, the user is prompted to type the next selection. This is where the main loop goes back to the beginning. In other words, the game starts another round of rock paper scissor.

This game is simple, but it is fun because anyone can win. The computer has a chance of beating you and there's also a real chance of ending up in a draw. Now that you understand how to create a random chance type of game, let's look at other examples to add to our game library while also learning Python programming.

Guess!

This project will be another fun chance-based game that will make use of the random module. The purpose of the game will be choosing a number between a minimum and a maximum and then the opponent tries to guess that number. If the player guesses a higher number, he will have to try a smaller one, and the other way around as well. Only a perfect match will turn into a win.

In this project the random module is needed because of certain specific functions. For instance, we know that we need to generate a random number, therefore we will use a function called "randint" which stands for random integer. The function will have two parameters, which represent the minimum number we can have, as well as the maximum. You can try out this function on its own. Just import the module and then type the following:

```
import random

random.randint (1, 20)
```

Python will now automatically generate a random figure between 1 and 20. Keep in mind that the minimum and maximum values are included in the number generation, therefore Python can also generate numbers 1 or 20. You can test this command as many times as you want to make sure that you are truly getting random values. If you execute it often enough, you will see that some values will repeat themselves, and if the range is large enough you might not even encounter certain numbers no matter how many times you run the code. What's interesting about this function though, is that it isn't truly random. This is just a side note that won't affect your program, but it is intriguing nonetheless. The randint function actually follows a specific pattern and the chosen numbers only appear to be random, but they aren't. Python follows a complex algorithm for this pattern instead, and therefore we experience the illusion of randomness. With that being said, let's get back to fun and games. Let's create our game with the following code:

```python
import random

randomNumbers = random.randint (1, 100)

myGuess = int (input ("Try to guess the number. It can be anywhere from 1 to 100:"))

while guess != randomNumbers:

    if myGuess > randomNumbers:

        print (myGuess, "was larger than the number. Guess again!")

    if myGuess < randomNumbers:

        print (myGuess, "was smaller than the number. Guess again!")

    myGuess = int (input ("Try and guess again! "))

print (myGuess, "you got it right! You won!")
```

That's it! Hopefully you tried to create this game on your own because you already have the tools for the job. Remember that programming is only easy as long as you practice it enough on your own. Just take it one step at a time. With that being said, let's discuss the code in case you need some help figuring the game out:

Just like before, we first need to import the random module so that we can use the random number generating function. Next, we use the randint function with two parameters. As mentioned before, these parameters are the lowest number we can guess, which is 1, and the highest number we can guess, 100. The random number generator will generate a number within this range. Once the number is generated, it is stored inside the "randomNumbers" variable which we declared. This number will not be known by the player because he or she needs to guess it. That's the point of the game.

Next up, the player needs to guess the hidden number. This guess will then be stored inside a new variable called "myGuess". In order to check whether the guess is equal to the number, we are using a while loop with the "not equal to" operator. We do this because if the player gets lucky and guesses the number correctly with the first attempt, the loop simply doesn't finish executing because there's no need.

Next, if the player guesses the wrong number, we have two if statements that check whether the guess is a higher value than the hidden number, or a lower one. An appropriate message is then printed for the player in each case. In either scenario, the player receives another chance to make the right guess. Finally, at the end if the user guessed the number correctly, the program declares victory by printing a message and then the program stops running.

To make the game more interesting you can challenge yourself to modify the random number generator to include different values. You can also add a statement that enables the game to print the score to see how many times the player tried to guess the number. In addition, since the game ends when the player guesses, you could write a main loop so that the player can choose to restart the game instead of automatically quitting. Have fun and don't be afraid to try anything.

Choose A Card

Card games are always fun and they also rely on random elements to some degree. No matter the card game, chances are quite small to have multiple identical games. This means you won't get bored any time soon. With what we tackle so far about Python programming; we can create a card game. It might not look good, unless you have an artistic friend to draw everything for you, but you could still create the graphics with the help of the Turtle module like we did for other projects. This will require some patience though. In any case, we can create a card game even without graphics by simply generating the name of each card. Instead of seeing a virtual card, we will see the name "four of spades", or "queen of hearts".

One of the simplest card games we could create involves a game with two players that battle each other to see who draws the card with the highest value. Each player will randomly pull a card from the deck, and the one who has the higher card will win. It is a simple game, but fun due to the random element.

Since we won't be using any graphics, we will have to create our deck of cards some other way. We are going to set them all up as a list of strings since we will be using their names instead. Next, we need to give the players the ability to randomly pull a card from the deck. This means that we are going to use the random module once again and we will add a choice function that randomly distributes cards to the players. Finally, we need a way to compare the two cards that are drawn by the two players. As you probably guessed, this is a case for comparison operators.

That is pretty much all it takes to create a card game. You can add more features, or remove some if you aren't interested in them. Whatever you do, design the game on paper so that you know your goals. Then work one those goals one line of code at a time. This way you will write your game in no time and whatever problems you encounter you will be able to fix fairly quickly.

CHAPTER - 12
HOW TO DEAL WITH ERRORS?

Spot and Fix Errors

The Python interpreter takes in every line and operates on that straightaway (more or less) when you press the Enter key. In hi World! You utilize Python's print feature. Print takes what's within the parentheses and outputs it to the program line (also referred to as the console).

Python is sensitive to each the synchronic linguistics and punctuation. If you spell one thing, the program will not work. If Python is expecting special characters and you do not place them in, then Python can fail. Some Python problems area unit shown here. Are you able to calculate however you'd fix them?

>>> print('Hello World!') Trace back (most recent decision last):

> File "", line 1, in Name Error: name 'print' isn't outlined

Here's another:

> >>> print ('Hello World!) File "", line one print ('Hello World!)
>
> Syntax Error: EOL whereas scanning string literal

Here's another:

> >>> print 'Hello World!')
>
> File "", line one print 'Hello World!')
>
> ^ Syntax Error: invalid syntax

Python tries to provide you the rationale it failing (that is, Name Error and Syntax Error).

Check Every Of Those Things:

All commands area unit properly spelled (fail 1)

Every gap quote mark features a matching closing quote mark (fail 2) each gap parenthesis features a closing parenthesis (fail 3)

Using print from Python two versus print() from Python three

The print () that you simply used for your 1st program during this project doesn't would like the parentheses. Python two features a totally different print syntax from Python three. In Python two, print may be a keyword. Before Python three came on, the hi World program was pretty simple and sounded like this: print "Hello World!"

This program doesn't have parentheses. For no matter reason that individuals guilty do what they are doing, the Python software package Foundation modified the Python three syntax to need the parentheses. once you're writing, bear in mind to place parentheses around what you wish to print.

For the code during this book, print can work notwithstanding you allow the parentheses out. (Don't believe me? act. Try it.) as a result of Python 3's syntax needs parentheses, I'm victimization them here therefore you'll be wont to them after you switch to Python three.

Work with Literals

In hi World!, the message that print is causation is named a literal. think about a literal as being one thing inside single quotes. (Single quotes area unit this ' rather than quotation mark, like this ").

Literals area unit the rocks (not rock stars) of the programming world. You'll choose them up and throw them around, however you cannot modification them. they'll exist by themselves in an exceedingly program, however they don't do anything: >>> 'Hello World!'

'Hello World!'

That's a program that has solely a literal and zilch else. It's simply a bit totally different from the hi World program. Therein program there have been no quotes within the text that Python written, however during this example the second line has inverted comma marks around it.

Python doesn't decide the content of a literal, meaning you'll spell it, fill it with weird words, and even fill it with weird, misspelled words. You continue to won't get a mistake message from Python.

The single quotes area unit necessary. If you allow them out, Python thinks the text is telling it to try to one thing. During this example, Python doesn't recognize what hi and World area unit speculated to do: >>> hi World!

```
File "", line one hi World!
  ^ Syntax Error: invalid syntax
```

The literals mentioned here area unit all string literals. String literals area unit scan like text, rather than sort of a range. (I do not know why they're referred to as string literals and not one thing else, like alphabetical literals.) You'll build a sequence of characters into a string literal by golf stroke one quote on every side: hi World! → 'Hello World!'

However, watch what happens after you build a literal from one thing that already features a inverted comma (like the word didn't) : >>> 'didn't'

```
File "", line one 'didn't'
 ^
Syntax Error: invalid syntax
```

Python reaches the second inverted comma and thinks that it marks the top of the string literal — however that's not wherever you needed it to finish you'll build a literal that has one quote by victimization quotation mark round the outside of the literal. you'll use quotation mark any time, notwithstanding there is not one quote concerned.

> >>> "didn't" "didn't"
>
> >>> '"I have an awfully eely ground-effect machine," he said.' '"I have an awfully eely ground-effect machine," he said.'

Ways you'll produce string literals embody such numerous components as single quotes and quotation mark. however, that is not all! you'll additionally use triple single quotes and triple quotation mark to form string literals. Seriously:
>>> '''This may be a literal created with triple single quotes.'''

> 'This may be a literal created with triple single quotes.'
>
> >>> """This may be a literal created with triple quotation mark [sic].""" 'This may be a literal created with triple quotation mark [sic].'

Make sure you'll produce a minimum of one literal that features an inverted comma, one that features a double quote, and one that has each one quote and a double quote.

Literally Save Your Strings in Variables

Okay, therefore you're a master maker of string literals. When Python defines a literal, it kind of forgets it (like you would possibly forget to try to your chores). Python stores literals in memory then thinks they don't seem to be being employed therefore throws them get into a method referred to as pickup. (No, I'm not creating that up.) kind of like after you leave one thing on the ground and it gets thrown within the trash as a result of somebody thinks you are not victimization it. However, does one stop Python from thinking your literal isn't being used?

Put a reputation to your literal. Then Python won't throw it within the garbage. It's kind of like tape a chunk of paper thereto with "Mine!" written on that.

You name a literal like this:

1. Concoct a reputation that follows the foundations (criteria) listed when these steps.

2. Place the name on the left aspect of AN sign (=).

3. Place the literal on the proper aspect of the sign.

Here area unit some of sample names:

```
>>> my_message = 'Hello World!'

>>> my_second_message = 'This name may be a very little long. Ideally, attempt to keep the name short, however not too short.'
```

Each name you utilize should suits (follow) these rules:

It ought to describe what the literal are used for. for instance, text_for_question may be a sensible name for a literal that has the text for a matter (if you're asking the user something). However, another_var may be a dangerous name for it, as a result of it doesn't describe the variable.

Start it with a letter or AN underscore. (Beginning with AN underscore, which is _, features a special that means. you'll avoid it for currently.)

It will have underscores (and ought to typically be manufactured from solely minuscule letters and underscores).

It Will Have Numbers.

It will have uppercase letters (but simply because it will doesn't mean you should; avoid uppercase letters in literal names).

It Cannot Have an Area.

It can't be a similar as any Python keyword. (This project features a list of keywords.)

Use a reputation to visit what you have named. When you utilize a reputation (except on the left aspect in AN assignment), Python acts like you've retyped fully the worth that's documented by the name.

A value is a few things that are documented by a reputation within the earlier examples, the sole values area unit literals. You'll see totally different styles of values within the later comes.

Whenever you provide a name to a literal (or the other value), you're creating AN assignment. In my_message = 'Hello World!' the worth 'Hello World!' is allotted to the name my_message.

You could rewrite your hi World! program like this:

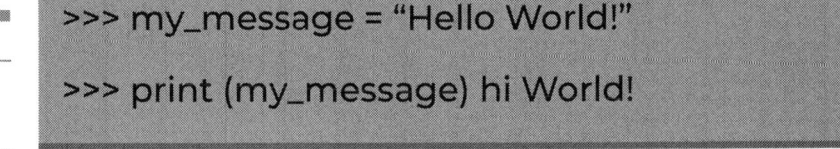

```
>>> my_message = "Hello World!"
>>> print (my_message) hi World!
```

This assigns the name my_message to the literal "Hello World!" (Remember, the name goes on the left aspect of the sign and therefore the literal goes on the proper aspect of the sign.) Then prints the literal that you simply named my_message.

When you've created a reputation, you'll modification what it names by victimization a similar naming method for a special literal. Or, use another name (since referencing the name is that the same as retyping it). To refresh your memory, this can be the code from earlier within the project:

```
>>> my_message = 'Hello World!'
>>> my_second_message = 'This name may be a very little long. Ideally, attempt to keep the name short, however not too short.'
```

Now, bend your mind and assign the second name to the primary name and print it:

```
>>> my_message = my_second_message
>>> print (my_message)
```

This name may be a very little long. Ideally, attempt to keep the name short, however not too short.

```
>>> my_message = 'A third message'
>>> print (my_message) a 3rd message
>>> print (my_second_message)
```

This name may be a very little long. Ideally, attempt to keep the name short, however not too short.

```
>>> my_message = 'Hello World!'
```

Also notice that the worth of my_second_message didn't modification. The sole issue that modified throughout AN assignment is that the variable name on the left aspect of the sign.

You can assign numbers to variables and add, subtract, and compare them:

```
>>> a = one
>>> b = two
>>> print (a) one
>>> print (b) two
>>> print (a+b) three
>>> print (b-a) one
>>> print (a> a = a+1
>>> print (a) two
```

Here, Python appearance up the worth of a, will increase it by one, and then stores it back within the variable.

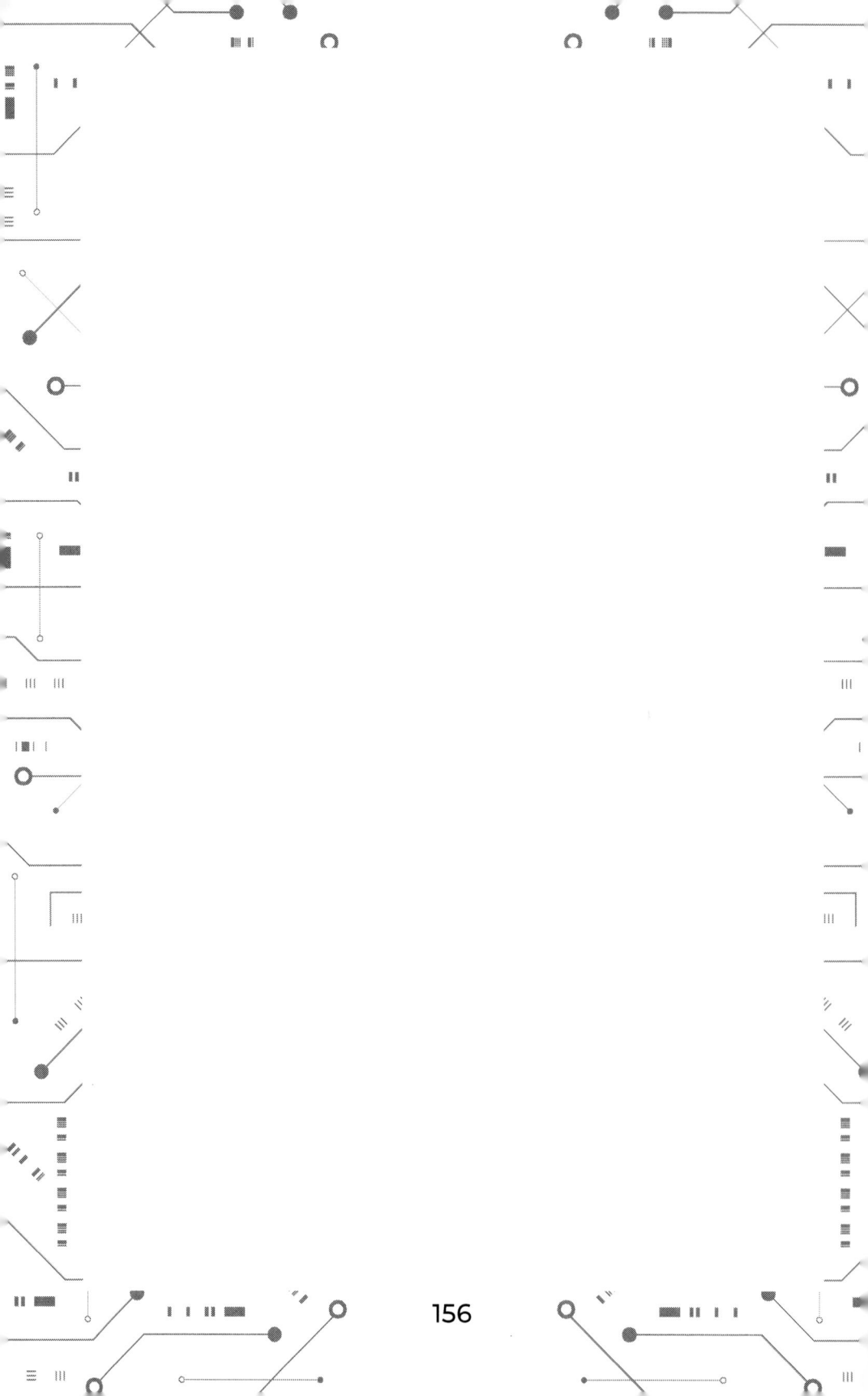

CONCLUSION

Learning how to get started with computer programing can seem like a big challenge. There are many different programming options that you can go with, but many of them are hard to learn, will take some time to figure out, and won't always do all of the stuff that you need. Many people fear that they need to be really smart or have a lot of education and experience in coding before they are able to make it to the coding level they want. Python has made it so easy to get started with coding whether you are a beginner or have been in this business for some time. The language is based in English so it is easy to read and it has gotten rid of a lot of the other symbols that make coding hard to read for others. And since it is user domain, anyone can make changes and see other codes to make things easier. This kid's book has spent some time talking about the different functions that you can do in Python and how easy it is for a beginner to get started. You will find that this process is easy and you can learn it with a little bit of practice. It is easy to use, works across a lot of platforms, and even the newer Mac systems come with this already downloaded.

When you are ready to get started on programming, or you want to find a program that is going to do a lot of great things without all the hassle, make sure to check out Python. This is one of the most popular options when it comes to programming and you are going to find that it is easy to read and learn, even if you have no idea how to start in the first place.

Working in Python can be one of the best programming languages for you to choose. It is simple to use for even the beginner, but it has the right power behind it to make it a great programming language even if you are more of an advanced programmer in the process. There are just so many things that you are able to do with the Python program, and since you are able to mix it in with some of the other programming languages, there is almost nothing that you can't do with Python on your side. It is not a problem if you are really limited on what you are able to do when using a programming language.

Python is a great way for you to use in order to get familiar and to do some really amazing things without having to get scared at how all the code will look. For some people, half the fear of using a programming language is the fact that it is hard to take a look at with all the brackets and the other issues. But this is not an issue when it comes to using Python because the language has been cleaned up to help everyone read and look at it together. This kid's book is going to have all the tools that you need to hit the more advanced parts of Python. Whether you are looking at this book because you have a bit of experience using Python and you want to do a few things that are more advanced, or you are starting out as a beginner, you are sure to find the answers that you need in no time. So, take a look through this kid's book and find out everything that you need to know to get some great codes while using the Python programming.

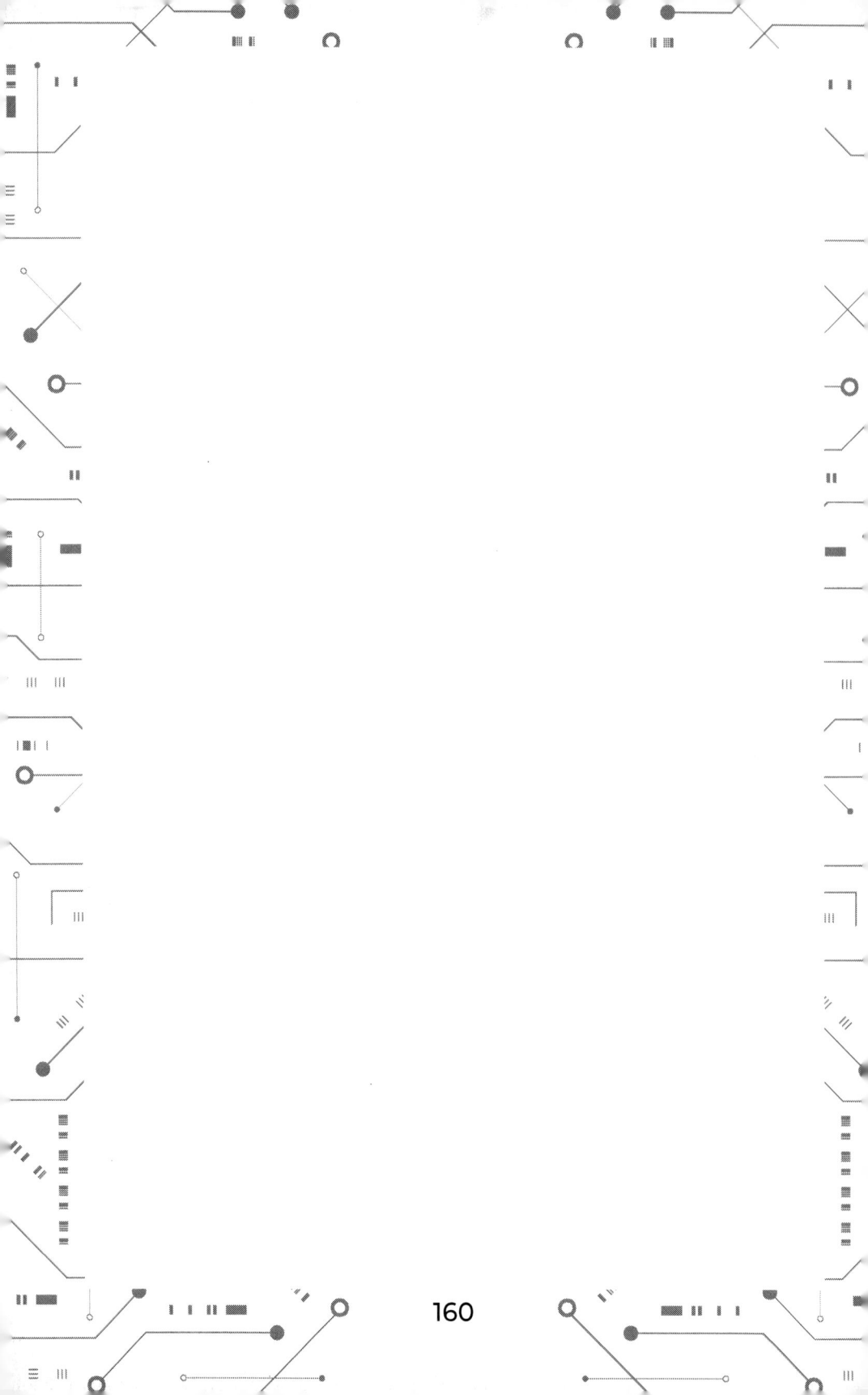

SCRATCH CODING FOR KIDS

HAVE FUN WITH COMPUTER CODING, CREATING AWESOME PROJECTS, ANIMATION AND SIMULATIONS. WITH THIS GUIDE YOU WILL BE ABLE TO CREATE YOUR GAMES IN FEW DAYS AND MASTER SCRATCH.

CHRISTIAN MORRISON

Copyright - 2020 -

All rights reserved.

The content contained within this book may not be reproduced, duplicated or transmitted without direct written permission from the author or the publisher.

Under no circumstances will any blame or legal responsibility be held against the publisher, or author, for any damages, reparation, or monetary loss due to the information contained within this book. Either directly or indirectly.

Legal Notice:

This book is copyright protected. This book is only for personal use. You cannot amend, distribute, sell, use, quote or paraphrase any part, or the content within this book, without the consent of the author or publisher.

Disclaimer Notice:

Please note the information contained within this document is for educational and entertainment purposes only. All effort has been executed to present accurate, up to date, and reliable, complete information. No warranties of any kind are declared or implied. Readers acknowledge that the author is not engaging in the rendering of legal, financial, medical or professional advice. The content within this book has been derived from various sources. Please consult a licensed professional before attempting any techniques outlined in this book.

By reading this document, the reader agrees that under no circumstances is the author responsible for any losses, direct or indirect, which are incurred as a result of the use of information contained within this document, including, but not limited to, - errors, omissions, or inaccuracies.

TABLE OF CONTENTS

INTRODUCTION   165

CHAPTER - 1
   GETTING STARTED WITH SCRATCH   173

CHAPTER - 2
   THE BASIC OF SCRATCH   191

CHAPTER - 3
   FUNCTIONS, IF STATEMENT,
   AND LISTS   201

CHAPTER - 4
   LOOP THE HOOP   223

CHAPTER - 5
   MOVE YOUR SPRITE!   233

CHAPTER - 6
   CREATING A PLAN FOR
   YOUR PROJECT   243

CHAPTER - 7
   ADVANCED CONCEPTS   253

CHAPTER - 8
   DAY AND NIGHT GAME   263

CHAPTER - 9
   PRACTICING WITH SCRATCH   283

CHAPTER - 10
   PROJECT-CONNECT FOUR   299

CONCLUSION   315

INTRODUCTION

What is Programming

Programming is a good and useful skill, which every child should learn. In later years, this skill may be used to create and develop great things. These things may be intended for entertainment during the childhood and teenage years. But, many of these things raise an interest in programming that can later be a solid basis for a career in computer science, engineering, or some other computer-related profession. These professions today are very popular among young people. Programming basics are something that anyone who will one day work with computers should have a good grasp of.

There are so many different programming languages, intended for creating different sorts of programs. The general rule is that any language can be used to make any kind of program. But, is it true? We will discover the answer to this question in this book. Some of these programming languages can be hard to learn, while others are as simple as the alphabet we learned as small children. It is entirely up to you to decide which one will be the best to pick for your students. Just keep in mind that every person (and this applies to children also) is an individual. Not all of us have the same interests, so consider allowing them input when it comes to deciding which of the programming languages, they like best. You should present them with a few, for example Ruby, Python, and Java, explain to them what the advantages and disadvantages are for each of them. Then, to keep it interesting, you might give them examples of programs and platforms they are familiar with and explain to them which programming language are they based on. For example, if you tell a child who has an account on Twitter that this social network was built using the Ruby programming language, they may become interested in learning more about Ruby, because this language is what made their favorite pastime possible. By learning about the programming languages that made their favorite games, applications and social networks possible, they will also learn how to behave safely when it comes to computers and data they post on the Internet. So, this is another good thing that will come out of the first coding course.

What is Syntax?

Computers are machines and, as such, they understand only what we type if we type it in the exact manner that the computer expects you to. This is a basic must if you want your machine to work properly and to give you your desired results. The expected way of writing in a computer program is called syntax. This means that syntax represents a set of rules in spelling and grammar both when using programs and also when creating them. This is, in other words, the grammar of programming. Without the knowledge and correct use of syntax, we cannot use any program, much less make one.

Programming syntax contains strings similar to words, somewhat similar to a human language we use in our everyday lives. Correctly formed syntax strings or lines result in syntactically correct sentences within a specific programming language, in the same way that correct sequencing and use of letters when you write them down form a word and correct sequencing of words make a meaningful sentence. When we're talking syntax, what we are referring to is a collection of rules governing the structure of the language. You'll find that syntax rules are unavoidable in programming, as not following the syntax of a language results in your program failing to run. In the first case, the document is treated as source code, while in another case, the document is essentially a set of data to be processed.

Lower-level computer programming languages are rooted in distinct sequences of symbols. There are also some higher-level programming languages, which often have visuals, which may be denoted by either text or a graphical interpretation. Syntactically invalid documents are said to have a syntax error. That means, for example, if we type an incorrect code or command, the program will send us a notification that a syntax error occurred and that, with an incorrect command, we cannot proceed without correcting that error--an error that could be as simple as an overlooked typo.

Syntax is divided into three equally important parts: phrases, context and individual words.

Words represent the so-called "lexical level," determining how characters form pieces of a line in a code, or the whole code;

Phrases, or the so-called "grammar level," narrowly speaking, have the function of determining and distinguishing parts of the code from phrases;

Context represents a function that is determining to which objects or variables certain names refer to, if their types are valid, etc.

Distinguishing between these differences in this way allows us process each level individually, rather than having to load up everything every time you start up the application.

Why is syntax so important in programming?

Without syntax, no programming languages can exist. It is as if you have a language but no letters.

It would mean that we can speak in that language, but we have no way of writing our thoughts on it. That kind of language would not have any sense and would serve little useful purpose. Some of the factors related to the syntax of a programming language are readability, writability, and program expectations. In most cases, regardless of what their opinion is on a particular syntax, programmers use any available syntax and enjoy trying different things. Nevertheless, we have to ask and answer two simple syntax-related questions: Why is syntax so important in programming? Can syntax be easily changed?

The answer to the first question would be that the syntax is important because it is directly related to many factors of programming. Some of these factors are readability, writability, and program expectations. It is the grammar of a computer program, after all, the very backbone of the code. In most cases, you will like a given syntax or you will dislike it, but some programs may use any syntax and in so doing, you will enjoy trying different things and seeing what works best for you and for the children in your life.

As for the second question, my opinion is that we have to learn the syntax before we get the idea of changing it. If we do not know the syntax well enough (or we do not know the syntax at all, in some cases, as with beginners) we cannot know whether it suits us. Before you aim to change something, you should get to know the thing (in this case, a language) you wish to change. However, being able to change the syntax of a given programming language depends on the design and implementation of the language. For example, in the programming language that is called the Ring, the syntax can be changed very easily. For the other programming languages this varies from language to language. Basically, they all have their settings and syntax rules. Knowledge of the syntax rules of every programming language is essential for their adequate and successful use in coding or programming. But before getting any ideas about changing the syntax, we have to consider how the codes are written. We should also have in mind what a particular function or syntax rule enables us to do.

One important thing to note is that you can (most often during the run-time) change the language's keywords as many times as you want to and you can create different, custom styles for your source code. Creating a custom style (or changing the language keywords) can be useful in many ways. Let's explore a few examples to bring this into context:

This includes language translation from English keywords to Arabic, French, etc. Most uses of this function are applied in translating programs and applications that allow you to translate a given text from one language to another.

Easy storage and updates needed for some of your old codes (in old programming languages used at the time when the particular program was made). This also means that you may not only store but also use the programs written in older programming languages. The only condition here is that the programs stored must be updated.

Freedom for different teams working on different subsystems in the project, where each team can use their favorite style, is also very important for any given programming language. Besides that, if more than one team is working on one project, they can function and work separately. That means that no team may interfere with the work of another.

Syntax changes are good for research and trying different styles before choosing the syntax usage best suited to your programming needs. This has an enormous practical value, since that way, we can test our changes in simple things and programs, before trying them with more serious and demanding programs, languages and/or projects. It is also a great way to learn and to test our abilities, which is highly valuable for both adults and children alike. Besides proving ourselves as good programmers, it is also a way to design something new and unique, something we can call our own. Just be careful. You might end up with something more complicated than you intended. However, even this can be a great opportunity for growth as a programmer. Changes, in general, are a good thing because there is always a chance to create something better.

Where do we start?

When writing about the syntax of a programming language, the big question is: Where do we start? Do we start within explaining what the syntax of a computer programming language is, how we use it and what we need it for, as well as their practical application, or do we start somewhere else? What is the simplest answer to the question of what syntax is and what the importance of syntax is for us?

Syntax can be described as a kind of bridge between the machine and you. You and your computer are connected by the syntax your computer needs you to enter in order for it to execute your commands. If the syntax is wrong, the computer is unable to follow up and execute any given tasks or commands. It "does not understand" (let me put it this way) what you are telling it to do, because you have "told" (a better term here might be "written," since we write our codes) it in the wrong way - you have used the wrong syntax, or, you have used the correct syntax, but in the wrong way.

CHAPTER - 1
GETTING STARTED WITH SCRATCH

What is Scratch?

Scratch is a graphic programming environment developed by a group of researchers from the Lifelong Kindergarten Group of the MIT Media Laboratory, under the direction of Dr. Mitchel Resnick.

This graphic environment makes programming more attractive and accessible for anyone who faces for the first time to learn a programming language. According to its creators, it was designed as a means of expression to help children and young people express their ideas creatively while developing logical thinking skills.

Scratch allows you to easily create your own interactive stories, animations, games, record sounds and make artistic creations.

The application of block programming languages allows a visual presentation of the paradigm and methodology of computer programming allowing to focus on the logic of programming leaving aside the syntax of programming languages (semicolons, parentheses, etc.).

Scratch, The Programming Language

It is a visual programming language, oriented to the teaching of block programming to children, without having to delve deeply into the development of the code.

It is a project created by MIT, launched in 2005, free and open-source; available for Windows, Mac, and Linux.

Scratching is an English term that means reusing code, and that means that the program allows you to use internal resources and modify them to the user's liking.

Characteristics and virtues

- You can handle it online or offline. The good thing about the first is that it is always updated, making the user experience never stop improving. Here you can download the software, in case you want to use it on a computer without an Internet connection.

- The Scratch programming language works with blocks, where the user places some bricks with certain conditions, which make the object move to one side or the other.

- It is a collaborative environment, where each user can participate in several projects, moving blocks and interacting with the object.

- Those same blocks are classified by colors, making operation even more intuitive.

- Based on the Logo programming language, developed by Danny Bobrow, among others.

- It is usually recommended for children between 6 and 16 years old, but as we said, it can be used by anyone who wants, without any type of cutter.

- Programs can be launched directly from a web page.

- Autonomous Learning.

- Benefits of this programming language:

- Free, free software.

- Ideal for taking the first steps in the world of code.

- Available in several formats: offline (download on Windows, Mac, and Linux), and online.

- Once the project is finished, it can be downloaded and shared on the internet.

- You can use it in many languages.

- With the Scratch programming language, you learn to program without typing code.

- Transmits to the child the need to solve problems in an orderly manner.

- Being a scalable learning method, a problem can always be further developed, increasing the level of the challenge, and consequently, expanding the creative ability of the student.

- Depth of mathematical concepts: coordinates, algorithms, variables, or randomness, among others.

- Develop the capacity of self-criticism, doubting any hypothetical solution.

Scratch, The Code Editor

The Scratch editor divides the screen into several panels: on the left are the stage and the list of objects, in the middle are the block palettes and on the right the program, costumes and sounds editor. The block palette contains a series of blocks that can be dragged and dropped in the Programs area to build the scripts that constitute our project. The block palette is divided into ten groups of blocks: Motion, Appearance, Sound, Pencil, Data, Events, Control, Sensors, Operators, and More Blocks (to create special blocks and other extensions).

Let's go by parts!

- Contents

- The objects
- Information about an Object
- The costumes
- The sounds
- The programs
- The blocks
- Stage
- Top bar

The Objects

The Objects area can manage the objects or characters that we have been adding to the program. We can select the object we want to edit or add a new object:

Both from the gallery of Scratch characters, and drawing a new one, uploading a photo that we have on our computer or taking a photo if we have a webcam installed:

Information about an Object

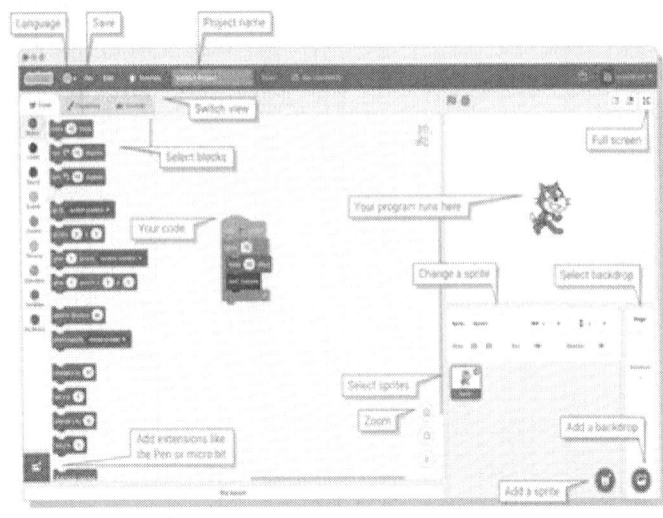

By clicking on the blue i in the upper corner of the object we can access the information panel of that object being able to edit among other things the name of the object.

The costumes

In the area of costumes we can add or draw different images for our characters as well as edit them. With the program we can control with what costume the character will be shown on stage.

The sounds

It allows you to add or edit sounds to our characters, both from the Scratch sound gallery and from files that we have on our computer.

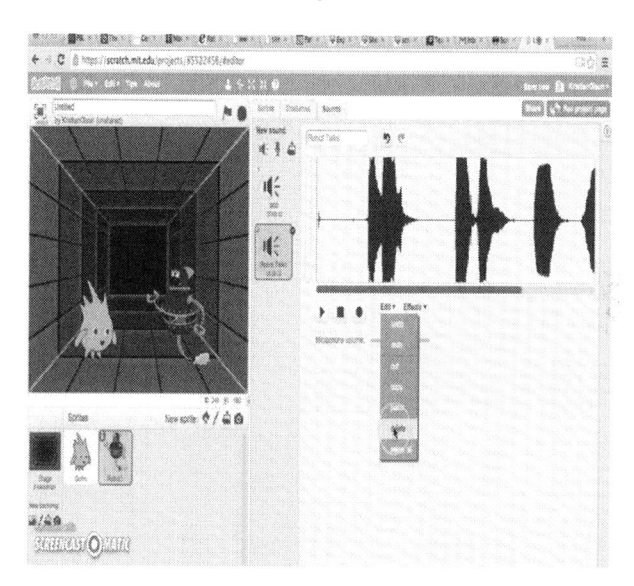

The programs

The Programs tab contains the instruction blocks assembled so that they give life to our object.

From the block area you can drag and drop the different blocks to the Programs area where they can be assembled together forming the programs of our project.

Each of the objects in the Object area, including the scenario, has its own programs that control only that particular object.

```
when  clicked
set Time to Wait ▼ to  pick random 2 to 8
say join join Press a key in  Time to Wait  seconds.
```

The blocks

The block palette contains a series of blocks that can be dragged and dropped in the Programs area to build the scripts that constitute our project. The block palette is divided into ten groups of blocks: Motion, Appearance, Sound, Pencil, Data, Events, Control, Sensors, Operators, and More Blocks (to create special blocks and other extensions).

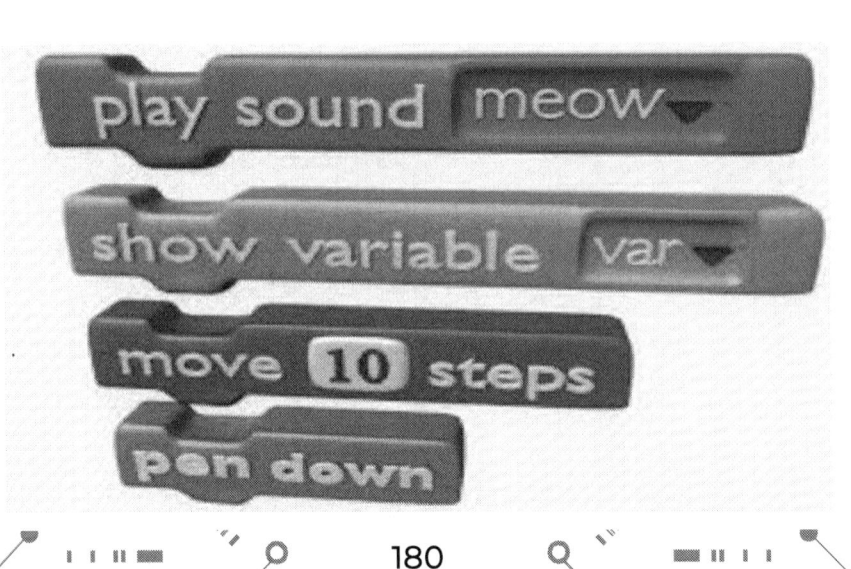

```
play sound meow ▼
show variable var ▼
move 10 steps
pen down
```

Stage

The scenario is a type of object that represents the background of the screen and is the place where all other objects interact.

As an object: that Programs, Costumes and Sounds can be added in a similar way to other objects.

As a place: where the rest of the objects interact, it represents a coordinate system where the center would be the point 0.0 (x = 0, y = 0) where the x correspond to the horizontal position and the y to the vertical position.

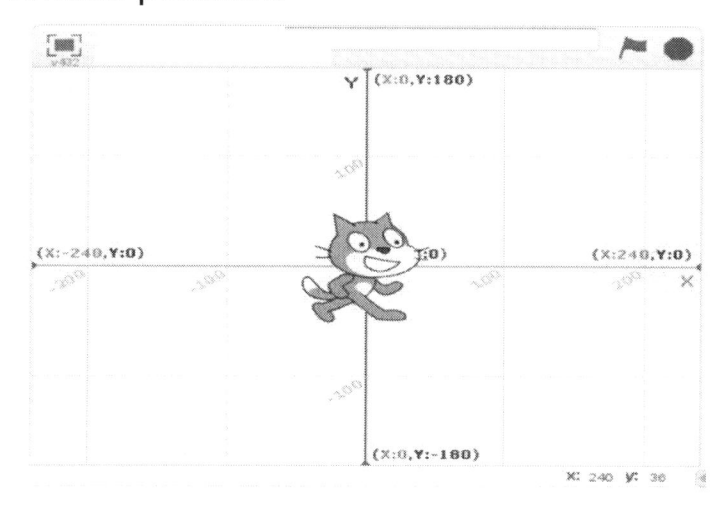

Top bar

Scratch button

Allows you to exit and return to the main page of the Scratch website

Menu file

New: Create a new blank project.

Save now: save the project in its current state

Save a copy: Create a copy of the current project to modify it.

Go to My Stuff: Link to the My Stuff section, where all your projects are.

Upload from your computer: Upload .sb2 projects you have saved.

Download to your computer: download the current project in .sb2 format

Revert: returns the project to its initial state before opening it the last time.

Edit menu

Undelete – Its function is to undo a sprite, costume, sound, or script that was recently deleted.

Small stage layout – Its funtion is to make the stage shrink to a s not a big size, i.e., a maller size.

Turbo Mode – It is where the code is executed very quickly. It is for setting the player into Turbo Mode.

Edit Buttons

Below you can find 4 buttons with which you can edit the Objects or Programs.

Duplicate: allows you to create a copy of the object or program we stamp

Cut: allows you to cut and eliminate the object or program in which we put the scissors.

Expand: allows you to enlarge the size of an object on the stage

Reduce: allows you to reduce the size of an object on the stage

Help: open the description, in English, of a block in the help section.

Building & Running a Script

As far as, Scratch will run one block from every script each tick. Let's say you had these scripts:

As soon as you click the green flag, the program will run the first block of the first script (go to 0, 0). Scratch will find the next running script (the second one) and run the first block there. So, loops such as forever and repeat count as blocks, so nothing would happen, except that the loop would start.

What scratch is going to do is to go back to the first script and check the next block (forever) and run that (again doing nothing). So, it will move to the next running script and run the other block, the next, in this case, in line (turn 25 degrees).

Look that, it will jump back to first script and move 10 steps, then go to script 2 and turn 25 degrees. And, there will be a continuity of alternative between moving and turning for the rest of the project.

The tricky part is that the order in which scripts are run (which is run first, the one with the moving block or the turn block?) is difficult to pin down. Keep in mind that, in scratch, it's up to you to place scripts wherever you would like them go first. That means, basically, the scripts run from the top to the bottom, with no concern for their x location.

So, one more time, the complications of the things get worse. You have to know which sprite you will fire first when there are multiple sprites involved.

Important: Make sure to not confuse sin the custom blocks with "run without screen refresh" checked are treated as just one block in the execution order.

Fortunately, the users who program in this way (rather than using, for example, broadcasts) are generally making projects simple enough that it doesn't matter the order in which events are fired.

Creating a Scratch account

Download and install directly from the project website: http://scratch.mit.edu/

In the zone "Download Scratch" we can find an installer for Windows and Mac. There are not yet specific packages for Linux (they indicate that they are working on it), but there are some instructions on how to make it work under different distributions of this system in the project forums.

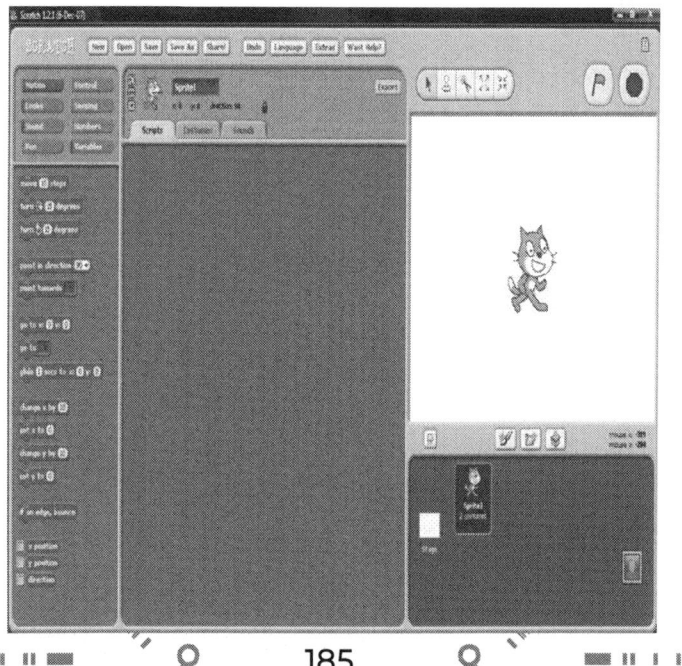

In the first execution of the program, the environment is in English:

For switching the language, you just need to make a click on the "Language" button. Select "the language you want"...

Scratch Installation

To download the latest version, go to http://scratch.mit.edu/ and follow the download link. After clicking the download link, this page will pop to your screen:

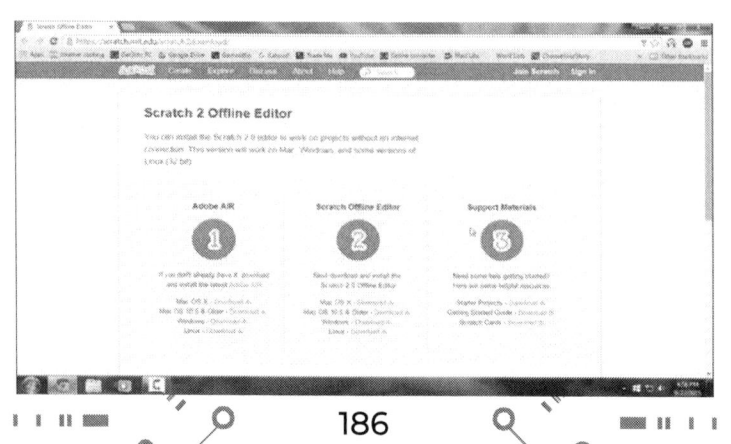

If you don't have Adobe AIR, you have to click and download it. Just follow the instructions to install it. After installing Adobe Air, click Scratch offline Editor Download depending on your OS.

After downloading the file, click the .exe file from the bottom left of your screen.

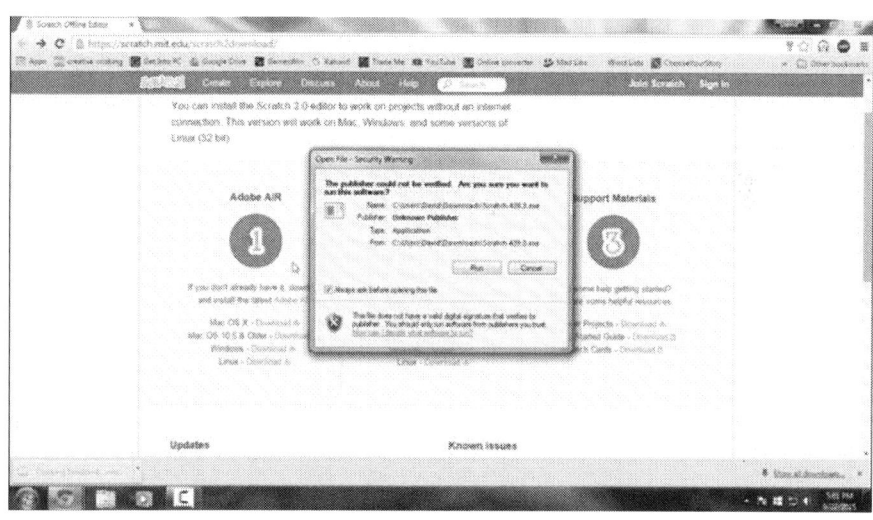

Click run to install Scratch to your PC.

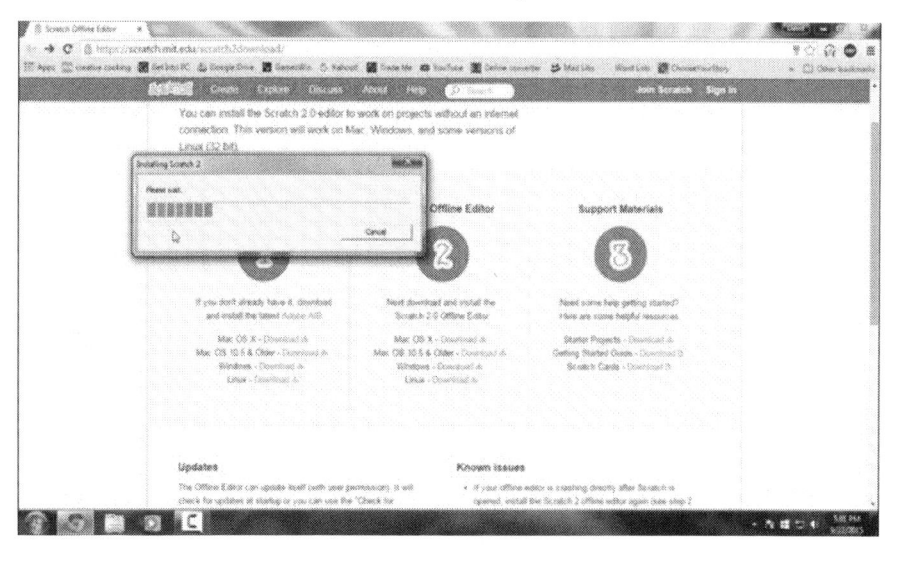

Wait the setup to finish.

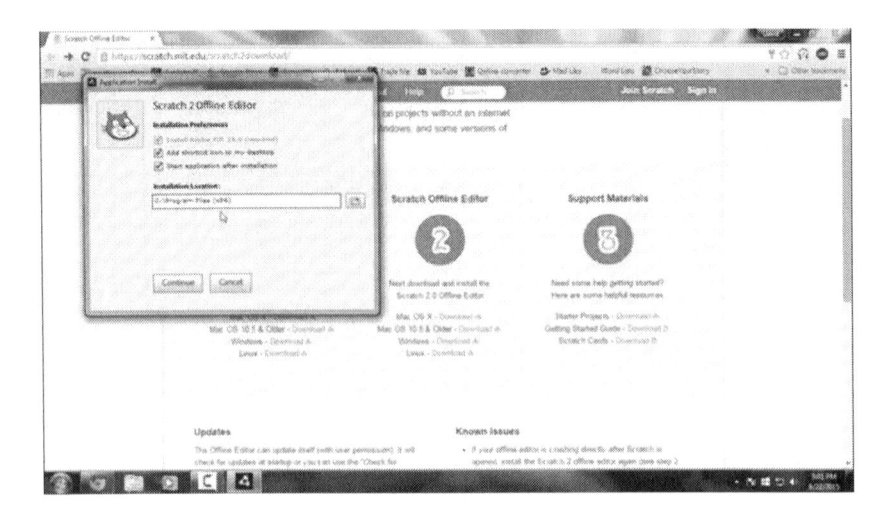

After the initial installation, click continue.

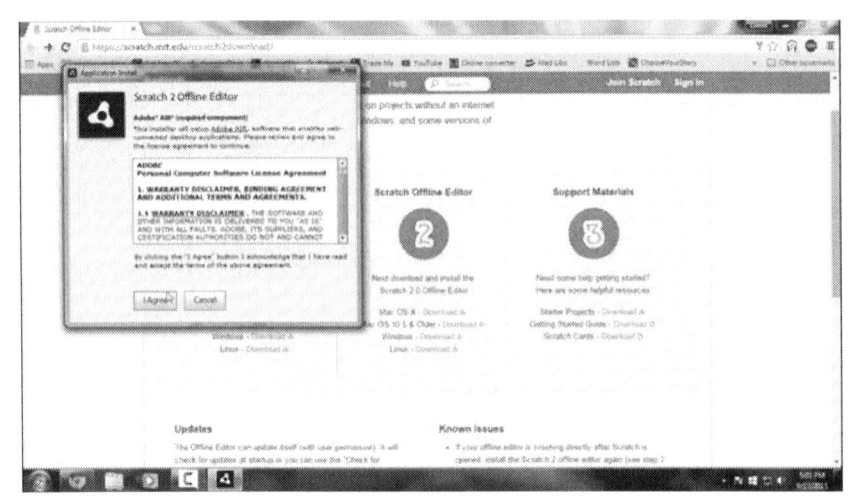

Click I Agree.

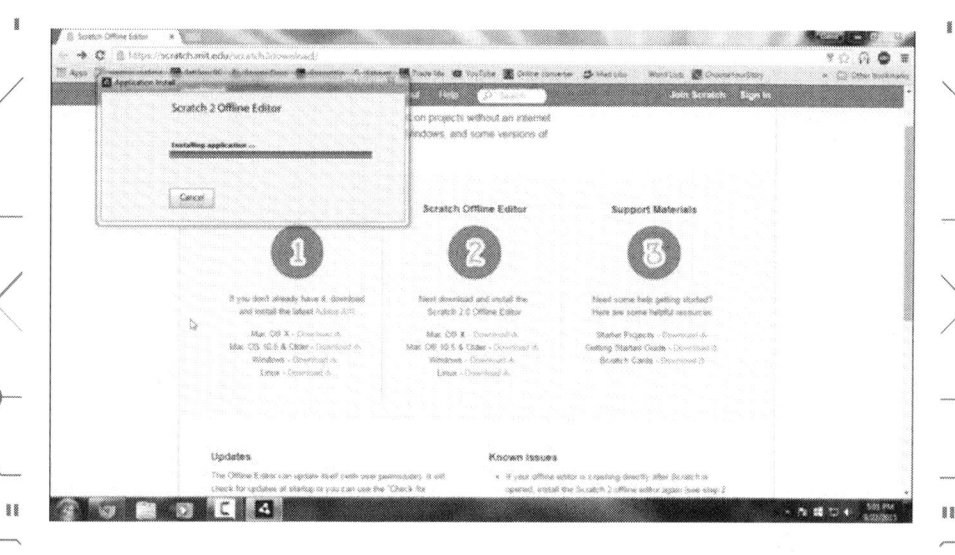

Wait for the installation to finish.

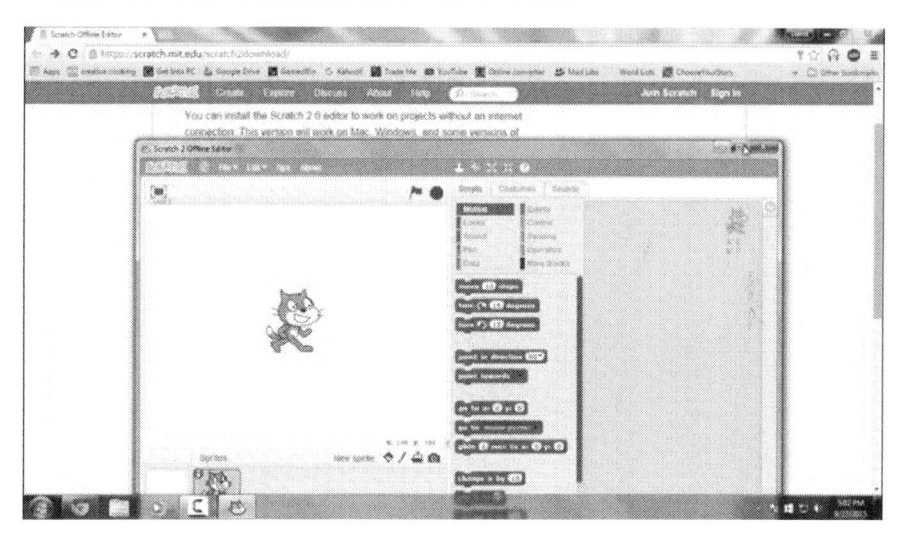

And your done!

CHAPTER - 2
THE BASIC OF SCRATCH

Variables

In Scratch programming, Variables are used to store values. We have already been using some variables in creating our project. For example, in the Up and Down project, we made use of the to check if the sprite was near the edge. In the project after this, we also used the and to change the position of the Sprite 1 to Sprite 2.

All these three palettes are examples of the variable used in Scratch programming. Scratch stores values in these variables; these values are what we use in creating our programs.

We also recall that in some of our project, we altered the values of some variables to fit into what we want. As much as Scratch already has its own variables, we can create our own variables and use this to keep value. A good example of a variable palette that can be altered is the more () block. We can use variables to keep the score of a game, to store speed and to determine the value of x and y in equations.

The two types of variables that would be considered:

- Numerical Variables
- String Variables

Numerical Variables

1. Project name: Times 2
2. Start a new project and title it Times 2
3. Go to the Data block and click on Make a Variable. Title the variable Number and select for this sprite only, then select the OK option

NB: You can share variables among all the sprites or use it with only one sprite. This type of variable can only be used to determine the position of x in a particular sprite. While is an example of a variable that can be used by any sprite. Local variables are variables you can use with only one sprite, while global variables are variables that use all of the sprites.

4. Run your program, when it starts running, go to the Sensing block and use the ask _____ and wait to ask for a number

5. Scratch keeps all the numbers you enter in the answer variable from the Sensing menu. Go to Go Data menu, open set _____ to _____ block. Use this to keep the answers to the variables in the number

variables. Below is how to achieve this:

- Create a local variable and name it Plus 2. After this, go to the Operator block, use the +operator to store the local variable created in the sum of number + 2

- Go to the Looks block, open the way ___ for 2 secs block to view the number + 2 score.

- Start your program, put in a number, and then confirm if it is showing the right answer.

- Make local variables to maintain the value of the number minus two and times two, determine these variables, and show their values. (We will observe that the multiplication operation makes use of an asterisk. This is so because, in programming, letter x is usually used as a variable. Using it again as a multiplication sign would be confusing).

- Test run your program to confirm it is showing the right answer.

It is noteworthy that this program cannot be written without variables because you are not aware of the number the user would choose, hence there is no way you would compute the value of the number without the use of variables.

String Variables

Name of Program: additional 2 (continued)

The user's number minus, times, and plus two were displayed. It would make sense to leave the user more informed. For example: making the number plus 2 = 7

Steps to adding more information to the variable

1. Start a new local variable called output.
2. Then put the plus2 variable to number + 2, after this determine the output variable by using the join operator in the Operators menu
3. Switch your 'say plus2' for 2 secs block so you can use the output variable.
4. Start your program and confirm it is working well.
5. Adapt your program to enable it to use the output variable to show the numerical values of 2 and times 2.

Algorithms

In Scratch programming, algorithms are a set of instructions that are used to complete a task. This task could be something unseen, like tracking the breakout of a dead and rotten dog through the air. However, whether seen or unseen, it is advisable to think of the algorithm you would be using before starting your program. A good example of the algorithm for graph is y = 4x +8. We will be creating a program and use algorithms for the program.

Program name: Sum of the Numbers 1 to n

Assuming you were asked a very simple question like, "What is the total number of 1 to 3?" This is quite easy; you would only calculate 1+2+3=6. The estimate of 1to 3 is 6. What if the question is 1to 7, you would calculate 1+2+3+4+5+6+7= 28? But if the question is 1 to 60? This is quite technical, to solve this, let's go into programming

1. Start a new project and title it Numbers 1 to n

2. Generate three local variables, title them Number, Summation and EndValue respectively

3. Initiate 3 as EndValue

4. Initiate the local variable Number to 1 and Summation to 0

5. Add the following repeat loops to your script:

- In the first loop iteration, the number (1) result derived is still less than the EndValue (3) we are aiming at. As a result, we keep running the iteration

- When the first block in the loop is iterated, the new total value is set to (0) plus number (1). This makes the overall value 0 + 1 = 1.

However, since the answer we are aiming at is number (3), we run another interaction with the second block in the loop. Our new value when the second block add 1 to the previous result is 1 + 1 =

2. After the second iteration, the result is still less than the required EndValue (3). We go inside again to carry out another iteration until we arrived at the desired number (3)

- Add blocks to display the output using the string "The sum of the numbers from 1 to n is: m", where n is the number we entered at the beginning of the program, and m is the Sum.

- Run your program to test what you have just done.

NB: The act of changing the value of a fixed amount is very common in loops. This process is called incrementing the variable.

Summation of the Even/Odd Numbers 1 to n

You find the sum of the even/odd number 1 to n; we would be creating a new program with the name " Sum 1 to n Even/Odd."

- Use the same method in the above program to write a program

- Request a number from the user and show the summation of all the odd numbers from 1 to n, and the summation of the even numbers from 2 to n. For instance, if the user puts in 6, the display would be 9 (that is 1 + 3 + 5) and 12 (that is 2 + 4 + 6).

Program Structure

Virtually all the programs that have been created so far are single script programs. Complex script programs are created with more than one script. Although single script programs seem easier, when a single script program becomes too long, any of these two problems can occur.

- Poor reading proficiency. The cluster of details in a single script program sometimes makes it too clumsy to read. It is easier to get lost while going through the clumps of details in the single script.

- The program becomes difficult to manage. The length of the program often causes this problem. To control the program Arranging length, the programmer would have to arrange and modify the program script. Doing this is always very difficult because each detail contains in the script of the program. This problem made it difficult to reuse parts of the script in creating another script.

We will examine how to use messages and more blocks to add structure to a program and how this structuring can be used to control the length of the script. Below are the steps to adding more blocks to a script.

1. Create a single script program and make the script do the following actions:

2. Open on the left side.

3. Move 10 steps at a time, making a total of 200 steps.

4. Jump up 25 steps (and fall) 3 times.

5. Turn and take 100 steps back, making sure you take 10 steps each time.

6. Turn 2 times.

7. Spin and take 500 steps, making sure you take 10 steps each time.

Adding Structures with Messages

Let's assume the program we created can perform all the actions mentioned above effectively; the layout of the script will be piled up with different instructions. These instructions would make it difficult to keep track of the series of instructions clustered in the program because the single script program is a lengthy set of commands devoid of a solid structure. In computer programming, this type of structure is known as spaghetti code. Spaghetti code is not only difficult to read but also hard to rearrange (moving first and jumping second) and to change (adding a second group of five jumps).

To fix this, each set of actions — initialize, walk, jump, run — would be replaced with a message and another script. For example, we would adjust the loop to jump three times with this broadcast ___ and wait block and the when I receive ___ script

After this action, it would be observed that the blocks we used in adding the structure to the program are the broadcast ___ and wait block and not broadcast ___. This is because when we use a broadcast ___ block without the wait block, it passes control immediately to the next block without waiting for the scripts that received the message to finish the process. For instance, the message in the program above is for the sprite to jump and then spin:

The next final step we would take is the replace step. Go to the Broadcast-and-wait block, then initialize spin to two times, jump to 3 times, walk to 200 times, walk to 100 steps.

How to Add More Blocks to a Program

After the first process, the sprite would look a lot better and easier to work on. The only difficulty we would encounter is with the walk block repeated about three times. Although each walk block has a defined number of times that determines how far the sprite would walk, we will be redefining this with the More block. In Scratch programming, the More block is usually defined by the programmer. The block derives its name "More" from the fact that the programmer is the one to define or determine how it would operate. In programming, this process of adding a block to a program is known as Function.

CHAPTER - 3
FUNCTIONS, IF STATEMENT, AND LISTS

Why Use Functions?

When you used the repeat command, it made drawing complex shapes real y easy. Now you will learn about functions, which allow you to repeat the same code over and over again without having to rewrite the code. A function may sound an awful lot like the repeat command, but functions are one of the most useful tools a programmer can have because it allows you to adjust certain parts of the code based on your needs.

The limitation of the repeat command is apparent when you want to draw a bunch of different size squares. Each square will be coded with virtual y identical code except 38

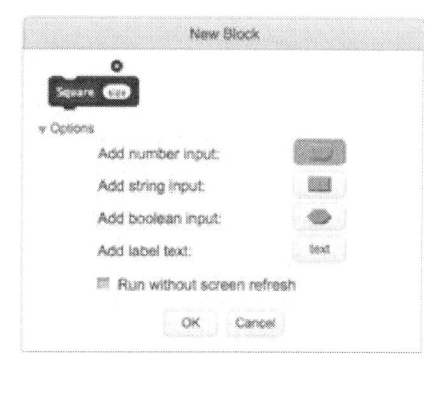

[define Square size]

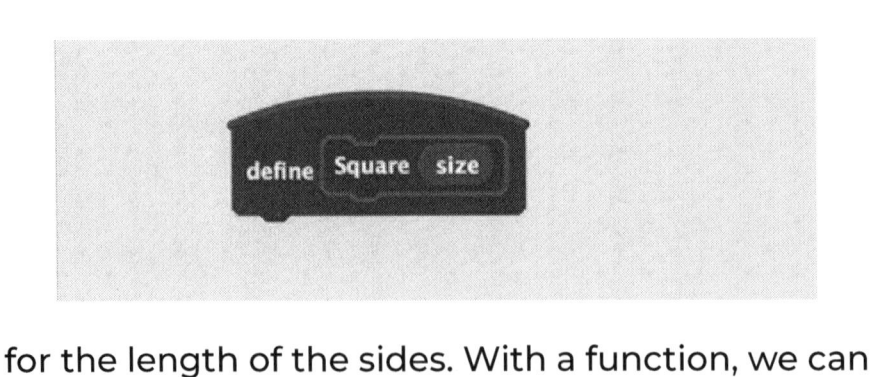

for the length of the sides. With a function, we can use one block of code to draw different size squares!

Formatting Functions have to be written in a particular way. A function must have a name and it may have zero or it may have multiple inputs.

Inputs Scratch offers three different types of inputs: number, string, and boolean. Strings are words like "hello" or

"program." Booleans can have only two values: true or false. Final y, numbers are values like 23.56 or 200.

Create a Function To create a function, go to the More Blocks section and click on the "Make a Block" button.

Then, enter a name for your function. If your function needs to use input values, click on one of the options and enter a name for the input.

Click to add the "size" input The input value

The function name

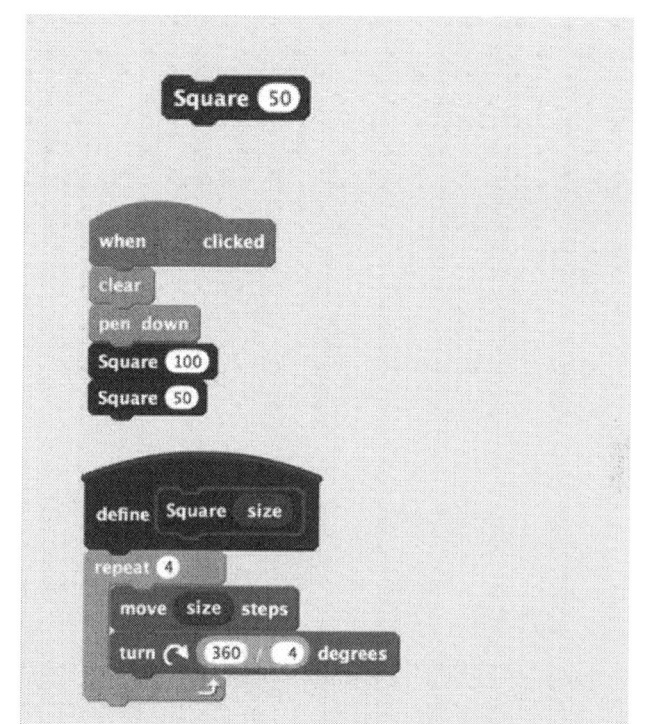

Calling A Function, you can make a script attached to a define block and click "run," but nothing will happen.

This is because you have to tell the computer to call the function. The way you call the "Square" function defined on the previous page is by using the following command block, which was created at the same time as the function.

In the example above, the input value is 50, but it could be set to any number.

Draw a square with a length of 100

Draw a square with a length of 50

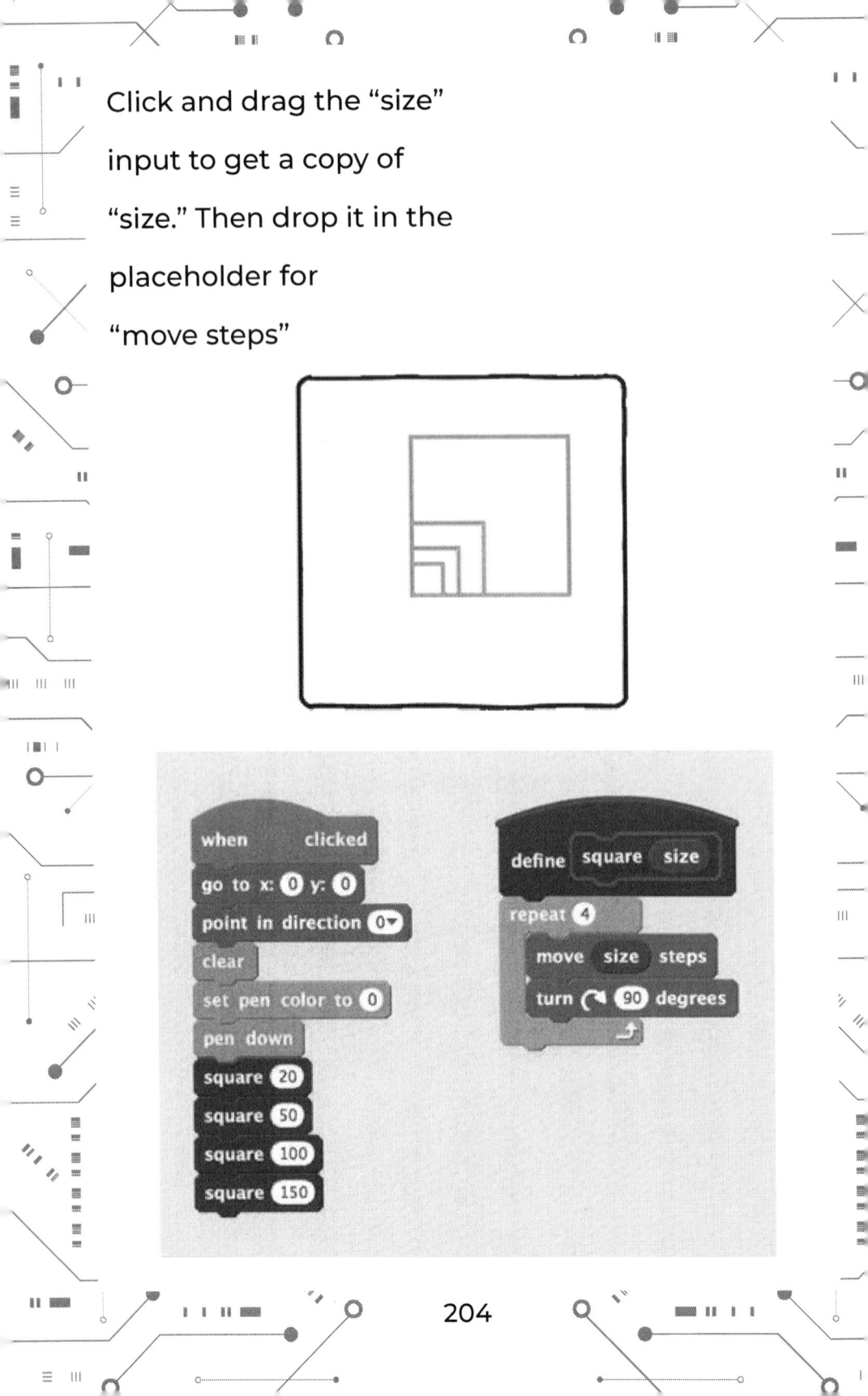

Click and drag the "size" input to get a copy of "size." Then drop it in the placeholder for "move steps"

```
when clicked
go to x: 0 y: 0
point in direction 0
clear
set pen color to 0
pen down
square 20
square 50
square 100
square 150
```

```
define square size
repeat 4
    move size steps
    turn ↻ 90 degrees
```

Project: Drawing Squares

Let's use a function to draw a bunch of different size squares. Can you draw some other size squares?

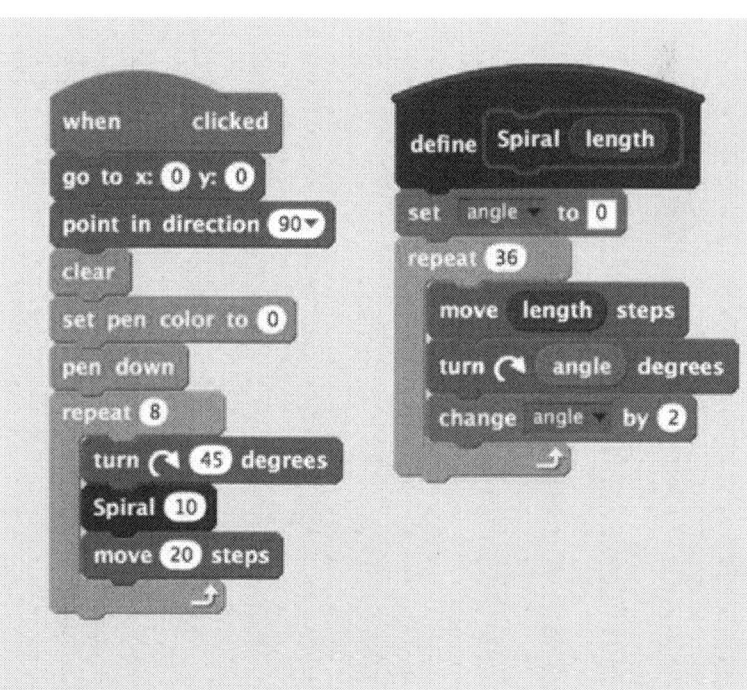

Project: Spiral Rose

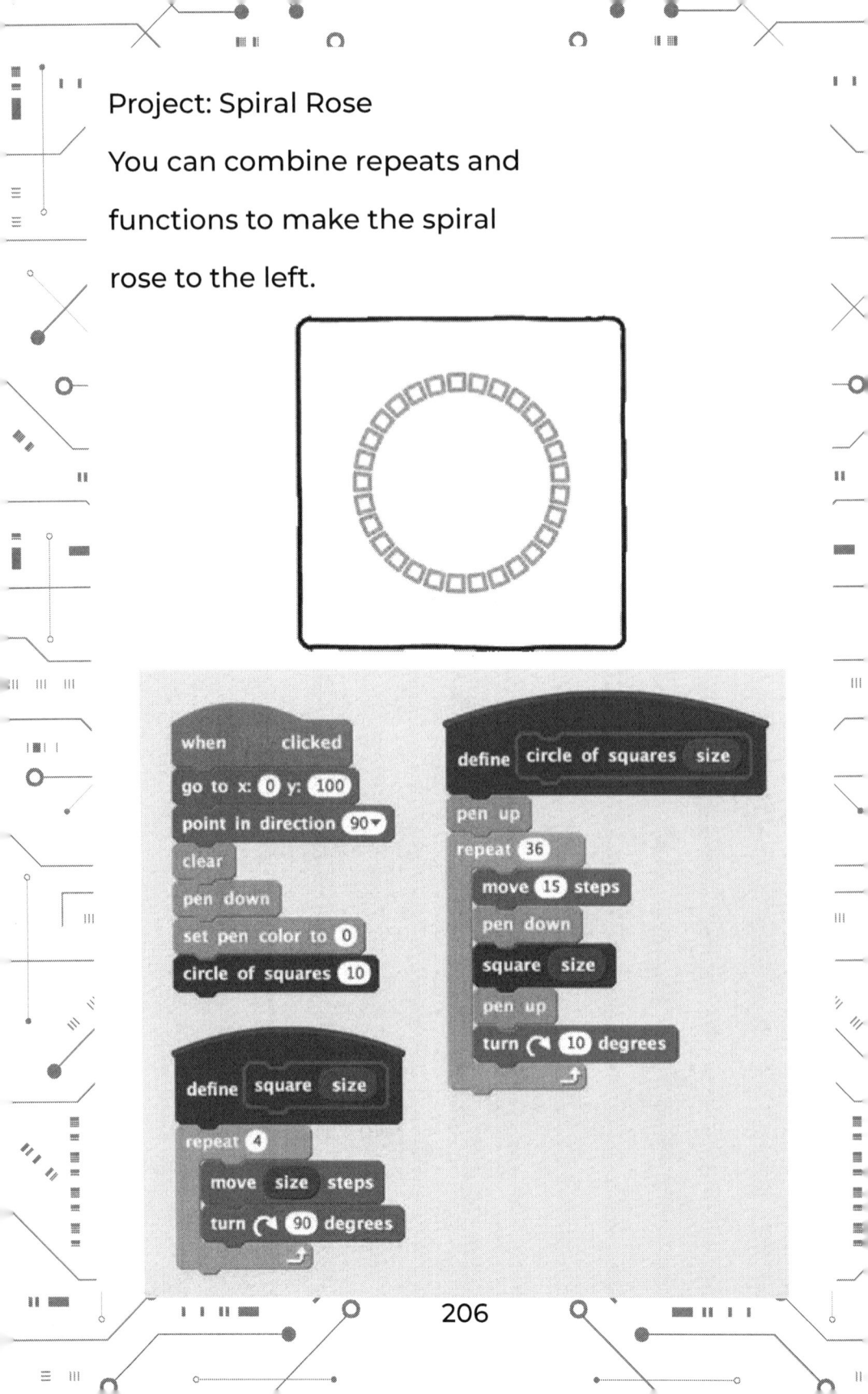

You can combine repeats and functions to make the spiral rose to the left.

```
when clicked
go to x: 0 y: 100
point in direction 90
clear
pen down
set pen color to 0
circle of squares 10
```

```
define square size
repeat 4
    move size steps
    turn ↻ 90 degrees
```

```
define circle of squares size
pen up
repeat 36
    move 15 steps
    pen down
    square size
    pen up
    turn ↻ 10 degrees
```

Project: Circle of Squares

You can make a lot of complicated things easily with

functions. In this function, the command penup is used to stop the pen from making marks while it is moving.

Ch 9: Practice Problems

1) Can you make a function that will help you draw different size triangles?

2) Make a function that will let you draw different size houses.

If Statements

What if you wanted your pen to do different things based on the current value of a variable? If the variable's value is greater than zero, the pen should rotate 45 degrees. If the variable's value is equal to zero, the pen should rotate 90 degrees. An easy way to program this is to use an if statement.

If Statement The if statement tells your program to execute a certain section of code only if a particular condition is true. If it is true, the code between the brackets will be executed. If it is false, Scratch will simply ignore the code between the brackets.

Compare "x" to 100

This code will only execute if the value stored in "x" is less than 100

Conditional Statements Scratch lets you compare values to see if one is greater than the other, less than the other, or equal to the other value.

Conditional Statements

Command	Example	Command In Scratch
equal to	5 = 6	
less than	10 < 3	
greater than	8 > 5	

Project: Radiating Lines

To make the image to the left, use two if statements to adjust the length of the lines.

The repeat command is going to run 73 times. You are going to use a variable called count to keep track of what number repeat we are on. If the count is less than 36, de-crease the line length. If the count is greater than 36, increase the line length.

You can use this technique to draw different shapes de-pending on your if statements. What will happen if you use four if statements instead of the two in the example?

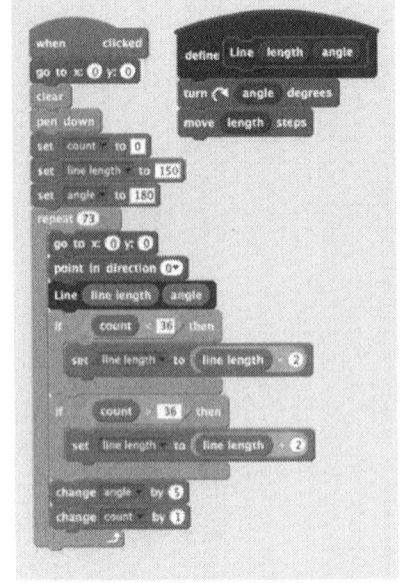

If the count is less than 36, decrease the line length
If the count is greater than 36, increase the line length

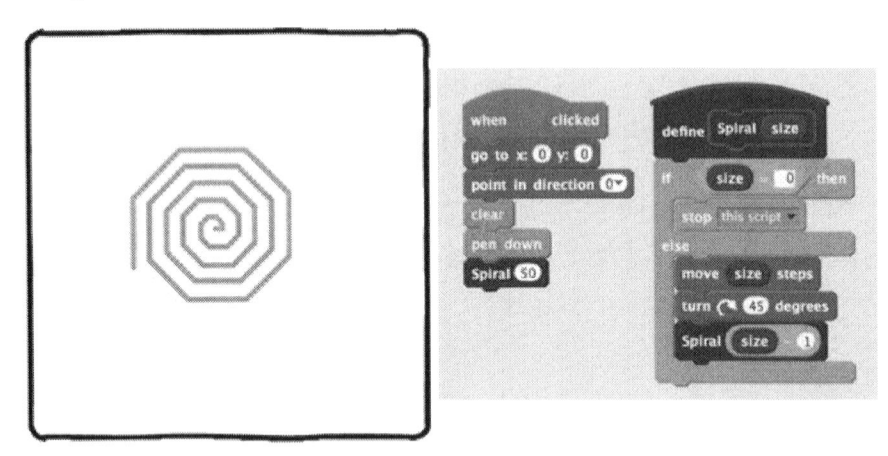

Project: Recursive Spiral

An interesting thing about functions are that they can call themselves. Whenever a function calls itself, it is called recursion. The only problem with this technique is that you need a way to stop the calling process or else the program will run forever!

If loops are helpful for stopping the program because you can tell the program to stop once a certain condition has been met. For example, you could initially call the loop with the variable "size" that has been initialized to 100. Each time the loop calls itself, the "size" decreases by 1. When the value of "size" reaches 0, the program will stop.

When size equals 0, stop the program

The Spiral function calls itself with size-1

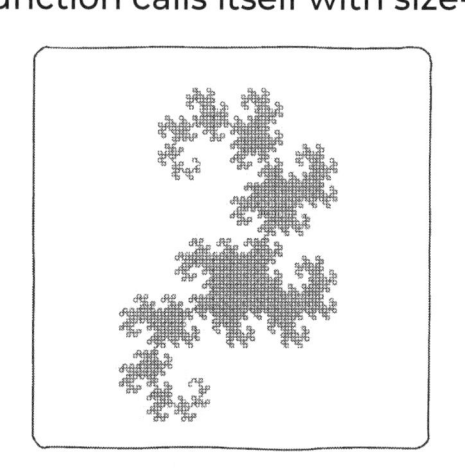

Project: Dragon Curve

Programmers like recursion a lot because it lets them make real y complicated drawings using relatively few lines of code. If you tried to draw the dragon curve above only by using functions and repeat loops, it would take you hours, and hundreds of lines of code, to complete.

Try experimenting with the code on the next page by calling the function with different inputs (for example call the function x with x 6 or x 13).

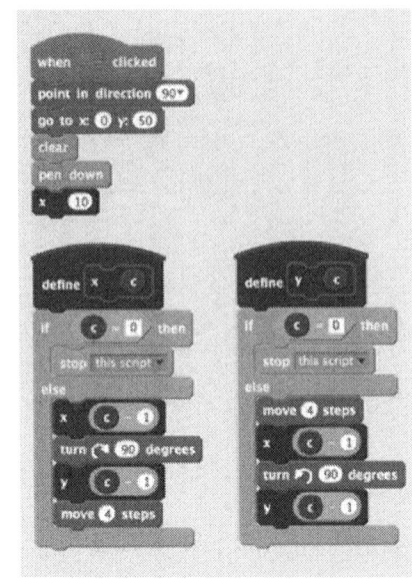

Try changing the input to a different number like 6 or 13

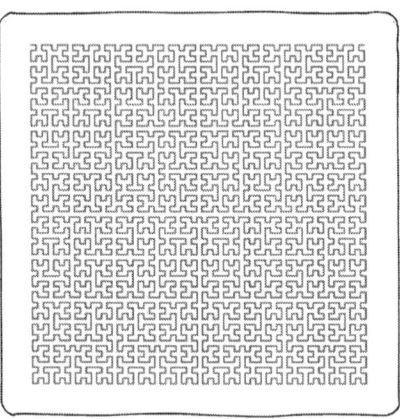

Project: Hilbert Curve

The labyrinth above is called the Hilbert curve. Like the dragon curve, it is real y easy to draw with a recursive function.

After you copy the code on the next page into

Scratch and run the program, try experimenting with altering the code. For instance, try changing the inputs for the lsec function call in the last line of code to lsec 5 5 or lsec 3 3.

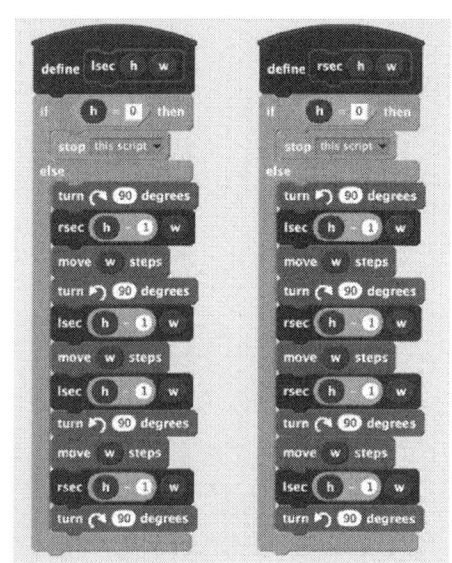

try changing the inputs to different numbers like (lsec 5 5) or (lsec 3 3) 53

Practice Problems

1) Can you make a recursive spiral triangle?

2) Use the spiral triangle code from above to make a star.

Experiment with different angles and lengths to create different types of stars.

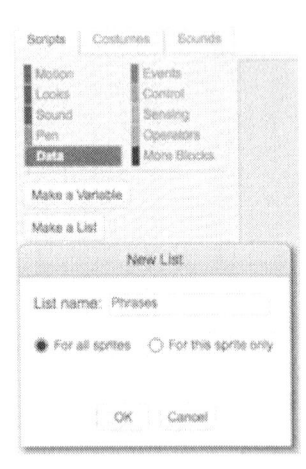

Making Lists

So far, we have only used Scratch to manipulate numbers and variables one value at a time, but we can also store and manipulate lists of things.

Lists Remember when you learned about variables? Variables are a way to store one thing in memory. Sometimes you need to store multiple things in memory but you don't want to do a lot of tedious typing. Lists let you store many values in a single structure.

Making lists is like making a variable.

Go to the Data Section and click the "Make List" button then enter the name of the list.

You can then use the add block to add items to the list.

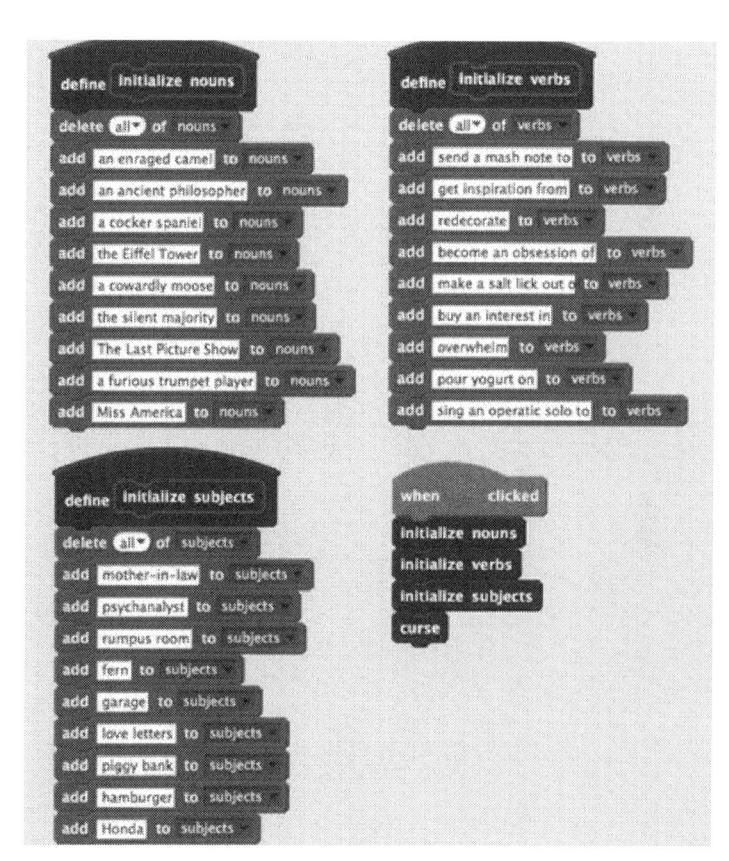

Project: Curses

This program is based on the work of Tom Dwyer and Margot Critchfield, who published a similar program in their book BASIC and the Personal

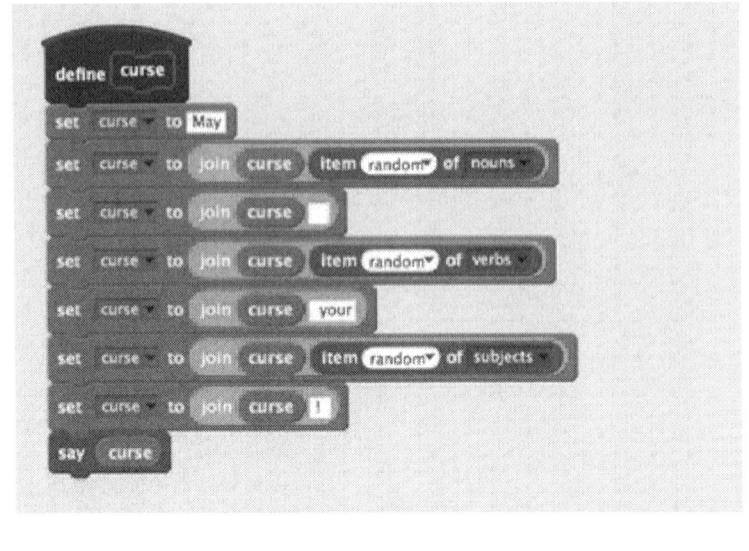

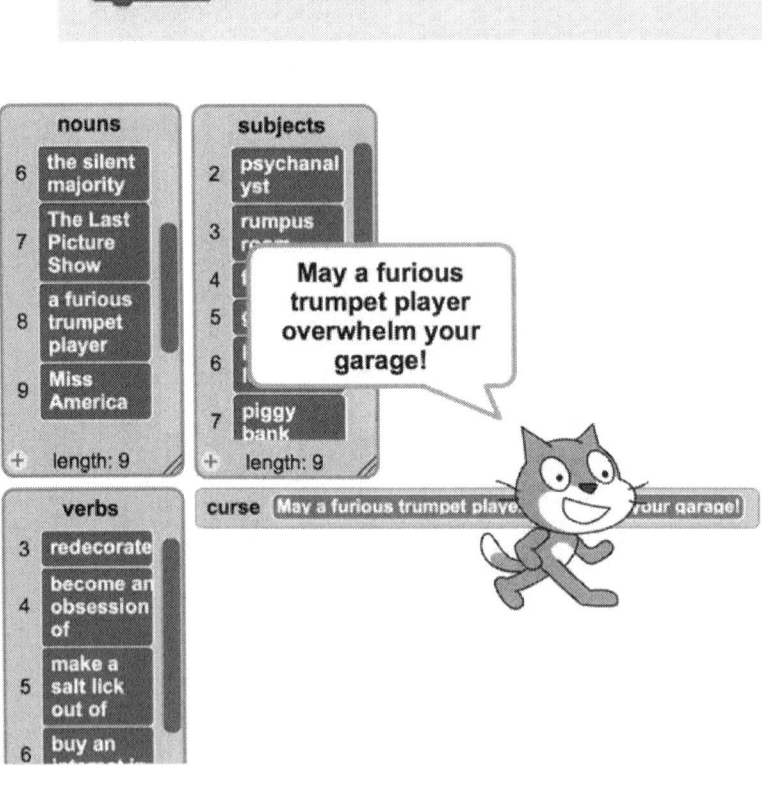

Computer in 1979. It uses lists to create a computer-generated poem.

Change this program to suit your personality. Add more things to the lists. Take some things away. Change the pattern used to form the curse. Is the pattern for a blessing different from the pattern for a curse?

Practice Problems

1) Many computer programs have been developed that generate poetry or music. Some of them use a technique similar to the curses program. These programs often have large lists of words that are arranged according to some predefined patterns.

For example, you might draw from lists in a pattern like this:

Title

Adjective Noun

Verb Noun

Noun Preposition Noun Verb Noun

Ending Phrase

How could you make your poem rhyme? How could you link the Title and Ending Phrase to give your poem a sense of order and completion?

2) Working in a group, modify your program so that it generates poetry instead of curses. Within your group, select your three favorite computer-generated poems.

3) Try making a program that generates haikus. A haiku is a short Japanese poem that consists of 3 lines. The first and last lines of a Haiku have 5 syllables and the middle line has 7 syllables. The lines rarely rhyme.

4) Make a Dadaist poem in the style of Tristan Tzara:
a. Take a newspaper.

b. Choose an article as long as you are planning to make your poem.

c. Make a list containing each of the words that make up this article.

d. Make a poem by randomly choosing each word. Remove the word from the list after it is used.

e. The poem will be like you.

*****Insert Poem here

Problem

Solutions

A1

2: First Program

1) There are many ways to draw a house. The code below shows one way to draw a house by first drawing the rectangle and then adding a triangle to the top of the image.

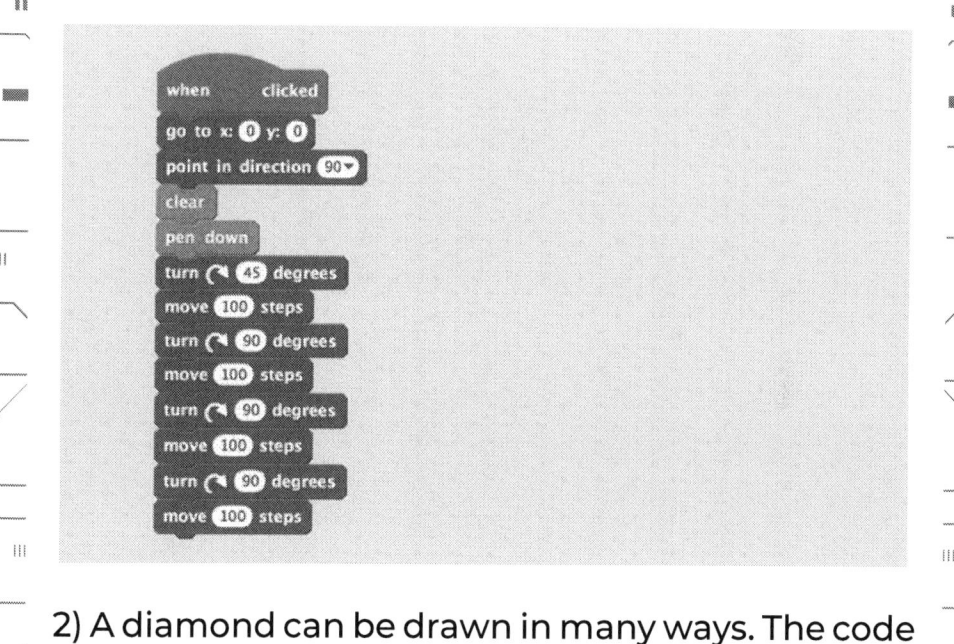

```
when clicked
go to x: 0 y: 0
point in direction 90
clear
pen down
turn ↶ 45 degrees
move 100 steps
turn ↶ 90 degrees
move 100 steps
turn ↶ 90 degrees
move 100 steps
turn ↶ 90 degrees
move 100 steps
```

2) A diamond can be drawn in many ways. The code below shows a simple way to draw a diamond.

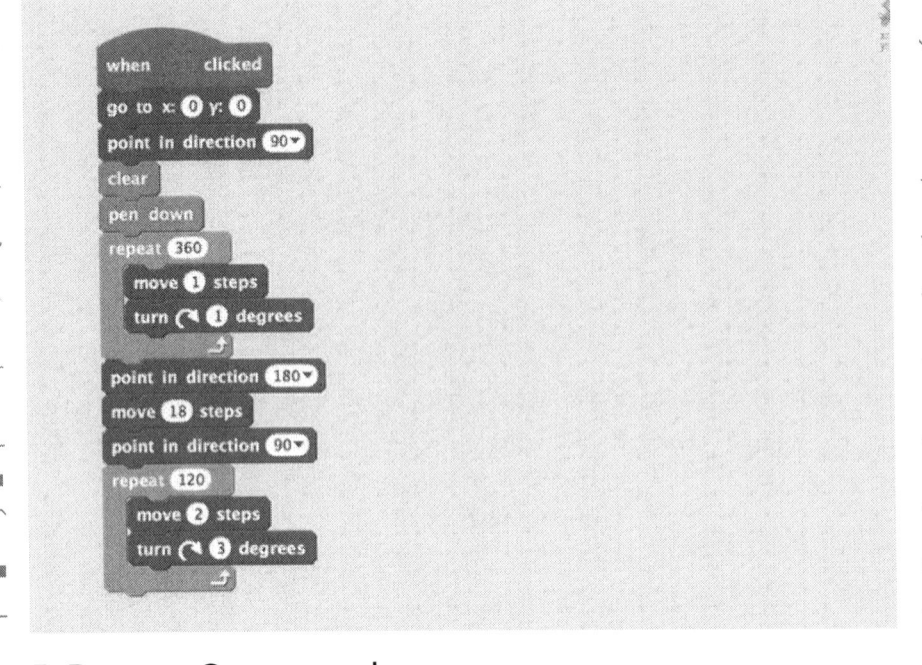

```
when clicked
go to x: 0 y: 0
point in direction 90
clear
pen down
repeat 360
    move 1 steps
    turn ↶ 1 degrees
point in direction 180
move 18 steps
point in direction 90
repeat 120
    move 2 steps
    turn ↶ 3 degrees
```

5: Repeat Command

1) There are many ways to draw different size circles.

The code below shows one way to draw two different size circles. The first repeat code draws the smaller inner circle and the second repeat code draws the bigger outer circle.

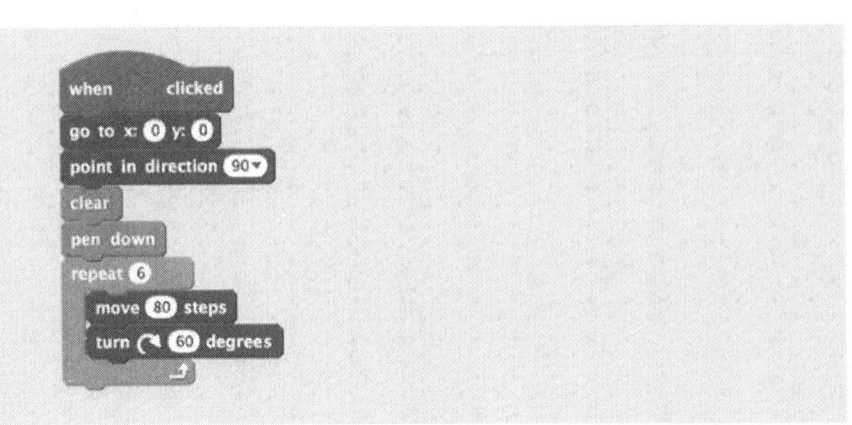

```
when clicked
go to x: 0 y: 0
point in direction 90
clear
pen down
repeat 6
    move 80 steps
    turn ↶ 60 degrees
```

2) The easiest way to draw a hexagon is to draw 6 lines with an angle of 60 degrees between each line.

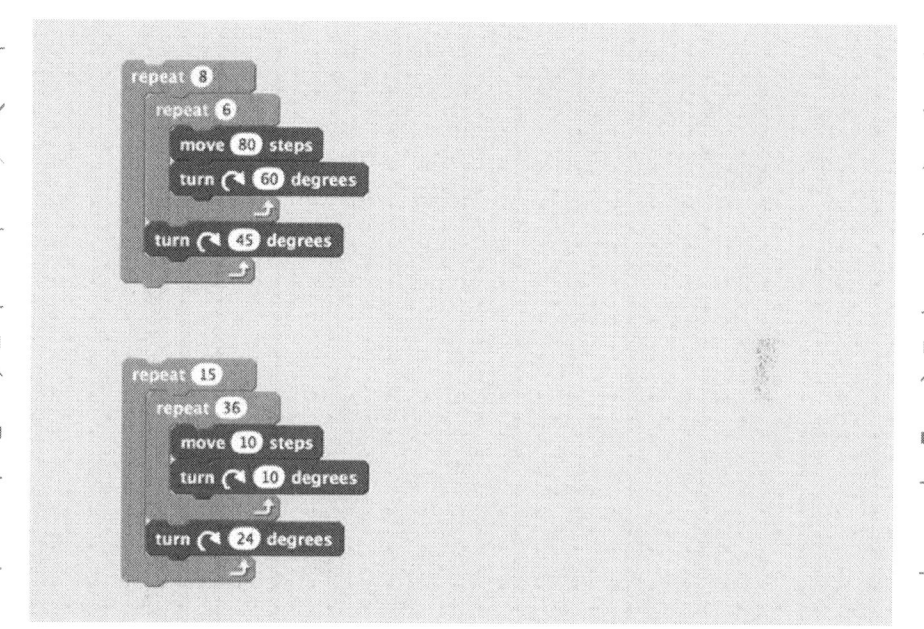

```
repeat 8
    repeat 6
        move 80 steps
        turn ↶ 60 degrees
    turn ↶ 45 degrees
```

```
repeat 15
    repeat 36
        move 10 steps
        turn ↶ 10 degrees
    turn ↶ 24 degrees
```

Nested Repeats

1) There are many ways to draw a shape consisting of hexagons. The code below describes one way to draw the shape.

2) The code below describes one way to draw a shape made out of many circles.

All About Variables 1) False. Since the computer thinks lower and upper-case letters are different, 'myFirstVariable and 'MYFIRSTVARIABLE do not mean the same thing to the computer.

2) The final value of w is: 12

3) The final value of w is: 16

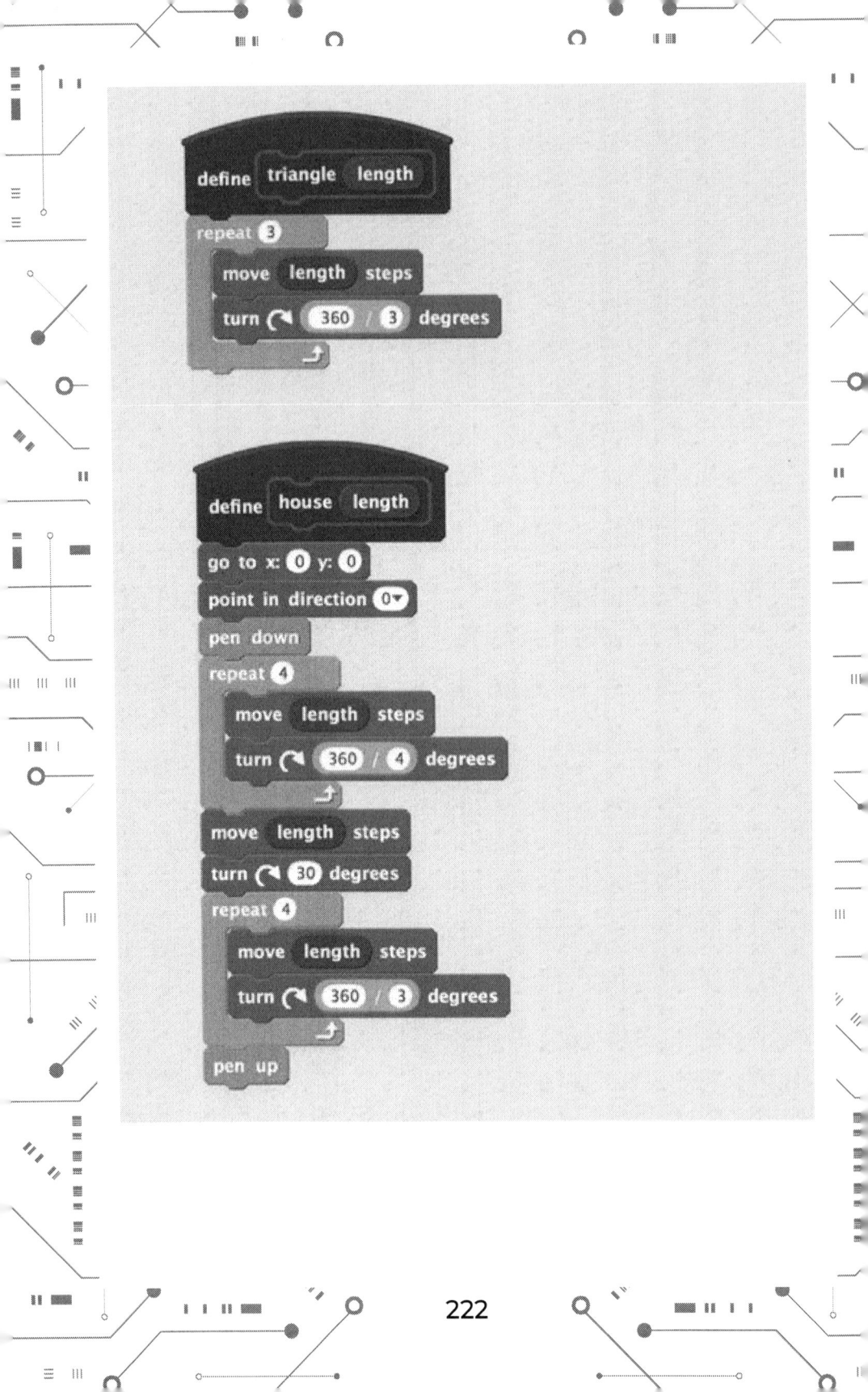

```
define triangle length
repeat 3
    move length steps
    turn ↻ 360 / 3 degrees
```

```
define house length
go to x: 0 y: 0
point in direction 0
pen down
repeat 4
    move length steps
    turn ↻ 360 / 4 degrees
move length steps
turn ↻ 30 degrees
repeat 4
    move length steps
    turn ↻ 360 / 3 degrees
pen up
```

CHAPTER - 4
LOOP THE HOOP

Have you been to a circus or a local festival where they have rides and things for everyone? Or you might have seen one on TV. The fancier merry-go-rounds have horse rides that also move up and down as you go around in circles. It was one of the things I loved the most when I was a kid. It was all fun and not scary at all! The ride goes round and round and round, endlessly and it has just the right speed.

In programming, we also have things that go round, round, and round! They are called loops. Yes, just loops, not the froot loops everyone loves! With loops we can do one or more tasks several times.

There are essentially two kinds of loops:

1. Loops that run for a specific number of times. We set the counter when creating the loop.

2. Loops that run until a specific condition is met. We define that condition when creating the loop.

We are going to work on two projects. Each project will focus on one type of the loop.

Loop #1

Have you ever taken a ride in a helicopter? Helicopters are so cool and scary at the same time. I loved helicopters. I have never been on a helicopter but as a kid, I used to be a helicopter enthusiast. I collected helicopter models and read books about them. I think I was inspired by the 80s TV show Airwolf. Okay, let me be clear. I am not that old and there's nothing wrong with watching very old TV shows, especially when they are as unique as Airwolf.

You know what's even cooler than helicopters? Spaceships! The first time I saw a spaceship was in a movie. I don't remember what the name of the movie was but it made a lasting impression on me. Well, not everyone can go on spaceships. Technology is still not that advanced! But, that doesn't mean we can't imagine hopping onto a spaceship and cruising along an alien planet's surface. You know what, let's do that!

Create a new project, name it "Third Project" and add a backdrop named "Space". Add a "Rocketship" sprite. Make sure it is selected in the "sprite and backdrop" section and change the direction of the sprite to 139:

Now, making sure the "Rocketship" sprite is still selected, start adding the following blocks (in the exact same order):

1. Add "when   clicked" block from the "Events" options in the Code tab.

2. Add "go to x:124 y:107" block from the "Motion" options in the Code tab. Change the x value to -176 and y value to 107.

3. Now, from "Control" options in the same Code tab, add the block that looks like this (change the 10 to 70):

   `repeat 10`

4. Inside the jaw of the above loop block, place a "change x by 10" block which is found in the "Motion" options in the Code tab. Change the 10 to 8.

5. From the "Sound" options in Code tab, drag the "start sound space ripple" and place it inside the loop block after the motion block.

The final stack will look like the image below.

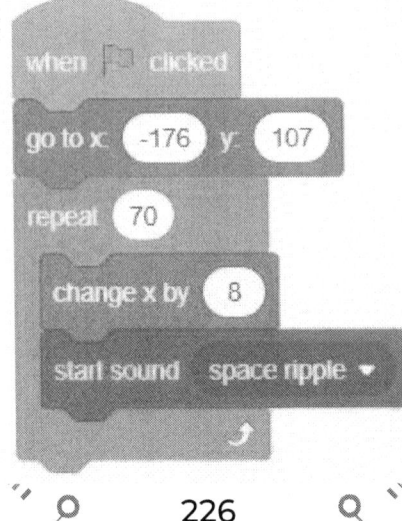

```
when clicked
go to x: -176  y: 107
repeat 70
    change x by 8
    start sound space ripple
```

The stage may look like this before running the project:

Now, run your project by clicking on the green flag and see the spaceship speed through the night sky of this alien planet with very mysterious sci-fi sound effects!

Loop #2

The loop we used in the previous project will run 70 times because we set that value in the loop. What if we don't know the exact number when creating the loop? For example, if you run the above project, you will see that the spaceship actually flies off the screen. What if we want to run the loop until our sprite touches the edge of the stage?

Let's see how we can do that. Let me introduce my health-conscious friend, Avery, who needs our guidance while walking around the city streets. Let's create a fun little project to help Avery walk on city streets without wandering out too far.

Let's create a new project. If the previous project

is still open, make sure to save it before creating a new project. Name the new project "Fourth Project" and start making the following changes.

1. Choose the "Colorful City" backdrop.

2. Select the "Avery Walking" sprite. Change the size to 40. Change the x and y values to x: -220 and y: -123. The sprite setting should look like this.

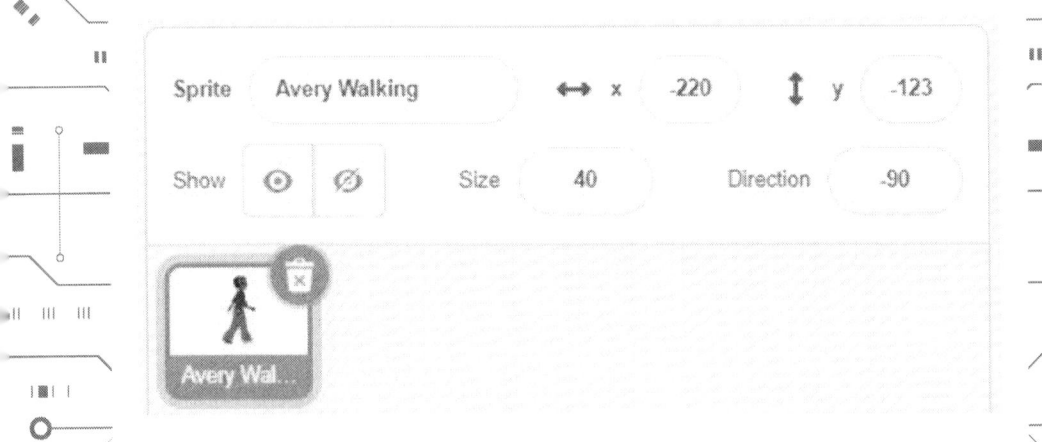

Sprite	Avery Walking	↔ x	-220	↕ y	-123
Show	◉ ⊘	Size	40	Direction	-90

Avery Wal...

Now, we have to add some blocks to this Avery.

1. Add "point in direction 90" block from the "Motion" options in the Code tab.

2. Add "go to x:124 y:107" block from the "Motion" options in the Code tab. Change the x value to -213 and y value to -123.

3. Now, from "Control" options in the same Code tab, add the block that looks like this:

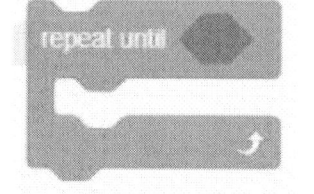

4. In the hollow box of this loop block, put the block "touching MOUSE-POINTER" block. Change MOUSE-POINTER to EDGE.

5. Inside the same loop block, add a "change x by 10" block from "Motion" options under the Code block. Change 10 to 2.

The block stack should look like this.

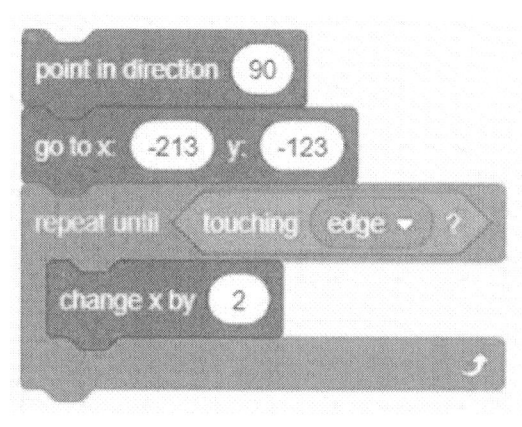

Now, we need to duplicate this whole block. Right click on this and select "Duplicate". It will create another block stack. Place it anywhere on the workspace with a left click. We need to change the settings on the second stack like below:

1. Change "point in direction 90" to -90

2. Change "go to x: -213 y: -123" to 216 and -123

3. Change "change x by 2" to -2

After the stacks are adjusted, put "when clicked" block from the "Events" options in the Code tab at the top of the entire stack. When you are done, the entire stack would look like this:

```
when clicked
point in direction 90
go to x: -213 y: -123
repeat until <touching edge?>
    change x by 2
point in direction -90
go to x: 216 y: -123
repeat until <touching edge?>
    change x by -2
```

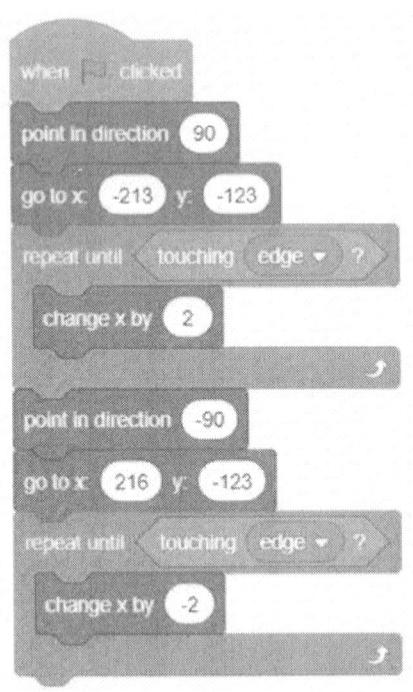

This whole stack will help Avery move from one end of the street to the other, turn around and then walk to the street end she started from. It is a very cool project. Save it with the name "Fourth Project" so you can help Avery whenever needed.

Loop within a Loop

The last thing we will learn is the secret of adding a loop block inside another loop block. Let's help Avery again because she wants to make at least 10 rounds on the street. Don't blame her, she wants to be healthy! We need to add one loop block to our Fourth Project and Avery will be able to walk up and down the city street.

We are going to use the loop#1 type and wrap most of the blocks inside them like shown in the image below. We are going to use 5 as the number of times the loop will execute.

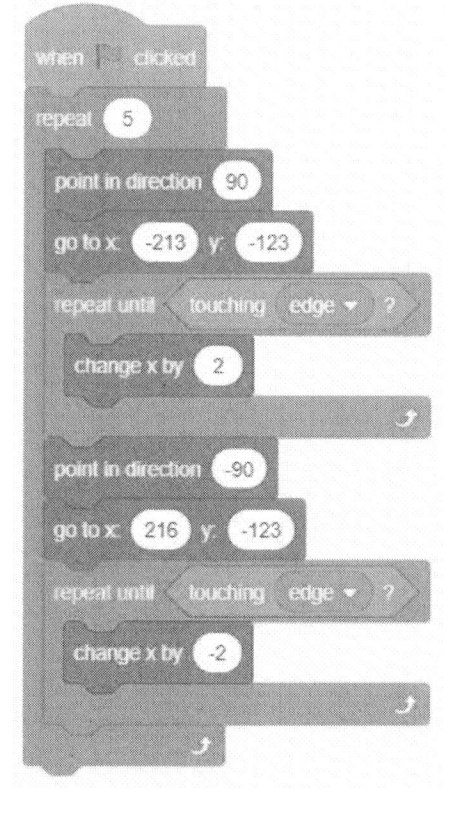

```
when [flag] clicked
repeat 5
    point in direction 90
    go to x: -213 y: -123
    repeat until <touching edge?>
        change x by 2
    point in direction -90
    go to x: 216 y: -123
    repeat until <touching edge?>
        change x by -2
```

CHAPTER - 5

MOVE YOUR SPRITE!

Sprite Information

Below the Stage area, you will find the Sprite information box. Here you will find the Sprites you have added to your game already. This box also has information about each of them. Each Sprite has a name, and it is displayed in this information area. Scratchy's name is written as Sprite1. Boring right? You can change this name to something more fun if you want. You can also find information about the position of the Sprite and the direction it is facing.

Task: Making A Sprite Move

Let us start with an easy one: making a sprite move. To make Scratchy the cat move, follow these steps:

1. Go to the blocks palette and select the "motions" palette. Drag a "goto x: 0 y: 0" block and drop it in the script area.

2. Next, choose the "move ten steps" block and add

it to the bottom of the block.

3. Change the ten steps to 100 steps. Click the green button and see what happens. Nothing right? What seems to be the problem here? By using the motions block, Scratchy can now walk. But the poor cat doesn't know yet. So how do we tell Scratchy he can move now? That's very simple too.

4. Go to the "events" pallet. We want Scratchy to move, but we have first to tell Scratchy when to run. If we don't do this, Scratchy will not be able to move.

5. Click and drag the "when the green flag is clicked" blocked into the script area. Attach the motion blocks to the base of this new block. By doing this, you are telling Scratch that he can move when someone clicks on the green button.

6. Now click the green button again and see what happens. Congratulation. You just got scratchy to move. Now let's go over what you just did again.

Now let's talk about the motion blocks you used. The first block: "go to x: 0 y: 0," tells Scratch to move on the same line as it is. This follows a rule known as the coordinate system. I will explain what the coordinate system does soon. The last block tells the cat to take 100 steps. You can edit this to be any number of steps that you want, and Scratchy will bring that number of steps in the direction you have selected with the first block.

Understanding Position and Direction In Scratch.

Before we make the cat turn around, let's learn about positioning and direction in Scratch. First, go to the box beneath the stage and choose a new backdrop. On the list of backdrops, you will find a sprite named XY-grid. Select this Sprite. You should notice the background of your stage area transform into a box with lines and numbers. This will help you understand the coordinate system that Scratch uses to position objects. What is the number at the center of the two lines crossing each other? (x:0 and y:0) right?

To understand what this means, you need to get familiar with the grid system. You've probably been thought that in school. But even if you have not been taught, it is straightforward to understand. Just follow along with In a grid system. Everything is positioned on two axes. The Y-axis represents the line that goes from up to down. This marks the up and down (vertical position) of any object. The Y-axis is labeled form -180 (at the lowest part of the lines) to 0 at the middle to +190 at the top of the page.

The X-axis represents the line that goes from left to right. This indicates the position of an object on a horizontal line. It has a range from -240 on the left and +240 on the right.

Task: Let's Try Some Positioning Examples

Now for some cases: if we set the value of Scratchy's position as (x: 0 and y:180), what does that mean? It means we want Scratchy to be positioned at the top of the page vertically without leaving the center. Scratchy will move up vertically without going left or right. Let's look at other examples:

(x:-240 and y:180): try to guess what this means; this says scratchy should be positioned at the top of the page and the farthest left side of the page. The Sprite will end up on the top left corner of the page.

Here's another example: (x:90 and y:50)- this

command says Scratchy should move by 90 places to the right and move 50 spaces up.

Let us look at one final example: (x:-100 and y:-80) try guessing what this command says: This command simply tells Scratchy to move to the left by -100 spaces while going down by 80 areas.

Before we proceed, let's try to change something in the previous code we wrote and see how this will affect Scratchy, the cat. Go to the Script area and select the "go-to" block. Edit the figures on the box to (x:90 and y:90). Do not change anything else. Click on the green button now and see what happens. Notice that the cat did not move in the same direction as it did before. You can try out different combinations of X and Y and see how your Sprite responds.

Now that you can see how scratch positions objects, we can proceed to learn more about moving the Sprites in different directions with the motion blocks.

Turning And Waiting

Let's add some more blocks to your code to make the Sprite change direction. For a simple task, we are going to make the cat move around in a square. This should be easy and fun.

Step 1: Go back to the motions block palette and select the "turn counterclockwise 15 degrees" block. Drag and add this to the bottom of the blocks you had before. Change 15 to 90 degrees. At this stage, you can click the green button to see how Scratchy reacts or continue with the rest of the instructions.

Step 2: Add three more blocks like this.

Step 3: Click the green button and see what happens. The cat moved in a square, but you probably didn't notice before it was quite fast. Let fix that as I introduce you to another category of blocks.

Wait For Blocks

Select the "controls" palette on the block tab. Click and drag the "wait for 1-sec" block into the script area. Do the same thing for each of the turns. Doing this will add a wait of 1 sec before the cat follows the next command. This will show each step as the cat changes direction more clearly. You can change the wait time to make it even slower if you want to. That was cool, wasn't it? Let's try some new tricks with the things we have learned so far.

More motion blocks

What if we wanted to make Scratchy glide about instead of jumping the way he did before? How do you think we can do that? Let's go back to the motions palette and see if there's anything there that can make Scratchy glide around. Can you find anything that helps? Yes. The "glide" block can be used to make Scratchy glide smoothly across the screen from one position to another.

To do this, follow these instructions:

| Step 1: Remove all the blocks we used earlier, leaving only the "when the green flag is clicked" block.

| Step 2: Now drag in the "glide _ secs to x:0 y:0".

| Step 3: You can edit x and y position as you want it. You can also change the time from one second to any time of your choice. This will change how fast the Sprite will guide to the position you have chosen.

Once you are done editing, click the green flag to see what happens. You can play around with other action buttons and see what other cool stuff you can make scratchy do,

LOOPS: MAKING THE SPRITE REPEAT AN ACTION.

Before we proceed, let's quickly learn a neat new trick that will be very helpful as you learn to code more with Scratch. Like every other programming language, the more you make Scratch do, the longer your codes you need to write.

For instance, remember the code we wrote to make Scratchy the cat moves in a square while waiting for 1 second after each turn. It was a simple "move-turn-wait" code. But the code became quite long because this action was repeated four times for scratchy to move in a square.

Imagine if we wanted the character to move like

these 100 times, we would need to join 1200 blocks to make that happen. That's a lot of hard work, right? We don't want to waste our time on that kind of hard work. Luckily, there is a neat little trick that can make your codes shorter and still make the character do what we want over and over again. In coding, this is what is called a loop. To do this in Scratch, all you need is a repeat block.

Remember the blocks we combined with moving the cat in a square earlier. Now we need it again. Along with the when the green button is clicked block, you should have five blocks. To make Scratchy repeat this same move four times, drag a "repeat" block from the "controls" palette into the script area. Put all the "move-wait-turn" blocks into the repeat block and set how many times you want the action to be repeated. Since we want the cat to move in a square, we can set this value to 4 instead of 10. now, when you click on the green flag, the cat will run on its own and repeat the action for the set number of times.

Let take things a step further. Let's take a look at our code and see any repeated action that we can set into a loop like this one. For instance. Remember that in the first motion block we set the cat to move 100 steps. How about we make it move 10 steps at a time. How many times will the Sprite move now to complete 100 steps? Yeah. You are a smart kid. The cat will run 10 times instead of 100 times now. But we don't want to waste our time repeating ten

240

move blocks. So what can we do? I know, we can summon the loop wizard again.

This time remove the moving block from the rest of the blocks. Change the number of steps to 10. Select a repeat block from the palette and drag it into the script area. Put the "move" block into the repeat block and set the number of times you want this action to be repeated. Join the other blocks as you had it before. Click the green flag to see what happens. You should see the Sprite move smoothly across the screen in a square.

More on Loops

Before we move on from loops. Let's learn another neat trick:

A wizard is in town and has cast a spell on Scratchy, the cat. Now Scratchy will keep on moving in a square forever. The wizard used Scratch to cast this spell, do you want to know how to do this too. It's very simple. You can make a character in your game do the same thing over and over again using a forever loop block. It is just like the repeat block, but it has no end. Let see this in action. Remove the repeat block from your script. Replace this repeat block with the forever block. Click on the green flag and watch scratchy go on forever.

CHAPTER - 6

CREATING A PLAN FOR YOUR PROJECT

Many people don't like this concept. The worst thing that you can do when starting a project is to just jump in and start working on it. Instead of doing that, you should think about your project beforehand.

The Importance Of Having A Plan

First, consider a story. You could just open up scratch and then build your story as you go. You could pull up character sprites, and just make up stuff for the characters to say. You could keep doing this until you had a large number of scenes worked out.

There might be a better way to come up with a story app for your scratch project. Suppose that instead of just working it out on the fly, you took some time to think about your story first. You could even use a pencil and paper. Start by drawing the main characters. Or you can just write down their names and what they look at.

Think hard about the characters in your story. Who

are they and where do they come from? What do they want?

Then build up an overall outline for the story. At this stage, you don't have to fill in all the details. Just outline the main points of the story. You could name each scene you would like to have, and then write out what is going to be said and how things are going to develop. You can also write down some ideas about how each scene is going to transition into the next scene.

Again, this does not mean that you can't change the story later on. You can even change it after you have built up all the scenes in scratch. It can be changed at any time. But by planning, we will find that we save a lot of time and energy, and our work usually turns out better than it would if we just rushed ahead with it on the computer.

The More Complex the App, The More Planning You Need

If you are going to design a complicated game, it can help to use the same procedure. If you are building a script that is going to be really complicated, then it is even more important to plan out how you are going to do it first. The worst thing that you could do is jump on the computer and just start trying to build a game or large application without having any idea about how it's going to work and progress.

Let's say that you wanted to make a maze game. A

good way to approach this is to draw out all of your mazes on paper before you even open up scratch. You might find that some mazes that look good on paper are too hard to get through when you actually put them up on the computer screen. But one thing for sure is that your building of the game is going to be accomplished in a much shorter time once you get on the computer in scratch than if you had not planned it out ahead of time.

Planning Is Best as A Middle Ground

You want to plan out your programs, but don't overdo it. You don't want to write down every last detail. Have you written any papers in school? The way to write a paper is to start by making an outline. You can think of that here. Think of your planning stages for coding as making an outline for your project. Then when you actually start working on it on the computer and building your scripts, you can fill in all the details and potentially make changes.

Use the Planning Stage To Hone Your Ideas

During the planning stage, talk to others that are using scratch, or to your friends. Discuss your ideas with them to see what they think and see if they have some ideas that can make your project even better. It is easier to work things out like this in the planning stage if you are working on a large project. If you dive in to building your project and have a large number of sprites and scripts, having to go into all that detail to make major changes to the scripts can be very time consuming and frustrating. If you are working on a really large project, the project can actually get so complex that it is nearly impossible to change.

Planning with Pseudo Code

When we are working with scratch, we create actual code in our scripts. It can be helpful to plan out your scripts ahead of time by writing what is called pseudocode on a piece of paper. All this means is that you write out the steps that are going to be used in your script. So, we can write something like this:

If a cat touches the green bar then

- Play meow sound

- Increase score by one point

So, in other words, we are basically thinking out and

writing down the steps that our program is going to take ahead of time. This is an informal process, and so you don't need to have all the steps laid out exactly.

Think of the time you will save by doing this, though. When you write all the steps out, then opening up scratch and actually building the scripts is going to be so much easier that you are going to be amazed.

Start with The End Goal in Mind

Start the planning process with two statements. First, write down the starting point of your project. Then, write down the endpoint or goal of the project. So, if someone were to use your application, what is the end result of them doing so? This exercise should be used each time that you decide to start a new project on scratch. Once you have the two endpoints clearly defined, then filling in the intermediate steps to get you from point A to point B is a lot easier.

Draw Scenes on Paper

Don't just write out pseudocode when planning out your project. You can actually draw out the scenes the way you want them to look. Are you a lousy artist? Don't worry about that if you are. The point of doing this is not to impress anyone with your artistic ability. You don't even have to show the drawings to anyone else if you don't want to. The point of doing the drawings is for you and to help you get organized and get your project done faster and more efficiently. People who don't plan things out this way can end up wasting a lot of time in front of the computer screen. Wouldn't you rather be efficient and get your work done fast? It will also help you reduce frustration because you can open up your project and start building it quickly, according to the plan that you have already laid out.

Scheduling Your Work

You can also create a calendar and schedule for your project. You can specify what you are going to do on each of the days on the calendar. This will help you work more efficiently, which means that you will get more done in less time.

Reasons to Code

There are many different reasons that we can put forward for kids to learn to code. The first is that there is a continued shortage of people who are able to fill STEM jobs. Millions of these jobs are going unfilled, and a shortage means higher wages for those that possess the needed skills.

Learning some coding skills early is something that children can do to help bolster their resume in these competitive times. Even getting into college, or at least the college that you want is something that can be made easier if the child can already demonstrate some practical skills.

Coding can also help children understand the technical world that is all around them. They can understand the internet, smart TVs, and smartphones they can't seem to put down. By understanding how things work, they can also begin to get inspired and think of their own ideas.

Coding Can Make You Smarter And Improve Your Self-Confidence

You have probably seen people that go to the gym and exercise a lot. People that lift weights gain a lot of muscle. Other people that run or ride bikes get stronger and healthier. It turns out that the brain works in the same way. Your brain is just like a muscle. If you sit around and don't exercise at all, your muscles will shrink from a lack of use, and the body becomes weak. Older people who never exercise get out of breath just walking around.

The same thing happens to your brain. If you don't use it, then it won't develop and become strong. But if you work your brain by challenging it, the brain becomes stronger, literally making you smarter. The more you work your brain, the smarter you are going to get.

You may notice that if you practice doing math problems, they get easier for you. Or the more you study for an exam, the easier it is to remember what you need to know. And you become more confident about the right answers.

Coding is one of the best ways to challenge your brain and help you become smarter. Although people who haven't gotten any experience doing computer coding find it scary, when you take it slow and learn it step-by-step, you find out how natural it really is. Computer coding is nothing more than doing what comes naturally to humans. Let me explain.

What made the difference? Our brains made the difference. In other words, we used our ability to think. People used their minds to think of better ways to do things. This led them to figure out that they could survive cold nights by using animal skins to make clothing. Then they devised strategies to hunt, allowing them to use thinking for hunting the animals they needed to eat rather than trying to track them down using sheer speed and strength. They also invented many tools, to help them hunt using spears and arrows, and to cut things so they could use what they found in the environment, including preparing food to eat. Long ago, someone figured out how to use fire as another way of staying warm at night, and also to keep dangerous animals away.

This has been going on throughout history. People have continued to find out new and better ways of doing things, and this helped create civilization. This process is still going on today.

It turns out that computers are a natural fit for the

human mind, even though at first people don't feel this way about them. Computers are really just an extension of the human mind, and coding is just step-by-step problem-solving. So, it's not any different than any of the activities people have always engaged in.

When you get to work building a computer program, you are exercising the muscles of your brain, engaging in problem-solving activities. The more you do it, the better you are going to get at problem-solving. Coding teaches you to think carefully and to consider everything that can impact the problem at hand. It will also teach you how to look at how things will change, as each step in a computer program is executed. Not everyone has the same abilities, so some people are going to be better computer programmers than others. But that isn't what's important. The thing to remember is that everyone is going to be smarter than they were before they tried coding if they devote some time to learning this valuable skill.

The more you learn, the better your programming and problem-solving skills become. You can start off building simple programs, and then each time you tackle a new problem. You can build a more complex program.

CHAPTER - 7
ADVANCED CONCEPTS

After completing more than 10 projects in this book, it is time to focus on a few concepts in theory. We are going to discuss some advanced things here kiddo, but you can do it! Believe me, even many adults find these concepts hard to grasp.

Scratch is one of a kind when it comes to programming techniques. In Scratch, you use blocks to solve problems and create new things, an approach called block-oriented programming. Do you know what the most popular programming languages are? According to Stackify, here's the top three from 2019:

1. Java

2. C

3. Python

Guess what? None of them use block-oriented

programming. There are other approaches to programming, and we are going to discuss them now.

Functional Programming

Functional programming revolves around, drum roll please, functions! Remember our "Fifth Project", where we helped Gandalf find his magic stuff? We duplicated the same set of blocks for all the four arrow keys. It was not very efficient, was it? Creating functions is a way to cut down the number of blocks (or number of script lines) and avoid repetition.

How do we do that? We identify the line of codes that we will be using more than once. We give it a function name so whenever we need to execute it, we just call that name. There's one other amazing thing about functions. You can give them input (multiple if you can) and they return an output. A real-life example is a washing machine. You put in clothes, liquid detergent, and sometimes coins. The machine also takes water from an intake and washes all the clothes. After a preset amount of time, the machine gives you the clothes washed, rinsed and sometimes dried. Keep in mind that a washing machine can wash different types of clothes.

It would not be wrong to say that functions are mini programs within the main program. Breaking a big program into smaller functions also improves readability. But sometimes it can make it harder to understand the flow of the program. The key is to identify if there's a need for a function.

Twist

Now, here's a twist. You can create a block in Scratch that behaves like a function. How do you do that? This is something you will have to learn after you become good at things we have covered in this book. For now, add this to your to-do list.

Object-Oriented Programming

This is another type of programming, where everything is considered an object. Variables, constants, and even functions are just objects, or part of an object. This concept is closest to real-life and most applications built to tackle real-life problems are built using this approach.

Now, let us take the example of Cooper, the dog. He has many characteristics: he's (super) cute, friendly, talkative, happy and lovable. When it comes to doing stuff (actions), he can wag his tail, jump, walk, eat, hug, kiss, and lick among many other things. In the world of programming, Cooper is an object. His characteristics are called attributes. His actions are called modules (a fancy word for functions). We can give the object instructions to get some output.

We can also use, change, and transfer the available attributes. I know there's a saying you can't teach an old dog new tricks, but Cooper is a young fellow and we can definitely teach him some new tricks. This is equivalent to adding new modules to an object.

Algorithms and Flowcharts

When you advance in programming, you will see that it is difficult to keep up with the details and flow when a code starts to grow big. To help programmers keep track of everything, there is an entire process used when writing complex programs. Programmers write what is called an algorithm before writing the actual code.

An algorithm is a list of instructions that is written before coding is started. It helps break down the problem into groups of actions. Algorithms are actually used to detail the solution of the problem in simple human language. It also helps programmers to remain on task because sometimes it's easy to lose focus. Algorithms can be written for any task. For example, write a step-by-step guide on how to get ready for school in the morning.

Although not as popular anymore, veteran programmers still work with a flowchart, mostly to show non-technical colleagues how the program/application will be created. This is a bit more technical than writing algorithms because the shapes used to represent each step must match the type of action happening in that step. But this makes much more sense to view a flowchart because it gives a clear understanding of the flow of a program. Flowcharts are also used by planning teams to lay out a plan. If you have used MS Excel, you might have seen the flowchart section when you opened the Insert Shapes menu.

Health is Happiness

Why are we talking about health? Because health does matter. Talk with an old person and they'll tell your health is the most precious thing in this world. Here's a secret for your kiddo: if you have health, you can do anything. Spending a lot of time in front of screens can lead to various health concerns, especially those related to the eyes. In today's world, kids are also not spending too much time outdoors. It may lead to weaker muscles and immune system.

I am going to tell you a few tips that you can follow to keep your health in top condition.

The 20-second Rule

The rule is simple: for every 20 minutes spent in front of a computer, cellphone or a tablet screen, you should look at an object that's 20 feet away for 20 seconds. Why is that a good idea? Because you use your eye muscles to focus on a certain object. When you focus on a nearby object, your eye muscles remain strained. If you keep looking for a long time, the muscles get tired. It is for this reason that your eyes feel weary after spending a couple of hours looking at a handheld device. When you look at an object that's far away, your eye muscles get time to relax. This will help you a lot because many adults spend around 15 hours of each day in front of a screen. It is possible you would be doing the same when you grow up even when you don't want to. This is because of work requirements. The 20-second rule will help you avoid strained and sore eyes.

Hydration is Key

How much fluid do you drink in a day? The best fluid you can drink is water, because it has no bad stuff such as sugar. Using a computer or handheld smart device is fun and many times distracting. You lose focus and sense of time. This can lead to reduced hunger and thirst which is very bad for your health. What we can do is whenever you take the break for the 20-second rule, drink some water. Now, everyone has different requirements depending upon their age. Ask an adult how much water you should drink in a day.

When you start drinking more water, you will need to pee more. This feels like a nuisance but is very crucial to clean your body. Do not hold up, you should go to the bathroom as soon as you feel the need to do so.

When I talk about hydration, it's not just about drinking fluids. Your eyes also require good hydration levels for proper function. Have you ever experienced redness or itching after spending a long time in front of a screen? The phenomenon is pretty unique. Do you know why you blink? Blinking is an automatic process where your body removes dust and other things from the eyes and rehydrates the eyes. Have you ever noticed that sometimes when you are focusing on a screen, you forget to blink and only realize it after a few minutes? When you don't blink, the dust doesn't get cleaned up and rehydration also doesn't happen. In short, don't forget to blink.

Running and Exercise

You might already be active enough, but make sure you allocate enough time for physical activities. When you sit for a long time, the muscles in your legs become weaker. The joints also lose their strength. These will take a long time to happen and that's why these are very dangerous. You will slowly slip into a routine and when you start to notice the bad things, the internal damage might already be beyond repair. Stretching exercises are a great way of relaxing muscles. I know it sounds wrong, but stretching does relax the muscles. A doctor can give a good answer on how it works.

Going out also changes your perspective. It is a great way to relax your mind so it can get out of pressure situations. Sometimes when you think too hard for too long, the creative process gets stuck. In such situations, it is good to take a break, go outside to play or run.

Now, I understand that as a kid it is very difficult to go outside because you need permission and company. That's not a bad thing kiddo, trust me. Talk with your parents and let them know you need some of their time so they can go out with you. It is not like going out for a vacation. It won't require a lot of preparation. 20 to 30 minutes a day is good enough. It will give everyone some more time together and it will also benefit your parents' health.

Perfect Posture

There is a good way and a bad way to do every job in this world. Many people do things the wrong way because it's just easier. Using computers and handheld devices with the wrong posture is also another very easy pitfall to fall into. There are many parts of your body that cannot handle stress for a long period of time. These parts include your neck, your wrists, your spine, and ankles.

When you sit in front of a computer, make sure of following things:

1. Your feet are grounded firmly on the floor
2. Your thighs should be parallel to the floor
3. Your calves should be perpendicular to the floor
4. Your back should be relaxed and have a natural arc. The chair should provide support to your

back but must not push into it

5. The computer table should be on the same height as your arms

6. The computer screen should be on the same height as your eyes

7. The mouse should be light-weight

8. Keyboard should be soft-touch so you don't need to press them hard

I know these are a lot of rules. But they are very important. It will take time to follow all of them without effort. It also means you have to use the right kind of furniture. Again, that's not something you will be able to do yourself. Understandably, this is again something you should discuss with your parents. Chances are they already know about these but are not following them. Tell them the importance and the problems that can happen if you don't follow them for a long time.

CHAPTER - 8

DAY AND NIGHT GAME

Algorithms

You will soon learn how to create your own computer games. But first let's talk about Algorithms.

Have you ever given someone directions? Or explained how to make a sandwich? If so, then you're already familiar with algorithms.

Let's say you want to teach someone how to make a Club Sandwich.

The steps are usually as follow:

1. Take two slices of bread

2. Place a slice of ham over one slice of bread

3. Place a slice of cheese over the ham

4. place a second slice of bread on top of the cheese.

That's it!

We have a sequence of steps. Let's call the sequence: A step by step procedure, or script

The ordered sequence of steps is called an algorithm. Algorithms describe the procedure for solving a given problem.

Here is the algorithm you created in your very first game.

Movement and Talk Algorithm

- When Flag clicked
- Move 100 steps
- Say Greetings for 2 seconds
- Say How are you for 2 seconds

Reset Position Algorithm

- When spacebar key is pressed
- Move to position 0, 0 (middle)

Conditionals

To game the Day and Night game, you will make use of conditionals

What Are Conditionals

A conditional, simply put, is a condition for something to happen.

Let's take an example. If you have enough money

then you can buy some cakes. If you don't have enough money, then you can't.

With conditionals, you can tell computers to perform an action. If user click the spacebar key, then position the cat in the middle.

Another example, If it is night, then tell me it's Dark Outside,

Conditionals in Scratch

Scratch provides specific blocks to add conditionals to your game. You will use some simple one to build the Day and Night game, the If < > then block:

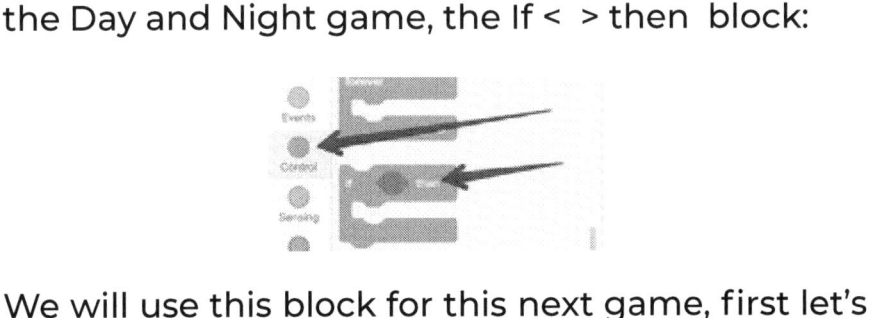

We will use this block for this next game, first let's create a new project.

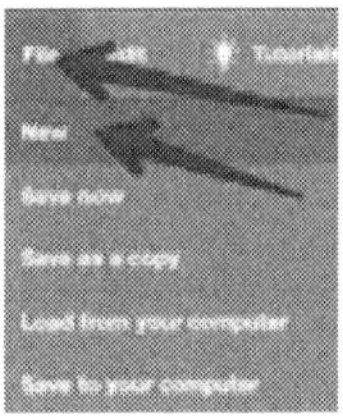

Create A New Project

Click on File the top left and New:

This will create a new project, give it a name, let's call it "Day and Night".

Sprites

Creating a new game will again place the Cat in the middle of the Stage.

We want to use a different character for this game,

Let's remove the Cat.

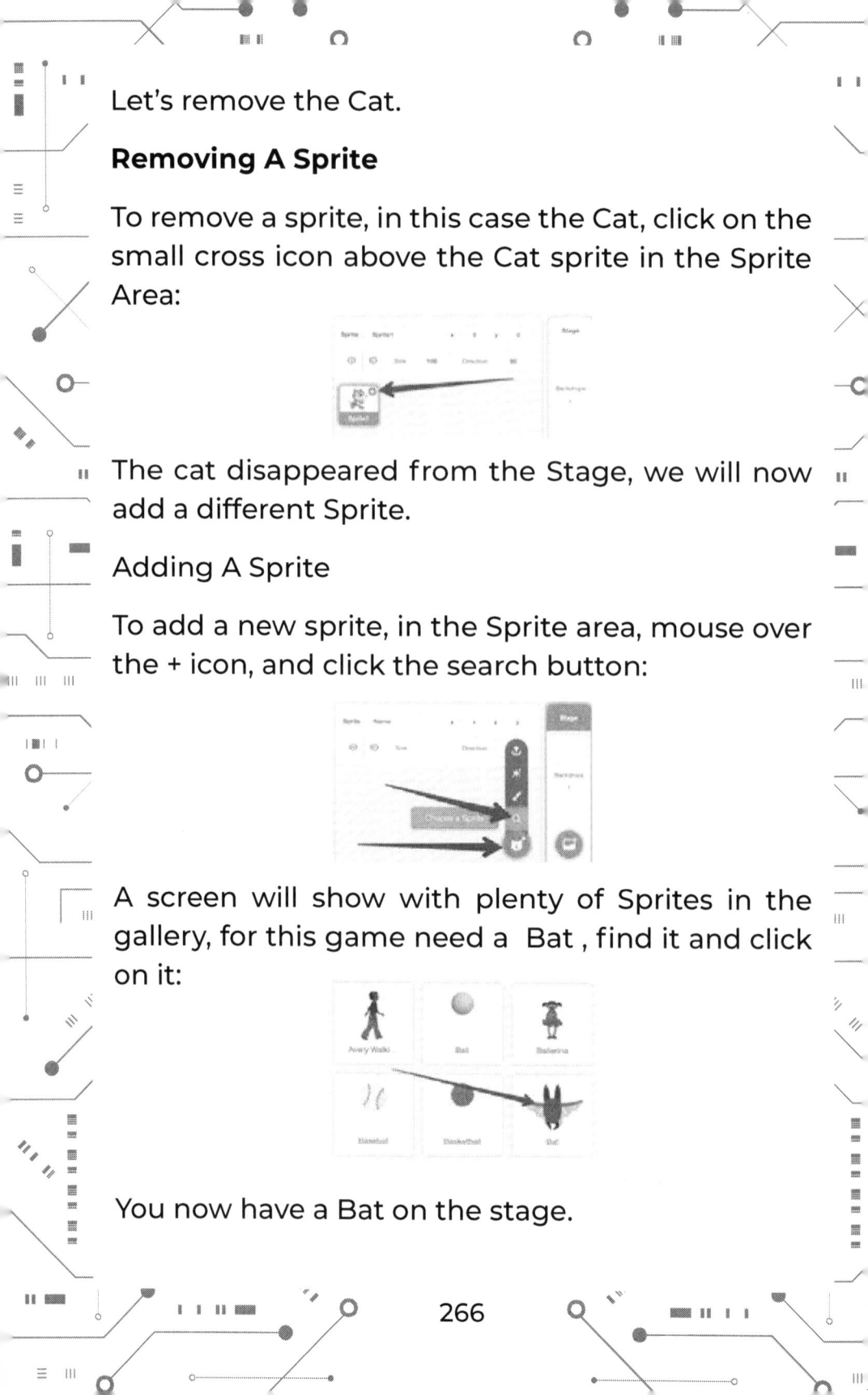

Removing A Sprite

To remove a sprite, in this case the Cat, click on the small cross icon above the Cat sprite in the Sprite Area:

The cat disappeared from the Stage, we will now add a different Sprite.

Adding A Sprite

To add a new sprite, in the Sprite area, mouse over the + icon, and click the search button:

A screen will show with plenty of Sprites in the gallery, for this game need a Bat, find it and click on it:

You now have a Bat on the stage.

Backdrops

The backdrop is the background of your stage, it's rather boring to have a plain background, so let's add some a Colorful City background.

Adding A Backdrop

To add a backdrop, find the + icon on the right of the Stage panel, below the stage panel, and click the Search button: .

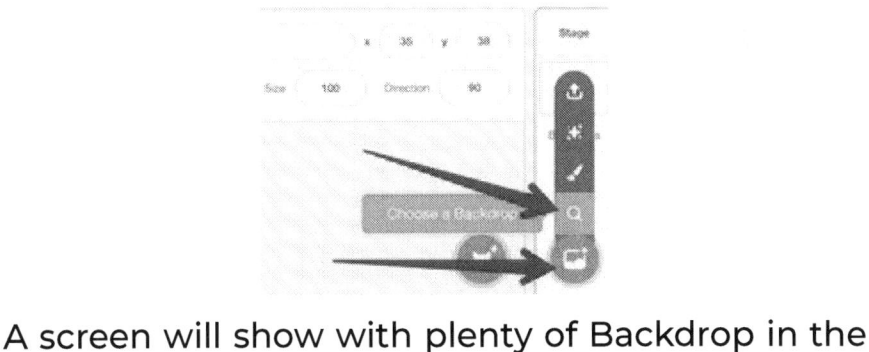

A screen will show with plenty of Backdrop in the gallery, this game needs a night and a day backdrop.

Search for a night image, find the Night City backdrops, add the it, then search again and find/add Colorful City:

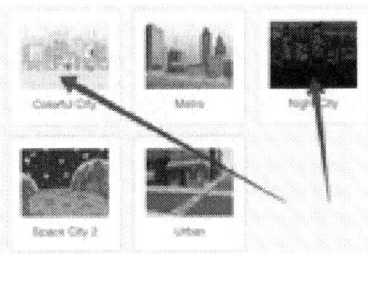

The stage will show the last drop you added. So, it should look like this:

Note: The backdrops can be found on the left side, just beside the Blocks panel, there is a Backdrop tab.

Click on it and see that there is a list of backdrops, one for the night city and one for the day city.

You can click on the backdrop you want by default, we want the Colorful City by default.

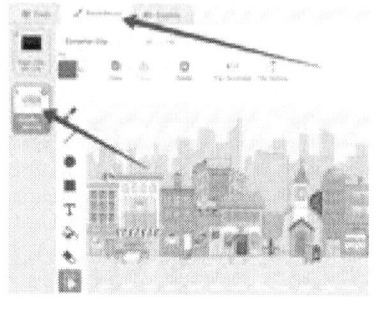

Game Logic

You now have all your arts put in the stage

A bat

A day backdrops

A night backdrop (not visible for now, but it's there)

This section is about making your backdrop change on a keyboard key press, and have the Bat tell you whether it is Bright or Dark outside.

First, let's go back to the Code tab.

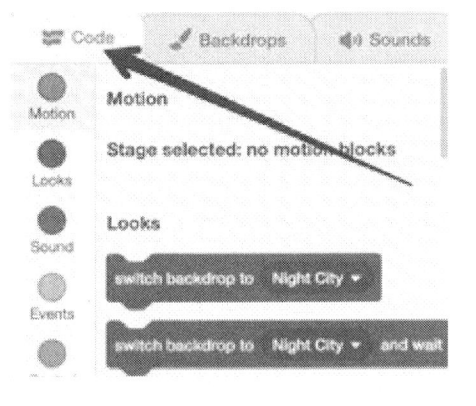

You will now Switch the backdrop on Event.

Switch Backdrop on Event

To switch the backdrop, we will use Event block called when space key pressed, to make the backdrop switch to the other image.

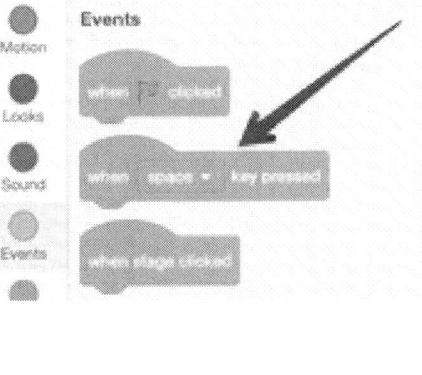

Drag it to the Scripting Area, then find and drag and plug, right below it, the next backdrop Looks Block:

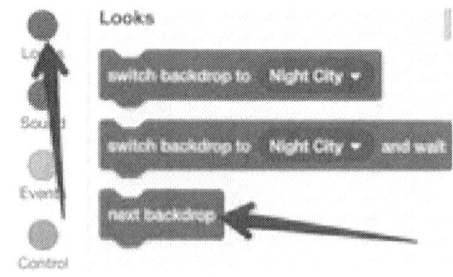

You should get a script like this in your Script Area:

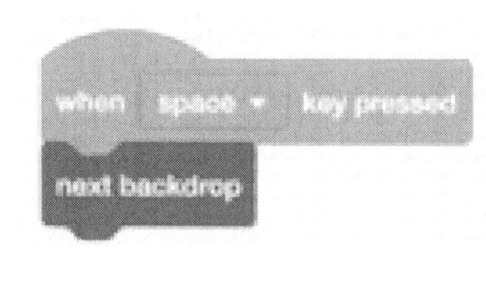

Test your stage, by pressing the spacebar key on your keyboard multiple times to make sure the backdrop changes from Day to Night and Night to Day.

A Note on Multiple Scripts

Observe that each script is associated with an element. When you created the script for the backdrop change, you selected the backdrop element, so the script is visibly only when the backdrop element is selected.

Click on the Bat in Sprite area, and you will see that the script you've created disappears,

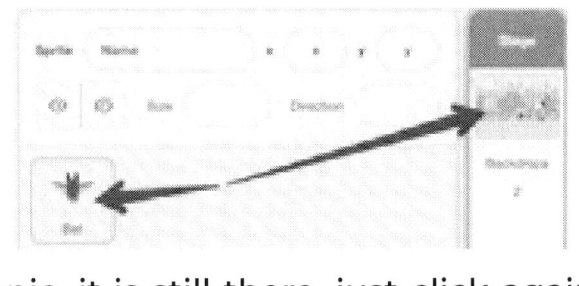

Don't panic, it is still there, just click again on the backdrop in the backdrop area (on the left below the stage) and you will see your script appear again in the Script Area.

Make the Bat Talk

- Click on the Bat sprite, in the Sprite Area.

  Then find and drag the Event block called when this sprite clicked into the Script Area:

  Then, find the say Hello! for 2 seconds block and plug it below the when this sprite is clicked block in the Script Area, you should get this:

Then test, to see that when you click on the Bat, in the stage, the bat says Hello! for 2 seconds

MAKE THE BAT TALK CONDITIONALLY

We now need to make the Bat say "Hello, It's Bright outside" or

"Hello, It's Dark outside" depending on the backdrop that is shown in the stage.

To do that, find the Control block if < > then block:

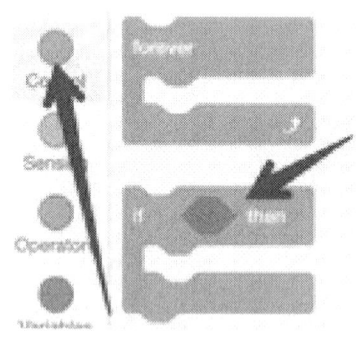

Then drag and plug it right blow the when this sprite is clicked block in the Script Area:

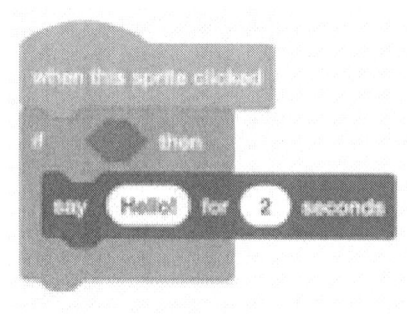

You might have to drag the Hello block away, to plug the If/then block, then plug the Hello block inside the If/then block, like shown above.

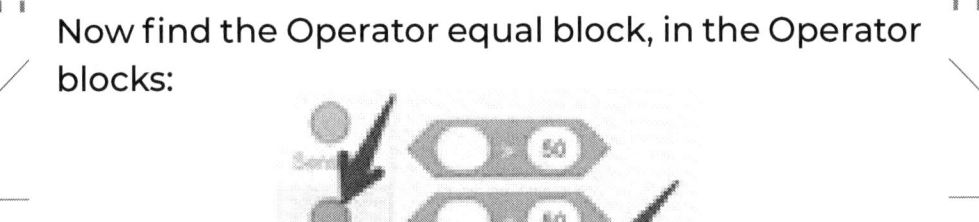

Now find the Operator equal block, in the Operator blocks:

Then drag and plug inside the < > space inside the if/then block, like so:

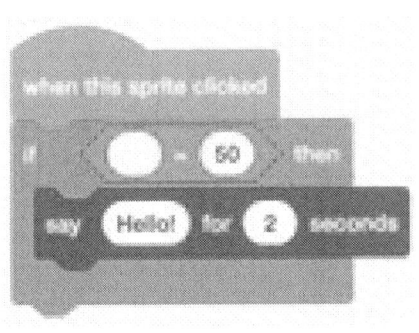

Then find the Look backdrop number block:

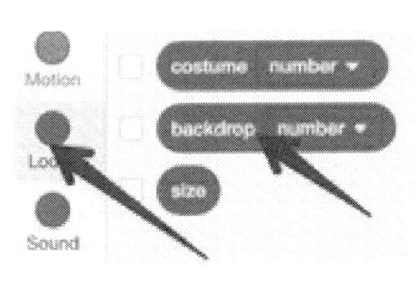

And drag/plug it on the left of the equal operator, like so:

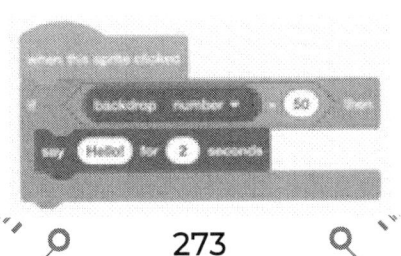

Finally:

Change the drop-down selected Number, to Name, on the left of the equal operator

Type Colorful City instead of 50 on the right of the equal operator.

Replace Hello with Hello, It's Bright outside

You should obtain this script:

[Script image: when this sprite clicked / if <backdrop name = Colorful City> then / say Hello, It's Bright outside for 2 seconds]

Now test, by clicking on the Bat with the night backdrop, and again with the day backdrop (remember it's the spacebar key on the keyboard to switch Backdrops).

The bat talks conditionally now, but it only talks when it's bright outside! Let's fix this.

Duplicate Script Blocks

The bat only has one condition: If it is the day backdrop, then   say Hello, It's bright outside.

We need to add another condition, which checks If the backdrop name represents the night backdrop, then the bat to say Hello, It's Dark outside.

To do so, let's duplicate the Bat script, and simply

change the name in the condition, and the message.

To duplicate, right click on the when this sprite clicked block, and click Duplicate:

Drag the duplicated script below, like this:

Now replace, in the duplicated script:

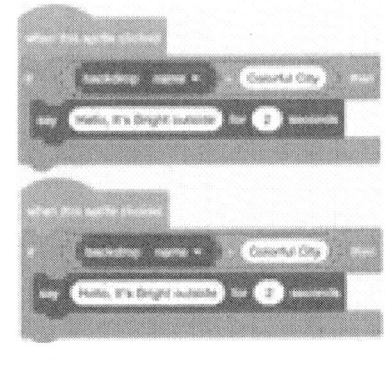

Colorful City to Night City

Hello, It's Bright outside to Hello, It's Dark outside.

You should get this script:

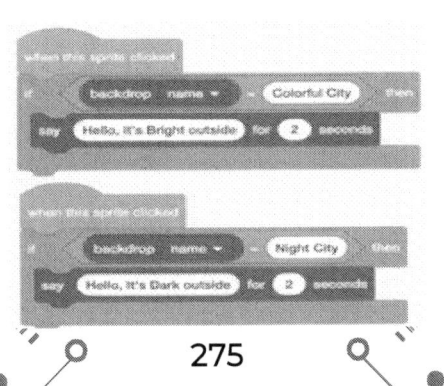

Event

Event blocks control events and the triggering of scripts. There are 8 Event blocks.

Input Events

when ⚑ clicked

when space key pressed

when this sprite clicked

When Green Flag Clicked — When the flag is clicked, the script activates.

When ( ) Key Pressed — When the specified key is pressed, the script activates.

When This Sprite Clicked — When the sprite is clicked, the script activates.

Situational Events

when backdrop switches to Night City

when loudness > 10

When backdrop switches to ( ) — When the backdrop switches to the one chosen, the script activates.

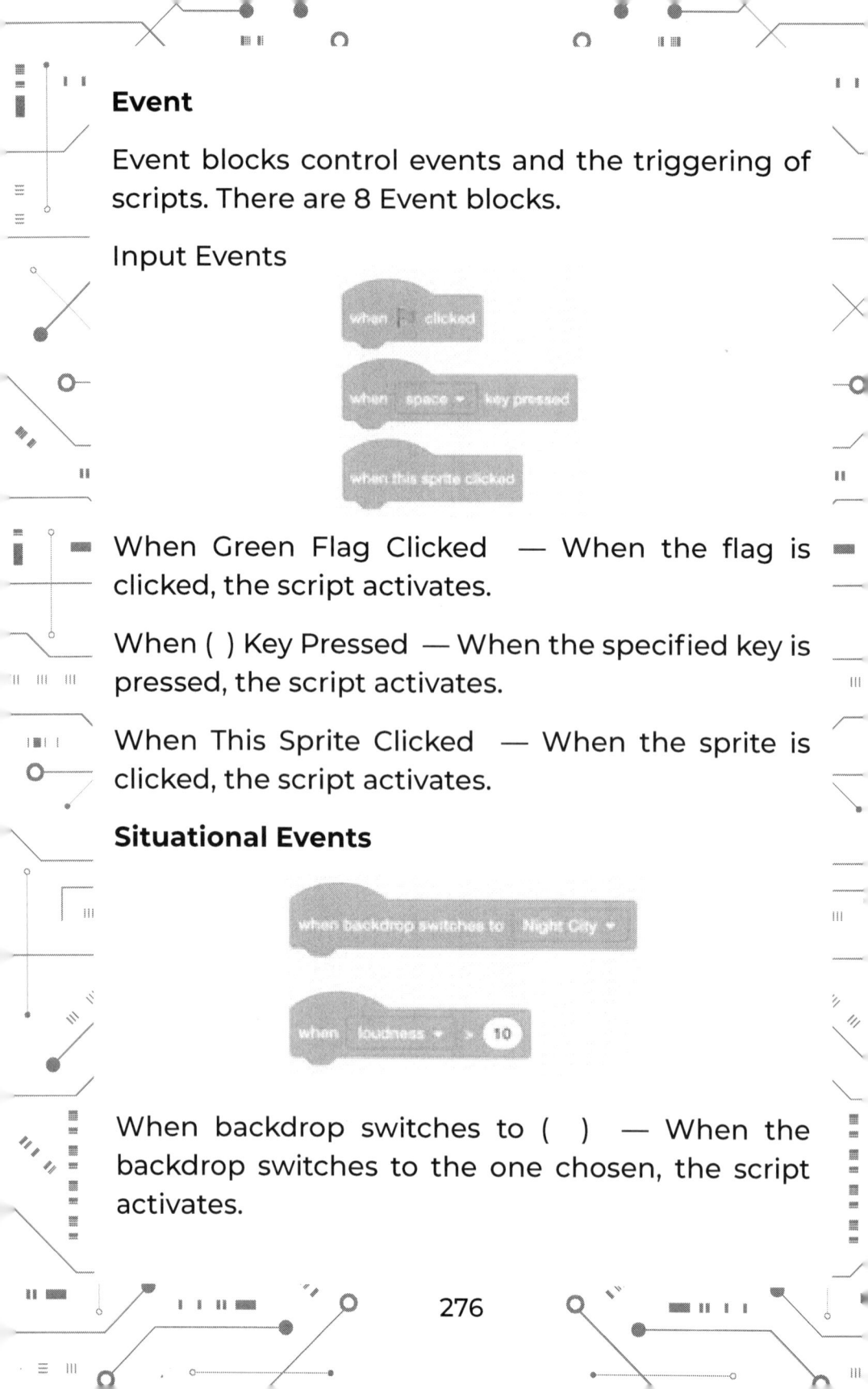

When ( ) is greater than ( ) — When the first value is greater than the second value, the script activates.

Control

Control blocks control scripts. There are 11 Control blocks.

Sprite Controls

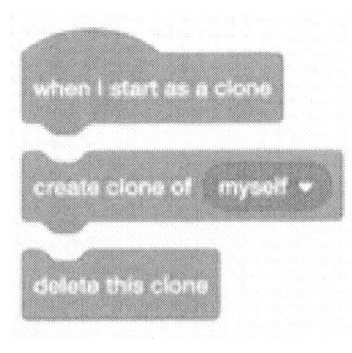

when I start as a clone

create clone of myself

delete this clone

When I Start as a Clone (sprites only) — This block is triggered whenever a clone is created, and will only be run by that clone.

Create Clone of ( ) — Creates the specified clone.

Delete This Clone (sprites only) — Deletes a clone.

Loop Controls

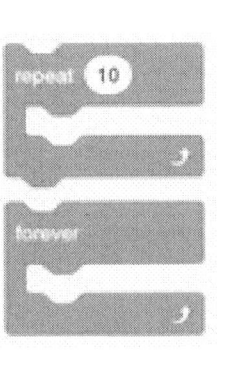

repeat 10

forever

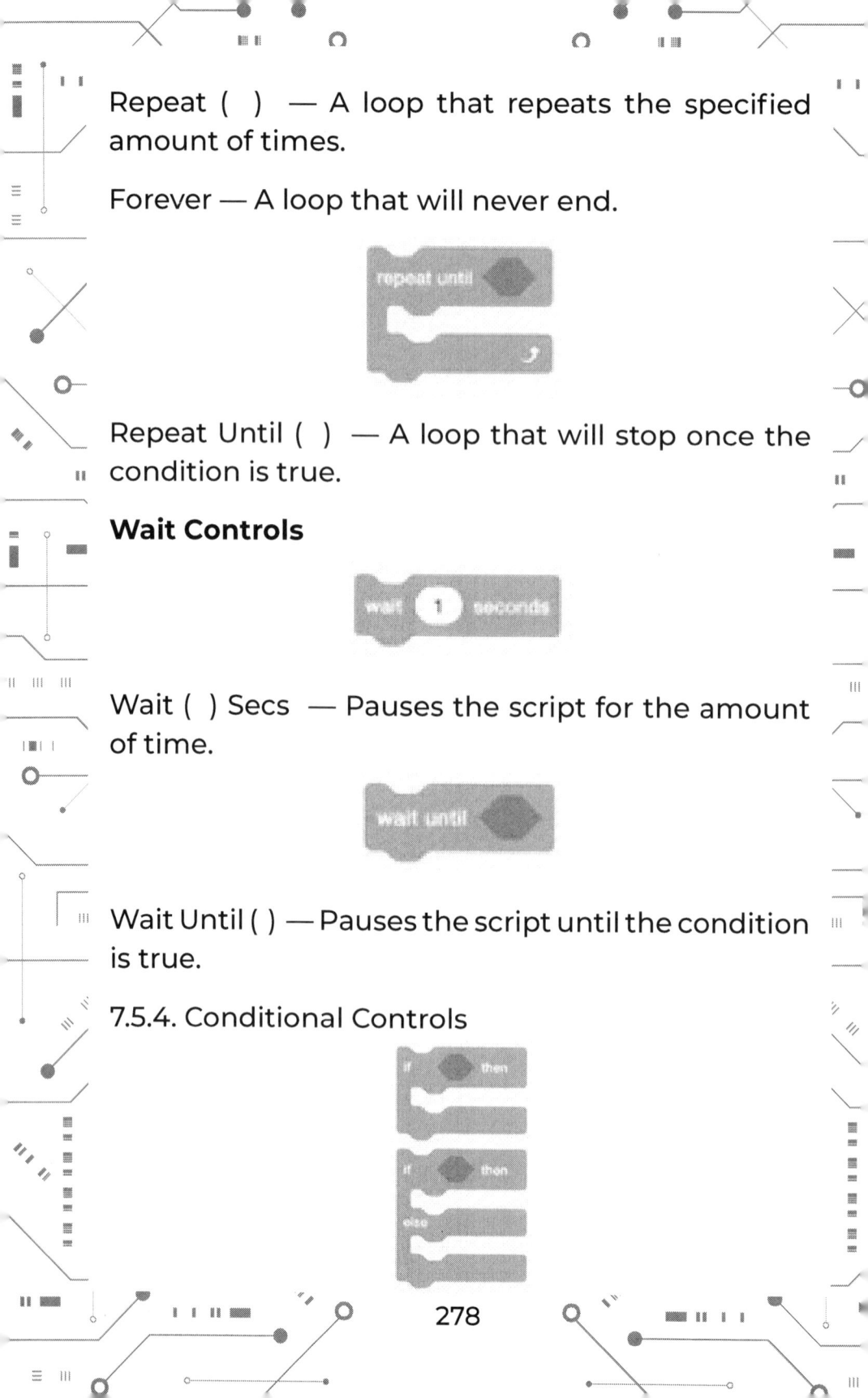

Repeat ( ) — A loop that repeats the specified amount of times.

Forever — A loop that will never end.

Repeat Until ( ) — A loop that will stop once the condition is true.

Wait Controls

Wait ( ) Secs — Pauses the script for the amount of time.

Wait Until ( ) — Pauses the script until the condition is true.

7.5.4. Conditional Controls

If ( ) Then — Checks the condition so that if the condition is true, the blocks inside it will activate.

If ( ) Then, Else — Checks the condition so that if the condition is true, the blocks inside the first C will activate and if the condition is false, the blocks inside the second C will activate.

Stop Script Control

Stop ( ) — Stops the scripts chosen through the drop-down menu. Can also be a stack block when "other scripts in this sprite" is chosen.

Sensing

Sensing blocks detect things. There are 20 different Sensing blocks.

Sprite Sensing Blocks

Touching ( ) ? — The condition for checking if the sprite is touching the mouse-pointer or another sprite.

Touching Color ( ) ? — The condition for checking if the sprite is touching a specific color.

Color ( ) is Touching ( ) ? — The condition for

checking if a color on the sprite is touching a specific color.

distance to mouse-pointer

Distance to ( ) — The distance from the sprite to the mouse-pointer or another sprite.

User Typing Input

ask What's your name? and wait

answer

Ask ( ) and Wait — Makes an input box appears, you type the value in and it stores the value in the answer variable.

Answer — The most recent input stored in the variable by the Ask ( ) And Wait block.

Keys And Mouse Input

key space pressed?

mouse down?

Key ( ) Pressed? — The condition for checking if the specified keyboard key is being pressed.

Mouse Down? — The condition for checking if the mouse click is down.

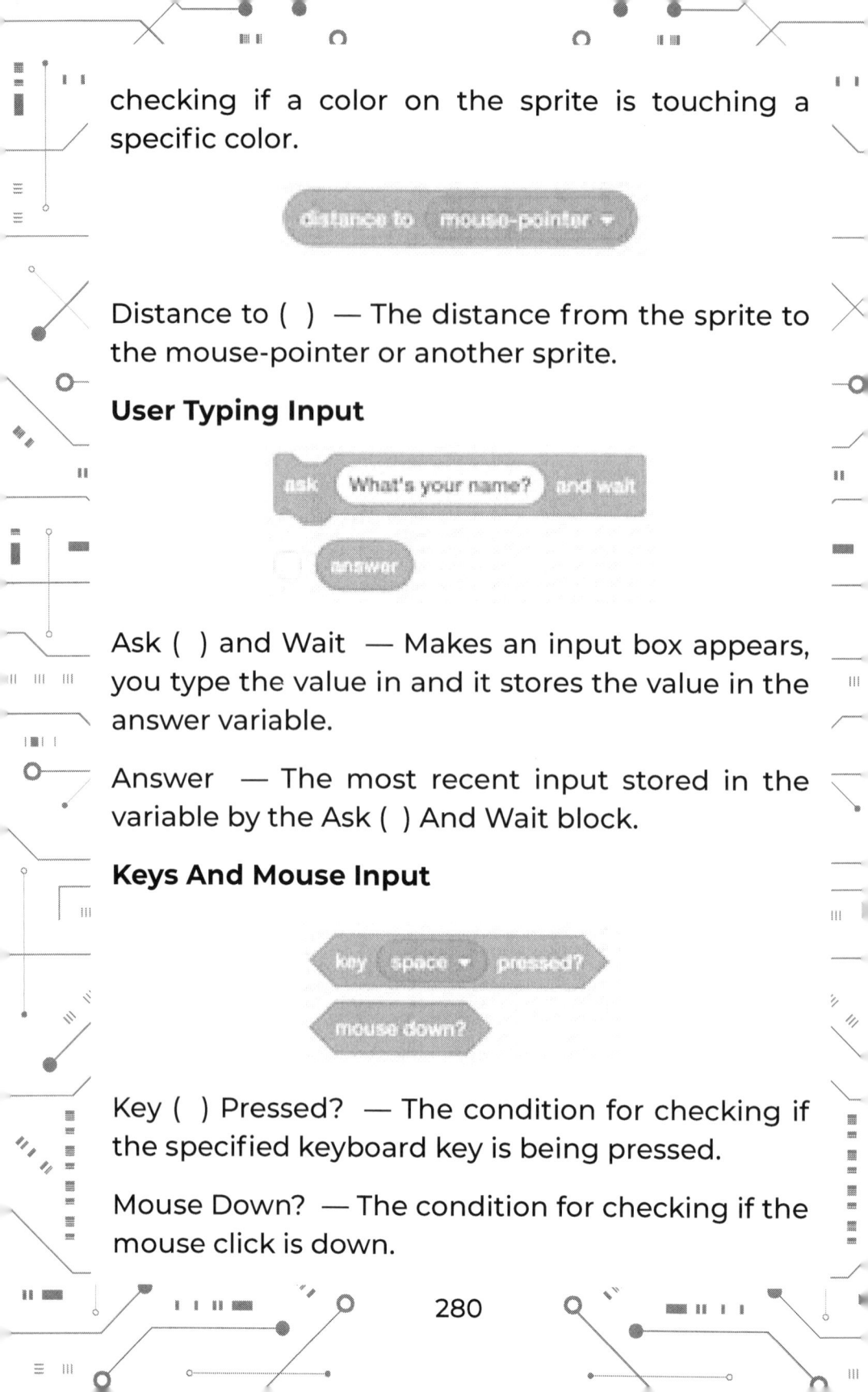

`mouse x`

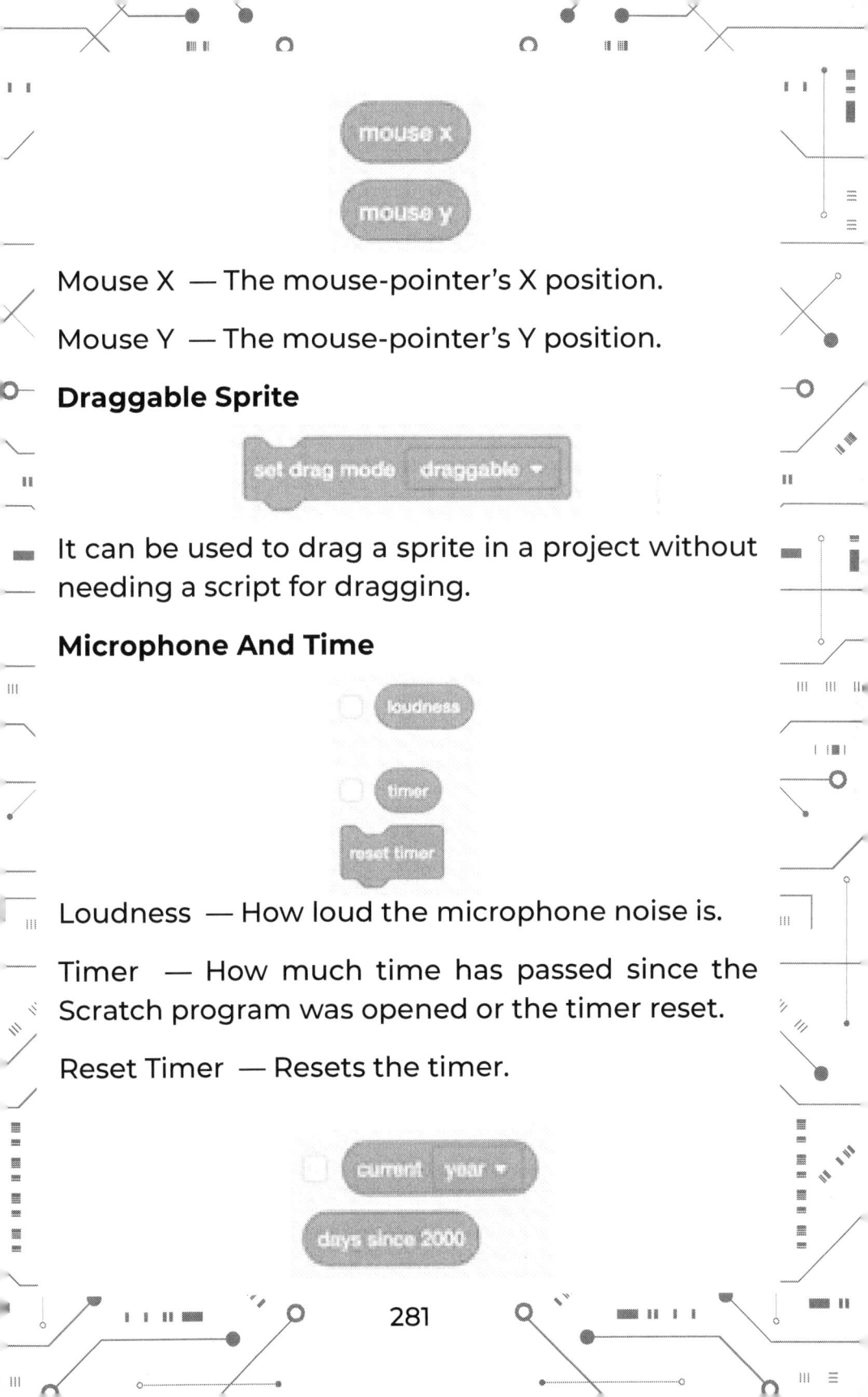

`mouse y`

Mouse X — The mouse-pointer's X position.

Mouse Y — The mouse-pointer's Y position.

Draggable Sprite

`set drag mode draggable ▼`

It can be used to drag a sprite in a project without needing a script for dragging.

Microphone And Time

`loudness`

`timer`

`reset timer`

Loudness — How loud the microphone noise is.

Timer — How much time has passed since the Scratch program was opened or the timer reset.

Reset Timer — Resets the timer.

`current year ▼`

`days since 2000`

Current ( ) — The specified time unit selected, can be from year unit to seconds. If ticked, it will display the value on stage.

Days since 2000 — The number of days since 2000.

Other Sensing Blocks

`backdrop # ▾ of Stage ▾`

( ) of ( ) — The X position, Y position, direction, costume, size or volume of the Stage or a specific Sprite.

`username`

Username — The username of a user.

CHAPTER - 9
PRACTICING WITH SCRATCH

Although the logic behind programming is important, what is the use of logic if it is not put into practice?

In this section, you will find basic projects that you can complete within an hour or two. Be sure to take the time to understand the challenges and try to do them on your own before coming back and reading the solutions from the book. Remember that in programming: the process is more important than the outcome.

There is no one true way to achieve an outcome in programming. Yes, there may be more efficient and optimal ways, but in truth, it all boils down to whether, at the end of the day, you've achieved your goal or not. Similar to mathematics, where there are hundreds of ways to achieve the equivalent of two, accomplishing a certain goal in the world of programming can be achieved through various means.

Fall in love with the process, and do not be too fixated into the outcome.

Listed below are some of the projects taken from the internet that you could start working on right now; it will only take around 1-2 hours to complete each project.

Tron

If you're familiar with the game of Tron, then you know the simple mechanics of the game. In this game, you simply have to make sure that your character avoids the trail emitted by the other light cycles as well as your own by outmaneuvering the opposing players.

Here a few of the variables that you would have to take into account when making the game:

1. Movement

The movement for the game is simple and basic. You simply use your arrow keys to move your character around the map. However, it should be that the two characters are moving at the same time; neither one slows down or goes ahead of the other. If the player doesn't click an arrow key, then the sprite should just continue on the path that it was already on.

2. Hitting the trails or other sprites

Once your character hits a trail or the other sprite, then the game ends, and you lose. This also holds true in the case that a sprite hits the edge of the map. All of these are programmable using the blocks in Scratch.

3. Character

Your character should be set to be an individual on a bike. If the game ends, then either your character or the opponent becomes an "explosion" costume. So, in simpler terms, you just have to program the two sprites, their trails, and their respective icons in case the sprites touch the trails, the other bike, or the edges of the window.

Space Invaders

Space Invaders is another simple program that many beginner programs complete.

In this program, you simply shoot the oncoming aliens while you avoid their lasers. You will have three lives, and each time you get struck by an alien laser, then you lose a life.

In contrast to the original Space Invaders games, the alien ships do not approach you. Instead, they simply sweep from right to left, and it your job to destroy them.

This program will require you to set up the following variables:

1. Characters

There are two essential characters here, namely:

the player and the opponents. Now, both sides are represented by differing ships

2. Movements

The movements of the ships are simple, just shift left to right.

3. Lasers

Like the players, the lasers are representative of the opposing sides. Now, these lasers can be of any color, but I suggest picking totally opposing ones as this creates a better graphical user interface and a better gaming experience for the user.

4. Lives

A player is given three lives in this game. A counter should be visible, and each time a player gets struck by a laser, then the counter goes down by one.

Moon Landing

This program is most certainly more difficult than preceding projects.

In this program, we have to simulate landing a moon lander on the surface of the moon. If you land on anywhere but the landing pad, then your moon lander gets destroyed.

To make it easier, here are the things that you will need to have in your program:

1. Movement

Obviously, the movement will be an essential component of the whole project. In this game, you will have to be able to move your spacecraft left and right as well as up and down, taking into account that there is no air resistance in space. Once your character starts moving in one direction, then it should keep gliding in that direction.

2. Crashing

This is one of the simpler things that you will be programming. You will essentially need two costumes: the lunar lander sprite and the explosion costume. Since all of the rocks will be grey, then you simply have to create the program so that when the lunar lander sprite touches something grey, then it switches to the explosion costume before stopping the program, essentially meaning you lost.

3. Gravity

Like all planets, the moon has gravity, and this gravity pulls things towards the ground. Try to incorporate that into your code.

4. Landing

The goal of this program is such that when the lander touches the landing pad, the game ends. However, you could make it so that if the lander lands too fast on the landing pads, the ship falls apart.

Solutions

Now, You will find the solutions, but please remember that these aren't the only correct solutions. If you have come up with your own solutions (as many of you should have), then I congratulate you on your grit and determination! However, regardless of whether or not you had completed the projects by yourself, I still urge you to read the solutions here, for you might find better and more efficient solutions than the ones you made.

Tron

Here's a possible solution to the game:

1. Player Starting Position and Trails

These blocks of code set the starting position of the characters. The sprites labeled 'bike' are set to the position of (-175,0) while facing the 90-degree direction. From here, the following lines of code make it so that when the character is moved, then it would leave a pen trail of the specified color.

2. Crash Checker

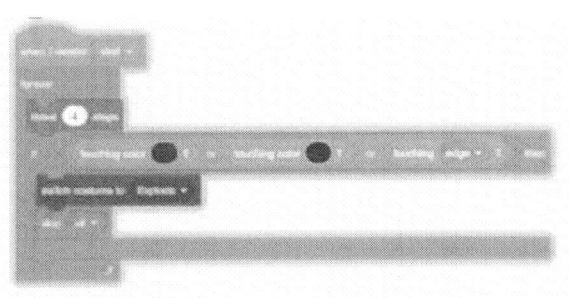

This is, as the name suggests, checks whether or not the sprite has "crashed." The blocks of code do so by checking the pen trail that the characters have left behind. If the character ends up touching his own pen trail or his opponent's, the sprite turns into the "explosion" character. If the character touches the other sprite, then they both transform into the "explosion" characters.

3. Player Movement

These lines of code control the movement of the characters. They control the direction that the character is moving. Because of the "pen up" and "pen down" blocks, the characters will continuously move unless told otherwise. As such, these blocks are meant more to direct the sprites rather than actually move them.

Space Invaders

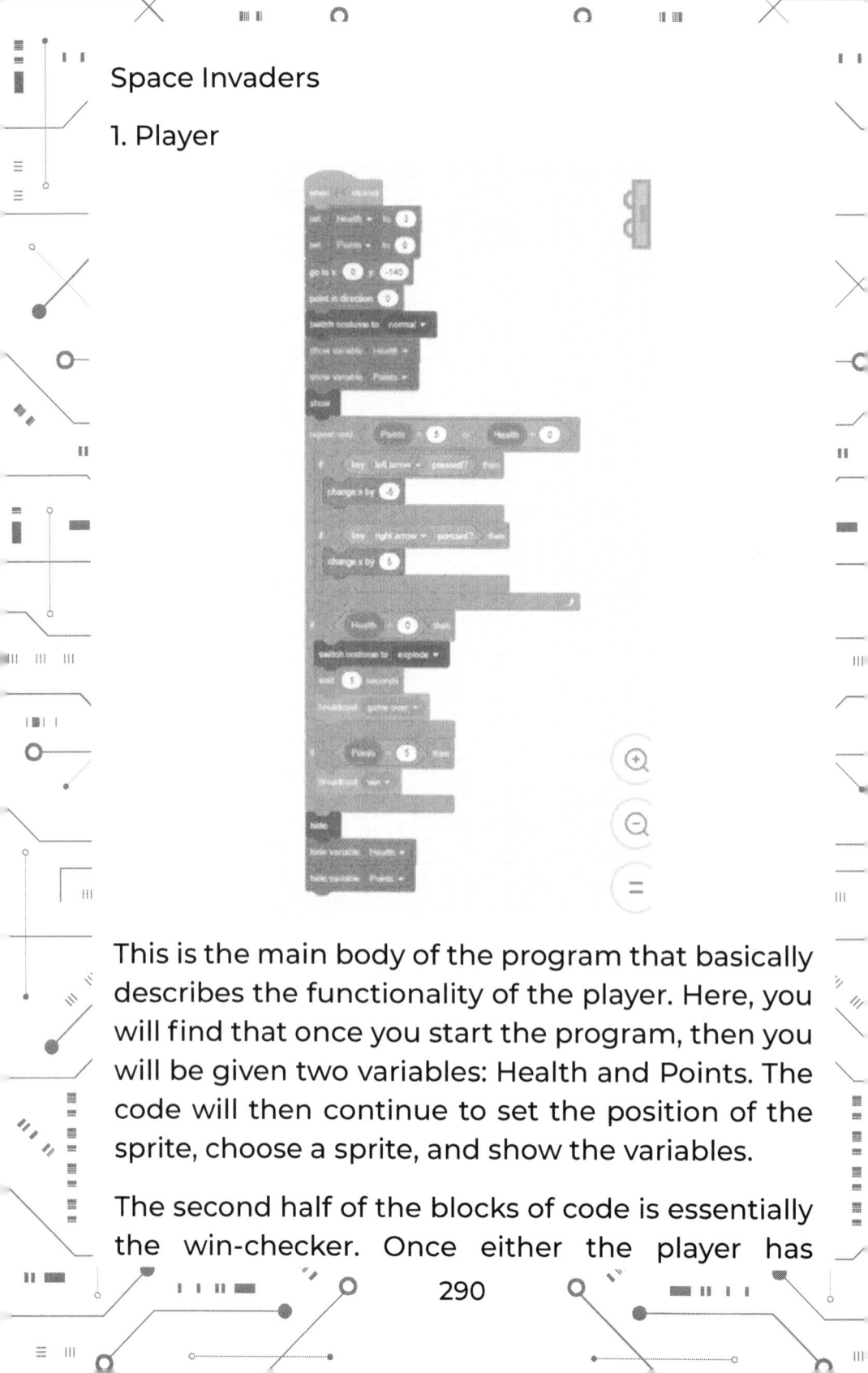

1. Player

This is the main body of the program that basically describes the functionality of the player. Here, you will find that once you start the program, then you will be given two variables: Health and Points. The code will then continue to set the position of the sprite, choose a sprite, and show the variables.

The second half of the blocks of code is essentially the win-checker. Once either the player has obtained 5 points, or the player has lost all his lives, the game ends. Until then, the player will continue to move around by either pressing the right arrow key or the left.

2. Your Laser

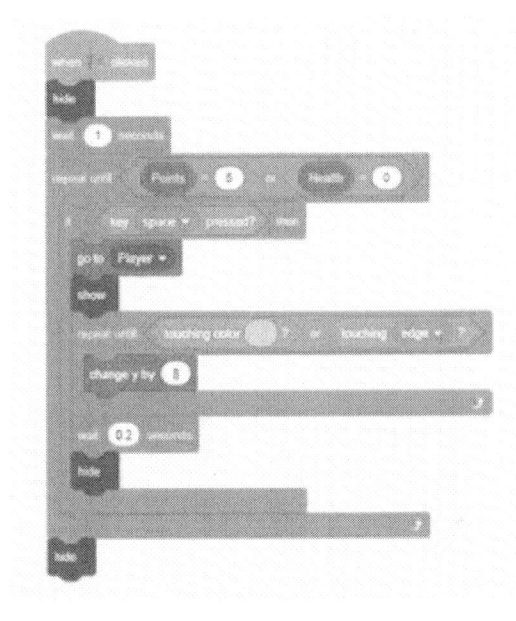

These lines of code explain how your laser works. Basically, if you press the spacebar, it will release a sprite in the form of the laser. If this sprite makes contact with the edge, it simply vanishes. If the laser makes contact with a yellow color, which is the color of the aliens, then it destroys them. Although it's not explicitly stated in this block of code, it will be stated in a different block.

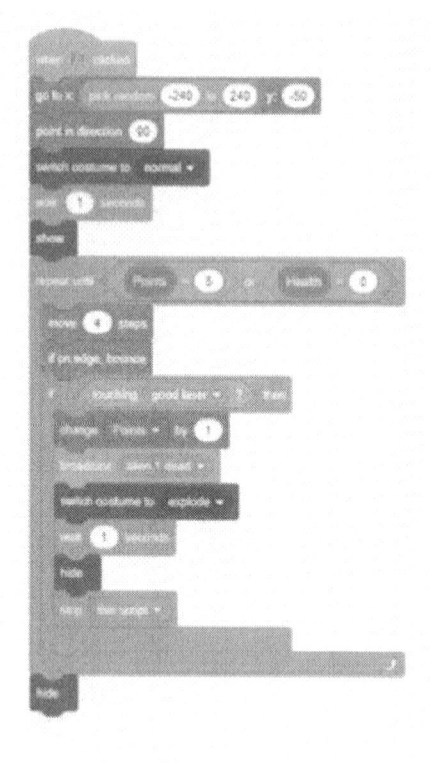

3. Opponent

This is the block of code wherein you will find the functionality of the opponent aliens. It sets the starting position of the alien and creates its functionality, wherein the sprite would continue drifting left to right in a single direction until it hits the edges of the game. If the sprite gets struck by one of your lasers, then your point tally goes up, the sprite is replaced by an explosion sprite before vanishing.

4. Bad Laser

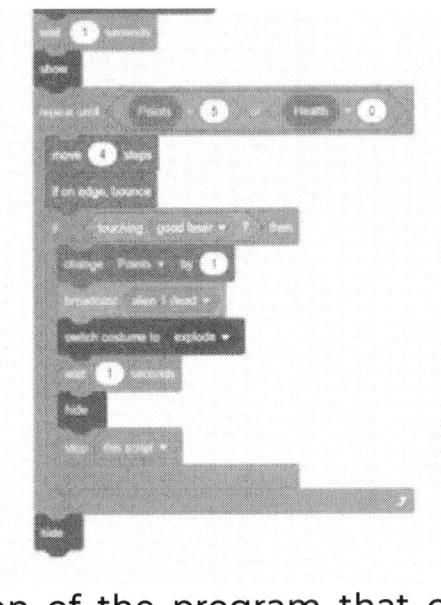

This is the portion of the program that controls the functionality of the "bad" lasers or, more appropriately, the lasers shot by the alien sprites. Essentially, the aliens shoot lasers at random intervals, and if they hit the player, the player loses a life. Otherwise, the laser simply disappears.

Moon Landing

1. Movement

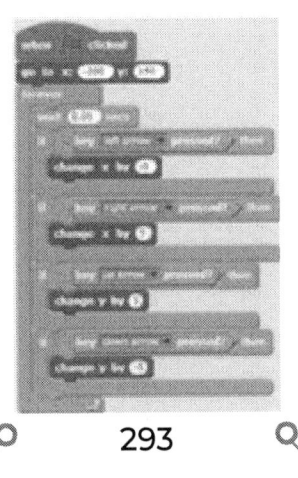

This block of code simply moves the character around using the left, right, up, and down arrow keys. The logic behind this code is very similar to the logic behind the blocks for movement for Tron and Space Invaders. After all, movement is movement, and in most games, movement mainly pertains to the change in position of the sprite in relation to the background of the program.

2. Crash

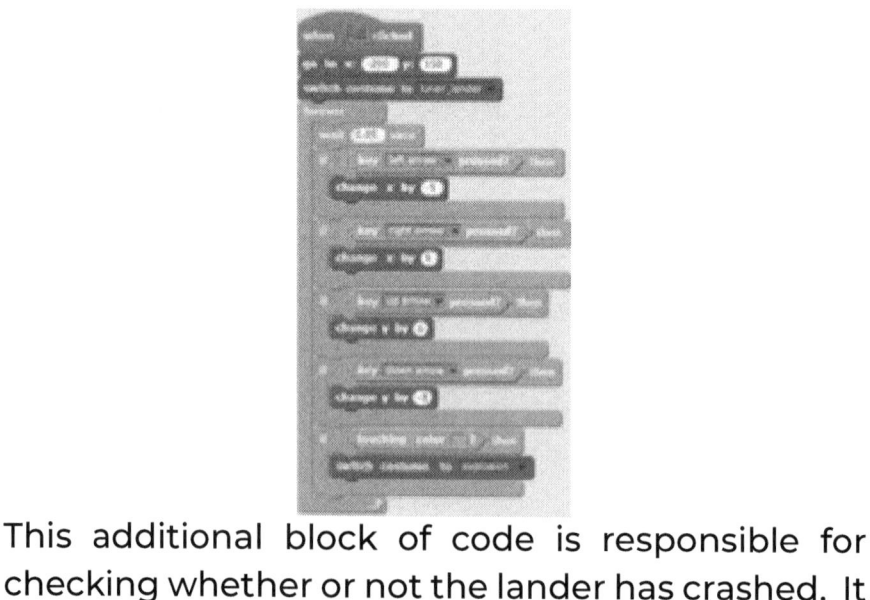

This additional block of code is responsible for checking whether or not the lander has crashed. It simply says that if the sprite touches the color gray, then it should switch to an "explosion" costume.

3. Movement

The change in these blocks of code simply shows that instead of changing the position of the sprite in relation to the background, we instead change the speed to simulate the presence of gravity in the program.

4. Up and Down

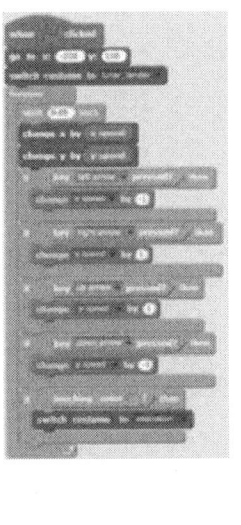

Similar to the change that you had input, you replace the code that is used for up and down movement so that instead of simply changing the position of the sprite in the program, we also try to simulate the presence of gravity in our program.

5. Landing

Finally, this separate block of code is used as a landing checker. It simply states that if the moon lander sprite touches a yellow color (the landing pad) but is moving slower than a speed of -2, then your sprite implodes on impact.

Looking at the solutions to the projects above, you'll find that the projects increase in difficulty. As you continue on your programming, you'll find that the projects that you create will require you to add more and more variables to your projects. The sheer complexity of the projects that you will soon be creating might seem daunting at first, but perseverance and determination will get you anywhere. Note, however, that these solutions above aren't the only solutions out there. It's best to try and come up with your own solutions! The library of programming solutions and concepts is so wide, and the variety of solutions that you can come up with are so plentiful.

Now this portion of the book has given you some increasingly difficult challenges. You do not need to accomplish the projects, but in doing so, you would have shown general mastery in the use of Scratch.

CHAPTER - 10
PROJECT-CONNECT FOUR

Connect Four is a 2-player game which consists of two sets of colored coins and a standing grid of rows and columns. Each player takes one set of coins and then by turn drops coins down any of the vertical columns (we will call them "tubes"). See the picture below.

The goal of the game is to get 4 coins of the same color to arrange themselves along a row, column, or diagonal. The first player to do this wins the game.

Do you want to check out a working Scratch version of this program? Click on the image below (or the URL just below it). I encourage you to explore the program and its various features. But, don't look at the Scratch scripts yet; we want to design this program ourselves!

How to Run The Program?

1. Click the "Green flag" to start the game.

2. Two users (blue and orange) will play the game by clicking alternately. The variable "Turn" shows whose turn it is.

3. Click the base of the tube in which you want to drop your coin.

4. Play until one of the players wins.

Scratch and CS Concepts Used

When we design this program, we will make use of the following Scratch and CS concepts. I assume that you are already familiar with these concepts.

Main concepts:

- Algorithms
- Arithmetic operators (+, -, *, /)
- Arithmetic expressions
- Backdrops - multiple
- Conditionals (IF)
- Events
- Geometry - parallel lines
- Logic operators (and, or, not)
- Looping - simple (repeat, forever)
- Looping - conditional (repeat until)
- Motion - absolute
- Motion - smooth using repeat
- Pen commands
- Relational operators (=, <, >)
- Sensing touch
- Sequence

- Sounds - playing sounds
- STAMP - creating images
- Synchronization using broadcasting
- User events (mouse)
- Variables - numbers
- Variables - strings
- Variables - properties (built-in)
- XY Geometry

Feature Idea # 1: Coins and the grid

Draw the coin sprites and the grid of vertical tubes.

Step 1: Draw the coin sprites.

Design:

To play the game we need lots of orange and lots of blue coins. But, how many sprites do we need?

Let us consider what happens to each coin. When a coin is dropped into a tube it just sits there until the game is over. So, we don't really need an actual coin sprite in the tube; an image would suffice. Does that give you some idea?

Yes, we can use the STAMP command to create an image of a coin when it is dropped in a tube. So, that means we just need two sprites: one for the orange coin and one for the blue coin. We will just draw the sprites.

Draw circle sprites with thick border. Fill them with gradient of the same color.

Resize them such that they fit the width of the tube.

Step 2: Draw the grid (series of tubes).

Design:

It is really up to us to decide how many tubes we should have. In my program, I have drawn 8 tubes. You can do the same or use a different number.

The grid, as you can see, has two parts:

1. A series of vertical lines which define the tubes

2. A solid base for each tube

The solid base of each tube will have to be a separate sprite, because, the players will select a tube by clicking its base. We can just draw one base and create duplicate sprites.

The vertical lines can be drawn as a sprite (or part of the background), but it is quite tedious to draw equidistant (equally spaced) parallel lines in the paint editor.

Instead, we will draw them in the program itself using the Pen commands and some simple geometry. First, we will draw the 8 bottom sprites and line them up in a straight line (see solution below).

The algorithm to draw the lines for the tubes is quite simple. Let's say "w" is the width and "h" is the height of each tube. Let's say point (x, y) is on the left edge of the first base.

Algorithm to draw the tubes:

```
Go to x, y
Repeat 9
    Pen down
    Change y by h
    Pen up
    Change y by -h
    Change x by w
End-repeat
```

Save as Program Version 1

Before continuing to the next set of ideas, we will save our project. This way, we have a backup of our project that we can go back to if required for any reason.

Compare your program with my program at the link below.

Connect4-1: includes idea 1 explained above.

How to run the program:

1. This program version doesn't do anything.

Next Set of Features/ideas:

Next, we will write scripts for dropping coins in the tubes. This involves the following features:

- choosing a tube
- choosing the right coin to drop
- positioning a coin on top of the selected tube
- dropping a coin down the selected tube

For this version, make a copy of your project (using "Save as") under a different name. For example, I am calling my copy as Connect4-2.

Let us get cracking with these ideas and features one by one.

Feature Idea # 2: Choosing tube and coin

Implement a way for the players to choose a tube, and have a way for the players to take turns.

Design:

Selecting a tube is straightforward. Since each tube has a separate base sprite, the players can simply click on the base to choose a tube.

To ensure players play by turn, we can have a variable called "Turn" which will indicate whose turn it is. If it says "orange" an orange coin will be dropped and if it says "Blue" a blue coin will be dropped.

Feature Idea # 3: Drop the coin

Write scripts to position the selected coin on top of the selected tube and drop it into the selected tube.

Step 1: Position the coin on top of the selected tube.

Design:

The variable "Turn" tells us which coin is to be dropped. The player will click on the base of the selected tube. In order to position a coin on top of this tube we need to know the X and Y co-ordinates of the point. We can pick some arbitrary value of Y which is somewhere above all tubes. How about X?

Well, we can use the X of the base sprite, right? Each base, when clicked, can save its X position in a variable.

Step 2: Drop the coin into the selected tube.

Design:

Making the coin drop into the tube is straightforward. We can make it move downward until it touches the base or another coin.

We don't need to leave the coin in the tube; we can leave its image. The STAMP command will come handy for that purpose.

Save as Program Version 2

Before continuing to the next set of ideas, we will save our project. This way, we have a backup of our project that we can go back to if required for any reason.

Compare your program with my program at the link below.

Connect4-2: includes ideas 2 and 3 explained above.

How to run the program:

1. Click the "Green flag" to start the game.

2. Two users (blue and orange) will play the game by clicking alternately. The variable "Turn" shows whose turn it is.

3. Click the base of the tube in which you want to drop your coin.

Final Set of Features/ideas:

We really have all the important features of the game working now. We will just add a few more features to make the program more tidy, robust, and user-friendly. Here are the things we will consider in this version:

- When a tube becomes full, don't allow coins to drop in it.
- Add a welcome screen.
- Add a help screen and sounds.
- Add code that will automatically place the pipe bases in a neat row.

For this final version, make a copy of your project (using "Save as") under a different name. For example, I am calling my copy as Connect4-final.

Let us get cracking with these ideas and features one by one.

Feature Idea # 4: Tube full condition

When a tube becomes full, don't allow coins to drop in it.

Design:

There are different ways to implement this feature. For example, you could keep a count of the number of coins inside each tube in a list variable, and check that count every time a coin is dropped.

I am going to use a much simpler idea which is as follows: Just start dropping the coin. After it reaches the lowest point, check its Y position and if it is more than a certain value (a point where the tube would look full), cancel the subsequent steps (i.e. creating its image etc.).

Do you like the idea?

If you do, modify your scripts to implement this idea.

Feature Idea # 5: Welcome and Help Screens

Add a welcome screen, a help screen and suitable sounds.

Design:

This should be a straightforward task. We will arrange the code such that the welcome screen appears when Green Flag is clicked and everything else is hidden at that time. After a short time (say 4 seconds) the game screen will appear.

The help screen will be optional – available when some key is pressed. It should go away when the mouse pointer is clicked anywhere.

What about sounds? Well, I have added one sound clip which plays every time a coin is dropped.

Feature Idea # 6: Placement of bases

Use a script to automatically place the bases in a neat row.

Design:

This is a matter of using the X-Y geometry and the "Go to x, y" command. Since all bases are at the same height, the Y position of all will be the same. Now, if you know the width of each base and the x position of the first base, can you calculate the x positions of the subsequent bases?

Here is the algorithm for these calculations:

```
Let x be the position of the first base.
Let w be the width of each base.
X position of the 2nd base = x + 1*w
X position of the 3rd base = x + 2*w
X position of the 4th base = x + 3*w
```

Do you get the idea? Now, since the sprites only move by themselves, each base will need to place itself when the Green Flag is clicked.

Save as the Final Program Version

Congratulations! You have completed the program with all the features we had planned. Save your program as "Connect4-final.sb2".

Compare your program with my program at the link below.

Connect4-final: includes ideas 4, 5, and 6 explained above.

How to run the program:

1. Click the "Green flag" to start the game.

2. Two users (blue and orange) will play the game by clicking alternately. The variable "Turn" shows whose turn it is.

3. Click the base of the tube in which you want to drop your coin.

Additional challenge

If you are interested, work on this additional challenge.

For idea #4 above, implement this alternate technique: Keep a count of the number of coins in each tube, and check that count every time. When the count reaches the upper limit, disallow adding any more coins. You could use a list variable for these counts.

Solutions to Feature Ideas

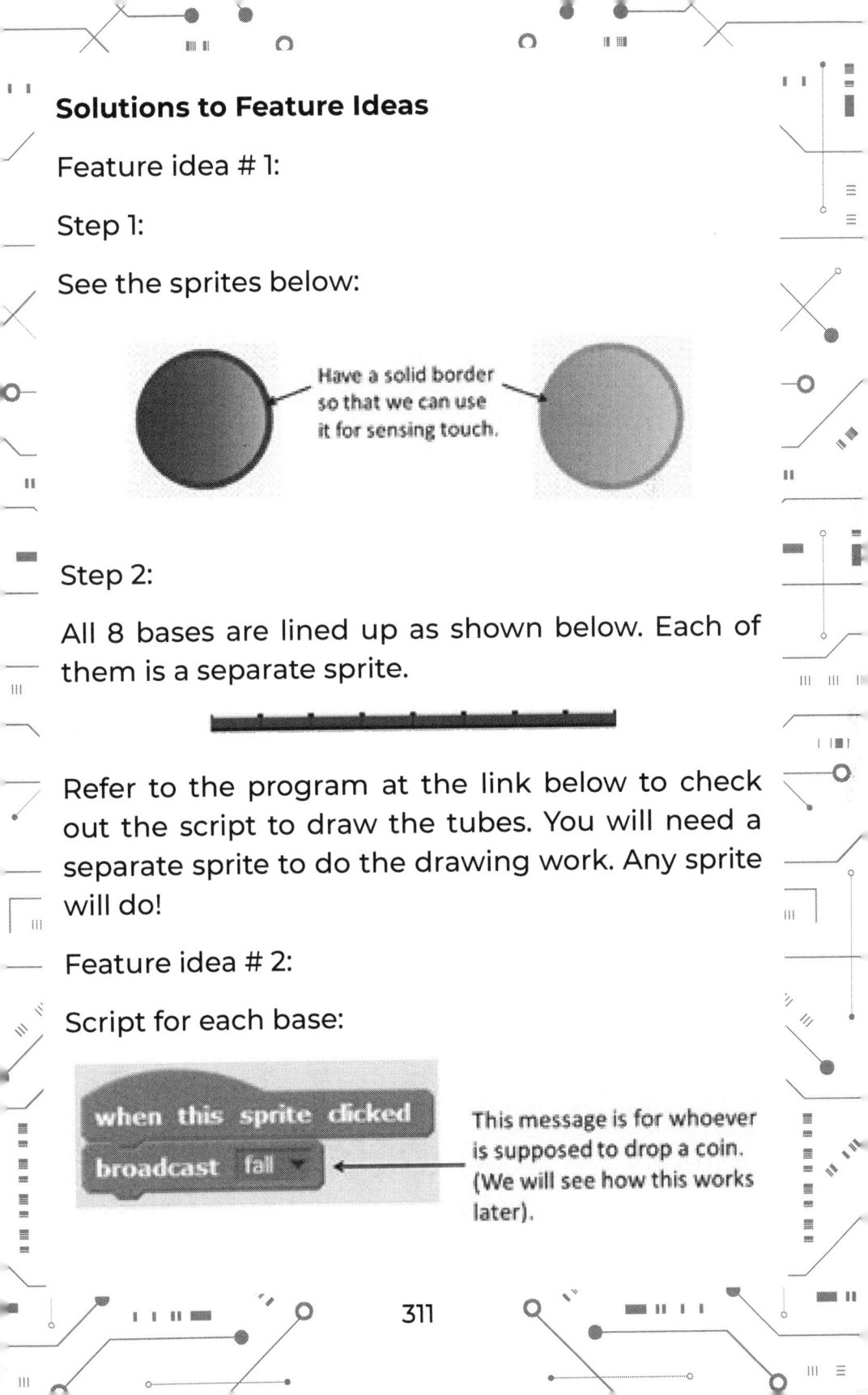

Feature idea # 1:

Step 1:

See the sprites below:

Have a solid border so that we can use it for sensing touch.

Step 2:

All 8 bases are lined up as shown below. Each of them is a separate sprite.

Refer to the program at the link below to check out the script to draw the tubes. You will need a separate sprite to do the drawing work. Any sprite will do!

Feature idea # 2:

Script for each base:

```
when this sprite clicked
broadcast fall
```

This message is for whoever is supposed to drop a coin. (We will see how this works later).

Feature idea # 3:

Step 1:

Modified script for each base:

```
when this sprite clicked
set tubex ▾ to  x position
broadcast fall ▾
```

Variable "tubex" would later be used by the coin to determine the X coordinate of the top point of the tube.

Script for the orange coin:

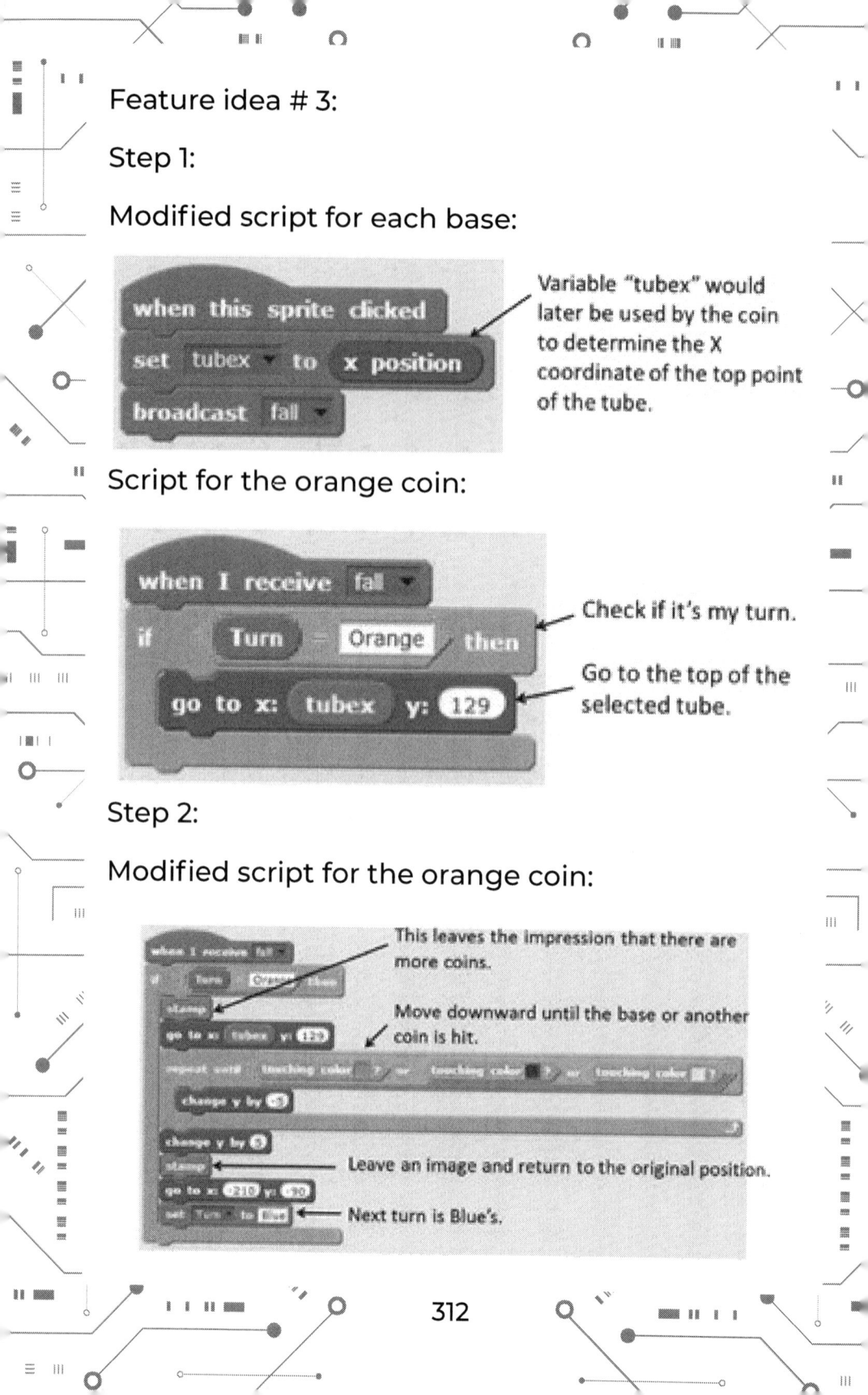

```
when I receive  fall ▾
if   Turn = Orange   then
    go to x: tubex  y: 129
```

— Check if it's my turn.

— Go to the top of the selected tube.

Step 2:

Modified script for the orange coin:

— This leaves the impression that there are more coins.

— Move downward until the base or another coin is hit.

— Leave an image and return to the original position.

— Next turn is Blue's.

Feature idea # 4:

Modified script of the "orange" coin:

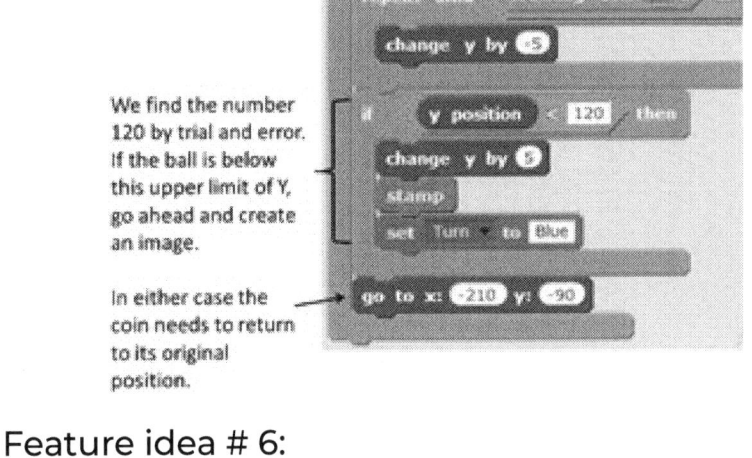

```
repeat until  touching color [ ] ?  or
    change y by -5
    if  y position < 120  then
        change y by 5
        stamp
        set Turn ▼ to Blue
    go to x: -210 y: -90
```

We find the number 120 by trial and error. If the ball is below this upper limit of Y, go ahead and create an image.

In either case the coin needs to return to its original position.

Feature idea # 6:

Script for base #2:

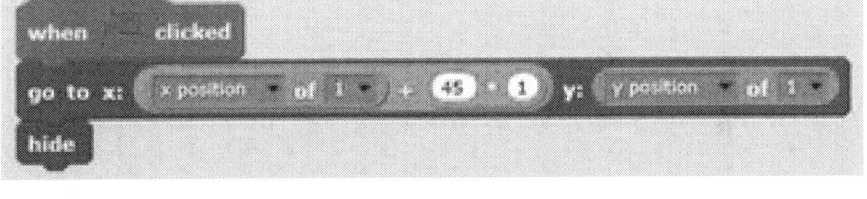

```
when [ ] clicked
go to x: (x position ▼ of 1 ▼) + (45 * 1)  y: (y position ▼ of 1 ▼)
hide
```

Script for base #4:

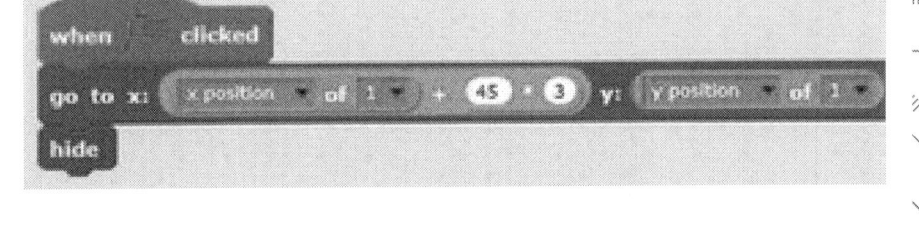

```
when [ ] clicked
go to x: (x position ▼ of 1 ▼) + (45 * 3)  y: (y position ▼ of 1 ▼)
hide
```

CONCLUSION

I want to thank you for taking the time to read this book! I certainly hope that you have found it informative and useful. The goal in this book was to keep things simple so that beginners can understand scratch and get started with using it, but hopefully, we've kept it interesting and fun as well.

Coding is a challenging and fun career, and since society is getting more dependent on computers and networks, the need for coders is only going to increase. Of course, even if your child is not going to be a coder, they can still benefit in many ways from learning some coding. First off, coding helps to train the mind to think carefully. Coding will help your child learn how to focus on and complete things that they have started. One lesson that all parents should strive for is making sure that children complete the projects that they start at scratch. This alone is a skill worth learning, even if they don't continue to code later.

Coding will also help children develop skills in logical thinking. You don't have to be a math whiz to do basic coding, but learning to code is going to improve the math skills of anyone who learns it and help them to think logically.

The best approach to use is to find simple tasks on the site, but tasks that are also interesting. One task that is good to try is one we touched on in the book. That is the animated letters. This is a fun task that children enjoy, and it lets them directly connect the commands they are giving the computer to the action that they see on the screen. The animation process can also involve several different methods, and so it also gives the children a chance to learn a lot about scratch, in a simple context.

There are many other good lessons to learn. However, if you are browsing around the MIT site, you are going to find that many of the projects posted on the site are quite sophisticated. Many of these have been developed by scratch fans in the general public. They can be instructive later, but they may not be suitable for beginners. The worst thing that can be done is intimidating a child by having them encounter codes that are complicated, and when they are just starting out, they may find that overwhelming. It will destroy the child's confidence. The site does provide many beginners tutorials. You can rely on those until the child has gained some experience. Then they can learn more complex programs that will take a longer time to figure out.

When guiding your children with scratch, it is important not to force them to do it. Not everyone is going to be inclined to do computer programming. If some children find it uninteresting, let them try something else. It is not going to be the end of the world if your child does not grow up to be a coder.

Again, thank you for reading my book. Please drop by Amazon and leave a thoughtful review, we'd love to hear how the book is helping you and your children!

Printed in Great Britain
by Amazon